SHERMAN
EXPOSED

SHERMAN
EXP**O**SED

Slightly
Censored
Climbing
Stories

by
John Sherman

THE
MOUNTAINEERS

Published by
The Mountaineers
1001 SW Klickitat Way, Suite 201
Seattle, WA 98134

Published simultaneously in Great Britain by Cordee, 3a DeMontfort
Street, Leicester, England, LE1 7HD

Manufactured in the United States of America

Edited by Paul Hughes
Cover and book design by Jennifer Shontz
Layout by Jennifer Shontz

Cover photograph by Jim Fagiolo

Library of Congress Cataloging-in-Publication Data
Sherman, John, 1959–
   Sherman exposed : slightly censored climbing stories / John
Sherman. — 1st. ed.
    p.   cm.
    ISBN 0-89886-605-7 (pbk.)
    1. Sherman, John, 1959– 2. Mountaineers—United States Biography.
3. Mountaineering. I. Title.
    GV199.92.S523 A3 1999
    796.52'2'092—dc21
    [B]

                                         99-6185
                                         CIP

To Thimble,

For her patience

For her love

And for never speaking ill

of my writings

Contents

Preface

ON MY VAN IS A BUMPER STICKER that reads "Sport Climbing is Neither." A friend threatened to add one next to it. It read: Climbing Journalism is Neither. I agree. Climbing writing can be fun, thought-provoking, stirring or boring, irritating or inspirational. Rarely is it an unbiased recitation of facts. In the end, it's just spewing about something we'd rather be doing.

At first, I wanted to entitle this collection "The Importance of Being Vermin." (Vermin has been my nickname since high school.) I was going to delve deeply into the media's role in the climbing community and my role in the media. I believe the climbing media holds the rudder that steers the sport. Other members of the media disagree and say that they merely hold up the mirror that the sport views itself in. The view in the mirror changes though, depending on at which angle it's held. My role has been twofold. First, by exposing a new generation of climbers to the values of traditional climbing—sheep, inebriation, and lowering after every fall—I hoped to give something back to the sport. Second, by providing lovably vulgar satire, I hoped to get climbers to take themselves less seriously. By fulfilling these roles, I've provided one more thing for my employers—a juicy target for outraged readers to go off on in the letters columns. Ethical defender, satirist, target, and squeaky cog in the mighty media machine—those are all the importance of being Vermin.

Scrutinizing the actions of the media and evaluating their responsibilities to the sport does not make for fun reading. Climbing should be fun, and I want this book to be fun. Therefore, we'll leave the media bashing and justifications behind. Instead, let go of that quickdraw, pop a cold one, forget about the importance of being Vermin, and welcome to the epic collection of climbing writings now titled *Sherman Exposed*.

Acknowledgments

FIRST OFF, I THANK ALL MY FRIENDS and supporters who have encouraged me to keep writing through the years—their names are too numerous to mention. Some, however, have gone above and beyond the call of duty (some might say sanity) to support my writing efforts. Neal Kaptain has been my biggest ally in this respect. Chris Dunn and Chris Jones are not far behind. Others who have gone out of their way to egg me on, cooperate in my writing endeavors, or make my life easier through the "starving artist" (read "sloshed journalist") years are Christian Beckwith, Bobbi Bensman, Barry Blanchard, Scott Blunk, Jim Bodenhamer, Tom Cosgriff, Maria Cranor, Dad, Dave Dornian, Amy Filerman, Jackie Gallen, Steve and Lisa Gorham, Donny Hardin, Brents and Arcy Hawks, Craig Hazelton, Dan and Lori Hershman, Bill and Pat Hoadley, Greg and Susan Johnson, Joe Josephson, Tami Knight, Craig Luebben, Bronson MacDonald, Mom, Catherine Mulvihill, Mary O'Connor, Mike O'Donnell, Bruce Pottenger, Doug Robinson, John Shireman, Robbie Slater, Geoff Tabin, Margot Talbot, Pancho Torrisi, Marc Twight, Lori Wagner, Annie Whitehouse, and Mark Wilford. Michael Kennedy gets the blame (and my gratitude) for publishing my first works, and John Long gave me a friendly shove toward the deep end. A special thanks goes to my editors through the years—especially Mike Benge—for weathering all those battles with me and still coming out as friends. Thanks also to *Climbing* magazine, and Mike Benge again, for helping collect the materials for this manuscript.

PART I

WHAT? NO EIGER?

TWO YEARS AGO I WAS 1,500 FEET UP the North Face of the Eiger, balanced atop a disintegrating dollop of snow the size of a large jack-o'-lantern, my ice ax hooking a rotting curtain of verglas on the bulge in front of my face. I was unroped and counting down the last minutes of my life. I'd like to say I stared Death straight in the face and spit in his/her eye, but I was too busy trying to freeze my glove to the polished limestone and buy a few more seconds. Many of the Nordwand's features have been named after climbers who perished at those spots. There were precious few unnamed features left. Fortunately, most Eiger fatalities had occurred higher up the face, so I still stood a chance of having my name attached to this otherwise nondescript bulge. Somehow I survived this epic and kept climbing up, but due to a foolish choice of stoves, came back down the next day. We had climbed but a third of the face, the easy third.

It's pretty much a given that a climber can't write an autobiography without an Eiger chapter. Even the mighty Bonatti had to chronicle his retreat from the Nordwand (I knew we had something in common). But as I backed off lower than Walter, my Eiger chapter would probably come up short. Hence, this book will not be an autobiography; rather it is a collection of writings based on my observations of the climbing world over the last 23 years. To put these into perspective, though, it will help to have some brief biographical content. First, however, let's sum up America's social and climbing history since 1975.

Back in the mid-1970s, disco gripped the nation while climbers embraced clean climbing. Cracks were king, and hangdogging was a grievous display of moral turpitude. Next came the Reagan "Me First" years of the 1980s, and the motto was "greed is good." Keeping pace with this philosophy was the sport-climbing revolution, driven by cordless rotary hammers and shiny tights. The American climbing community split between Trads and Sports. Bolt wars flared repeatedly, with the Bosches eventually overpowering the crowbars. Now it's 1999. Awash in low interest rates, domestic peace, and a balanced budget, the nation, starving for amusement, desperately clings to a low-grade White House sex scandal. The *Brady Bunch*, the *Addams*

Family, and all-around climbing have all made comebacks. Land managers, corporate interests, and the media have taken an increasing role in charting the course the sport takes. That most climbers are just along for the ride is evidenced by the apathy shown in the battle for access. Climbing is now decidedly mainstream, as proven by the media's insistence on calling it "extreme."

What happened to me during those thrilling years? Hall of Fame climbing journalist Frank M. Bellisher tells the story in the following three-part interview.

A Brief History of Vermin

By Frank M. Bellisher

PART 1—1982

IT'S LATE ON A SUNNY WINTER AFTERNOON when I first meet John Sherman at Hidden Valley Campground in Joshua Tree National Monument. Sherman, aka The Vermin, aka Verm, ponders a puzzle cap off a bottle of Lucky Lager as he sits on the corner of a picnic table. The campground is surrounded by rock formations and twisted trees straight out of *Lost in Space*. Reggae from the Wailing Souls blares from inside his beat-up silver Honda Civic, keeping beat with the hacky-sack players nearby. Along with a *G* pinched from a Ford Galaxy, the letters on the hatchback have been scrambled to read *GONAD*. Sherman gets up from the table and limps over to greet me.

"Funnel?" he asks, handing me a beer bong. I kindly refuse, but he hands me the plastic quart funnel with hose attached anyway. "'Course if you're some kind of fairy hangdog you don't have to do the full quart," Verm says. "One or two beers?" The hacky game stops and everyone looks to see how I respond. I relent and go for one, blowing about half the beer out my nose. Vermin gets a good laugh out of this, hands me another beer, and not too subtly rattles the empty short case. It was my cue. I produce a sixer, then sit down with my dinner. Verm takes the offensive and fires the first question.

V You're not one of those sellouts writing for the magazines?

FB Er, no. I just thought it would be a good idea to get some of your thoughts down before you get the chop. I see you've come close again. What's with the limp? I heard that a year ago you'd be hacking till dark.

V Screwed up in the Gunks a few months ago. Broke a hold, broke a pin, then broke my pelvis in four places.

FB So what about the name Vermin? Where did that come from?

V Mr. Shadoan, my high school biology teacher. He called my brother Sherm the Worm. A few years later Uncle Shad got even more clever and dubbed me Sherman the Vermin.

FB So this didn't have to do with any particular incident?

V No. This is nurture, not nature. I got the name, then kinda just grew into it.

FB I'd say you've done a good job, but did you have to peel that gobi off and flick it on my salad?

V Baco-Bit, dude.

FB So were your parents gross too?

V No. It wasn't until I started climbing that I learned the art. It helped hanging out with Harrison Dekker. He's a pro at grossing people out.

FB How long have you known him?

V Since high school.

FB Did he teach you to climb?

V No. That would be Keg Hazelton, Trainer of Champions. Harrison was a . . . (At this point Verm's eyes jerk to the side and he starts screaming. I wonder if he's snapped. Beer foams copiously from his lips.) FRIGGIN' HANGDOG!

FB Dekker's dogging?

V Uh, what was that? No, Harrison's true to the sport. He'd never dog. I'd bet a case of beer on that.

FB But you just yelled . . .

V LOSER! (Verm's words echo off the cliff face. Veins swell in Verm's neck as his face goes red.) Look at that sackashit, will you. (Verm points at a climber hanging from a nearby bolt. Now I see what set him off.)

FB It's just some guy working a move.

V No fuckin' respect I tell you. I bet he tells his friends he's a rock climber. I hope he dies of an impacted stool.

FB (Attempting to change the subject) So you're twenty-three and you've been climbing for eight years?

V Yep. PANSY! (Verm screams at the cliff again.)

FB You started at Indian Rock in Berkeley, correct?

V Yep. DICKWEED!

FB Did you crank hard right from the start?

V No, I sucked. It took me a week to climb *Beginner's Crack*. YOUR MOTHER SLEEPS WITH SASQUATCH!

FB Geez, that's only 5.5.

V I was so fat I couldn't do a single pull-up. UP YOUR ASS WITH A BROKEN GLASS!

FB So climbing whipped you in shape? Or did you train like a fiend?

V Pretty much just climbing. I'd go bouldering every day after school. Stay at The Rock until dark. As far as training goes, that's just for climbers who want to be as good as me. (Verm laughs at his own joke. Finally he seems to be calming down.) And for queers like that dude.

FB I hate to break it to you, but that's the way the sport is heading.

V No way. Maybe in Europe, but California will never cave in. PARLEZ VOUS YOU SUCK?

FB C'mon, you went to college in Boulder, you see what's going on in Eldo, you read the magazines.

V But I wouldn't be caught dead in one. The second your name appears in print, you've sold out.

FB Seems I saw your name in the info section of *Mountain*. (I wave a copy at Verm.)

V Let me see that . . . Oh shit, I'm done for. I knew I should have never climbed with a correspondent.

FB It sounds like you and Alec Sharp put up some good routes.

V Great routes. (Verm corrects me.) None of that sissy bolt clipping. Goddam bolters are ruining things. Did I tell you about trying to free *Fire and Ice* in Eldo before they added that first bolt? Popped off the skinny mantel edge and went flying. I hit my feet on that ledge a few feet off the deck and that flipped me headfirst toward the ground. Just before I cratered, a #2 and #3 stopper stacked in a flared pin scar stopped me. Now some cretin drills a bolt by the mantel and turns it into a homo route.

FB I heard about that fall. Didn't you rip out some RPs?

V Different climb. That was on *Tubesock Tanline*, a direct start to the *Wisdom*. I got out to the crux overlaps and placed six of the seven #0 RPs I'd borrowed. I couldn't find a slot for the seventh and the nuts looked pretty shaky, so I backed off. While I lowered to the base, four of them ripped. Once my feet were on terra firma, I yanked on the rope and the other two came flying out.

FB So what did you do then?

V I asked Alec for the pin hammer. Sneaky prick took it out of the pack the night before. Anyway, I ran down to the parking lot, scrounged a hammer, and went back up. I drove a knife blade upwards under the roof, climbed around one bulge, dynoed over another, missed the hold, and took a 20-footer on the knife blade.

FB And it held?

V Probably just because my feet hit a ledge on the way down. It flipped me over backwards, just like on *Fire and Ice*. This time, though, I went back up and bagged the first.

FB So where did the name come from?

V One day that hangdog Jim Collins shows up in Eldo without his tubesocks. His legs were so pale from the knees down, they looked like slats from a white picket fence.

FB I take it you don't respect Collins much?

V How can you take a guy seriously who (cringing as he wiggles two fingers from each hand, Verm sets the next word in quotes) "free-climbs" *Genesis* and renames it *God's Golden Hour of Power*?

FB What about climbers you respect? Can you name a few?

V Sure. Purists like Nat Smale, Scott Frey, Harrison, and most of the boulderers at Indian Rock. Well, except Vanjiver. Every time you look away, that dude is stealing a handful of chalk from your bag. Fifty cents a block, that shit ain't cheap.

FB And in Colorado?

V I'd have to say Skip Guerin for his barefoot prowess; Rufus Miller for the full-rope-length, no-leg-loops whipper he took off *The Nose*; Rick Doerksen and Eric Eriksson for their sub-two-second funnel times; Bill Hoadley for his no-hands rest finding ability; Neal Kaptain for his crimp strength; and Robbie Slater for his drive.

FB Any Europeans?

V Yeah, some of the Brits. Andy Parkin and Alec Sharp can hang in forever to dick in pro. I think it's a gritstone thing. If there are any climbers I'd like to model my climbing style after, it's Andy and Alec. They stay cool and never seem to get pumped. Just get the gear in and keep going. Same with that Moffat kid. Just did *Hercules* with him a few days ago. Watched him lieback the whole thing. If he ever learns how to jam, he'll be dangerous.

FB So pretty much you just respect the people you've actually climbed with?

V Yeah, I guess so.

FB What about old-timers?

V You mean like Bachar and Kauk?

FB Those guys are only a few years older than you. I mean Robbins, Chouinard, Kor, Pratt.

V Yeah sure, those guys too. Who was the last one?

FB (Verm's sense of history seemed rather scant. It was time for a new line of questioning.) So, what's with all the sheep toys on your dashboard?

V What kind of question is that? Are you sure you're a climber?

FB I mean, have you spent much time in the Wind River Range?

V Nope. Sierra East Side. Ever met Bob Harrington? He's from there. He's another big influence on me.

FB How so?

V Bought me beers in Tuolumne when I was underage and turned me on to Frank Zappa. One day I told him I was ready for him to take me up my first 5.11. I said, "Let's make it an easy one." He said, "No way. We'll do a real one." Drags me up *Dreams, Screams*. I thought right then that I'd never do another 5.11 in my life. I needed my kletterschues for the edging pitch, then my EBs for the runout friction. I fell at least six times. Later I saw it in the underground guide as 5.11 with three pluses after it. Bob taught me a good lesson that day. Besides, Bob knows sheep.

FB I'm sure he does.

V You know where they get virgin wool from?

FB Is this a joke?

V Ugly sheep. (Verm guffaws.)

FB What are your future plans?

V Funnel the rest of your six-pack.

FB No, I mean in the upcoming years.

V Years? Shit, I dunno. I'm heading out to Texas in a few weeks. I hear there's good climbing near El Paso.

Upon hearing that, I figured Verm had had one funnel too many. For such a proud and idealistic climber, he sure is daft—everyone knows there's no climbing in Texas. The interview concluded with another funnel shoved in my hand. At least that's the last I remember.

PART 2—1990

The next time I track Sherman down, I'm visiting Hueco Tanks in Texas. Damned if it isn't one of the finest climbing areas I've ever been to. Verm is one of a handful of climbers spending his entire winters here. He hasn't tied into a rope in years and has gained a rep as the local bouldering guru. At 6'1", 161 pounds he looks like he crawled out of Auschwitz, but his arms look like they've been hanging at Gold's Gym. His hair reaches his shoulders. Chalk smears his face, arms, and shorts as he sits on the steps outside the funky Quonset hut that houses Mexican Pete's Store. He looks rangier and a bit weather-beaten compared to the first time we met, but one thing hasn't changed—his chalky paw is clenched around a frosty one.

FB So you're writing for the mags now. (I couldn't help rubbing it in.)

V Everyone's got their price. I'm not proud of it, but it beats having a real job.

FB You can't tell me you bought this nice van by penning articles.

V Nope. Vestige of the oil days.

FB Oil days? That's not a trust-fund ride?

V I wish. No, I dropped out of grad school and went to work as a petroleum geologist. Did consulting work at oil wells. It paid great. Anyhow, I didn't know what to do with the money, other than quit swilling cheap beer. Then the Gonad died and it was time to move up.

FB But why an American van? I figured you for a VW bus, a real climber's rig.

V Those are fine if you live in the Camp 4 parking lot, but if you ever need to drive anywhere . . . Besides, foreign cars don't go over big in the oil patch.

FB So why write for the mags when you can work geology?

V You seen the price at the pump? Know how you call a geologist in Boulder?

FB Ummm.

V Hey, waiter!

FB So what are you? Sponsored by Playtex? No visible means of support.

V The van's paid for. People see me traveling around climbing all the time, not punching a time clock and they think I must have married a Rockefeller. Not true. Living in a van is dirt cheap and simple. No rent. No bills. No phone. No boss. One-third food, one-third gas, one-third beer. Every once in a while splurge for a dollar movie or a box of chalk. Like Eric Beck said, "at either end of the social spectrum lies a leisure class."

FB So what about those Fires. You get those for free?

V Yeah, I only worked thirteen years for this pair. Same with the chalkbag.

FB So you sold out to the media and to sponsorship. What's with the ice bags on your elbows?

V Roasted them in Arapiles. Hanging on too long trying to dick in those RPs. Awesome climbing there. I was on so many painkillers for my hips that I didn't feel my elbows go south until it was too late.

FB How's that affect your climbing?

V It helped me focus on bouldering again. Back in '81 I trashed my fingers tree-planting in Oregon—couldn't lift a twelve-pack with one hand. That put bouldering on hold for a couple years. So I did a load of roped climbing. Hung out in Yosemite a bunch, did a lot of cracks—*Nabisco Wall, Astroman, Tales of Power*—you know, the standards.

FB Dog any of those?

V Fuck no. What kind of question is that? Fuckin' hangdogs with their fuckin' power drills in their fuckin' girls underwear are ruining this sport. Derek and Croft are the only climbers with balls anymore. Nobody runs it out anymore. This is turning into a pansy sport and you know who's to blame? The media. They dropped the ball on this one.

FB You're one of them, what have you done?

V If I thought the mags would go under if I stopped writing for them, I'd quit in a heartbeat. That simply isn't the case. So I keep writing so at least there's some traditional climbing values represented.

FB Like dating strippers?

V She's an underemployed microbiologist. Eat your heart out anyway.

FB You've poured a lot of energy into the boulders here.

V (Shrugs, munches on a taco.)

FB Some folks say you act like you own the place.

V Because I tell them to pick up their trash?

FB They say you're a snob because you won't climb with them.

V I end up bouldering by myself a lot, because few people want to explore. I offer to take people to new boulders where they could put up classic FAs, but all they want to do is climb on the Mushroom Boulder. Do you know how many times I've done the *El Murrays*? When guys like Chris Hill, Mike McCarron, or Donny Hardin show up we go on a rampage. There's a lifetime of first ascents waiting out there. I'd rather do those than repeat stuff. Besides, the Mushroom Boulder is low angle.

FB What about the tasteless route names? I heard you just put up a climb called *Devil's Butthole*.

V That one is sooo classic. You gotta check it out. It features the deepest hueco in the whole park. You chimney up it into the dark and it keeps getting warmer and stinkier the higher you go. I won't tell you how deep it is, or what lives at the end. You gotta find that out for yourself. Nobody who has ever been there has suggested that the name wasn't 100 percent appropriate. We're not talking bad taste, we're talking accuracy. Now naming climbs after Gordon Lightfoot songs, *that's* bad taste.

FB Don't you find the *Lesbian Love Grotto* to be offensive?

V Well, there's one problem there where you have to thrash through an overgrown bush, but otherwise I find the climbing there to be quite pleasant.

FB No, I mean the name. It picks on a minority. That's not politically correct.

V In this case, the name was based on historical fact—just ask Ranger Dave. As far as political correctness goes, that's just for people who are afraid to have fun. Do you know how long it's taken me shake off my liberal Berkeley upbringing? The oil patch and El Paso have been good to me. They've really helped me get in touch with my inner redneck. I have more fun now than I ever had exploring intellectualism.

FB You didn't look like you were having fun when you saw that chiseled hold this afternoon.

V (Turning red, fists clenching) Ball-free bastards are destroying the sport. They don't deserve to be called climbers. Not only did the media never distinguish between sport climbing and free climbing, but they're rolling over on this issue as well. They publish highfalutin editorials saying they won't print photos or accounts of chiseled routes, then they run an article that gushes about some hold called the Chippadeedoodah. They even hire Mr. Leave the Chipping to Masters Like Me to be their equipment editor. I've seen gastropods with more backbone. (Verm looks like he's about to kill. I figure I'd better defuse this walking time bomb.)

FB Here, have a beer. What will you do when it gets too hot to stay here?

V Head over to the East Side of the Sierras.

FB What's there?

V Boulders, man. Lots of boulders. And sheep.

FB So what is it with you and sheep?

V Like I said—traditional values. Haven't you ever read *Vulgarian Digest*?

FB No.

V You ought to. Hey, do you know where virgin wool comes from?

FB Wait a minute. I know this one.

V Ugly sheep.

Verm slaps his knee over this one. He then grabs a funky homemade carpet and foam sandwich called a sketchpad and limps out toward the boulders. Overall he seems pretty loose about life, but incredibly intense about bouldering and "the right way" to climb. If his spotter so much as brushes Verm's shoelace during an ascent, Verm will have to climb the problem again "cleanly" or he won't count it. On the rock he seems at ease, at one, doing what he does best. Off the rock he is bitter and defensive, watching the sport he has poured his life into go down a path he doesn't approve of. One senses that he takes the sport far more seriously than he takes himself.

PART 3—1997

It's winter and I am interviewing Verm at his house in Estes Park, Colorado. He seems almost as surprised as myself at the size and quality of his abode, and at the fact that he ever bought a house in the first place. Climbing books and memorabilia line the shelves and Sportscenter plays its endless loop on the big screen TV next to the stone fireplace. Outside, elk mosey through a forest of ponderosa pines and granite boulders.

V Have you met my wife?

FB I didn't know you were married. (I hear a scuffling sound from the bedroom and out rushes a fifty-pound shepherd/Doberman mix with one ear flopping at half-mast. She jumps up and darts her tongue in my mouth before I can react.)

V Easy, Thimble, you don't know where that mouth's been. Ain't the missus great?

FB Whatever possessed you to buy a house?

V I'd been living out of my van on and off for over a decade, living off savings, royalties, slide shows, and some stock my grandmother left me. Then I ran into my old boss's kids at Brents's rock gym in Jackson. They got me to call their dad and he set me up with geology work again. Pretty soon, I had a stack of money saved up. I figured I'd go climbing for three years and not work a day, but I got injured with no quick fix in sight. I reckoned if I was ever going to buy a house that this was the time.

FB I have trouble picturing you as a homeowner. Do you feel like a prisoner here?

V Sometimes I feel tied down by the bills, but this place is just a pool table short of being as posh as a white-collar prison. And I don't waste time suing the department of corrections for not giving me cable TV.

FB You mentioned you were in a rock gym. So you're sport climbing now.

V Lick rim, pussnuts. Verm don't dog. I was in there eating Ruffles and drinking beer in front of the bolt huggers. It really throws them off. All the blood rushes to their salivary glands and their fingers butter off.

FB Rumor has it you're alpine climbing.

V It's a logical progression. One can only crank so many hard boulder problems before the connective tissue is trashed. The good thing about alpine climbing is you don't get injured.

FB You just get killed.

V Precisely. Plus it's one of the only climbing venues left where adventure and self-sufficiency are still of prime importance. I don't care to fall anymore. Falling is still bad style in the mountains.

FB What about the approaches? As I recall, you have a severe aversion to hiking.

V Damn, I must be getting old. I actually enjoy hiking now. Plus whenever allowed, I let Thimble come too.

FB I've heard folks in Canada say you abuse that dog.

V (Indignant) What?

FB They say you fill her doggy pack with beer and make her haul it to the base of ice climbs for you.

V That's not abuse. That's a dog showing love to her partner. You don't mind, do you Thimble?

T (Wags tail upon hearing her name)

V See. Besides, I haul her Milk Bones in my pack.

FB Why the name Thimble?

V She's named after the rock in the Needles that Gill made famous. She and the rock are both short, tough, and hairy. Moreover, it was either Thimble or Vanna. I figured Spot was not a safe name for a boulderer's dog.

FB Which means more to you? Thimble the dog or Thimble the climb?

V I must have dreamed about doing the *Gill Route* on the Thimble for over ten years. To me, the Thimble, the *Ripper Traverse*, and *Midnight Lightning* were bouldering benchmarks I felt bound to do. Of the three, the Thimble was the most intimidating and exclusive. Climbing it was one of the greatest thrills of my career. However, what I gained from the climb doesn't compare to what Thimble the dog has given me. She's taught me a lot about how to approach life in a positive fashion. She's really mellowed me out. And she's made me far more forgiving.

FB You forgiving? So you forgive the climbers who chiseled holds in Hueco's boulders?

V Forgive might be too strong a word there. I haven't been to

Hueco for two winters. Injuries are just part of it. It just wasn't fun to go there and see holds chiseled into problems I did the first ascent of years before. I used to take that shit very personally. I wanted to find the bastards responsible, knock their teeth out, then Krazy Glue their gums together. Partly I got mad, because it was so obvious to me that the chipping was wholly unnecessary. One winter I put in the effort to climb past all the chiseled moves without the chiseled holds. I succeeded, but when I'd announce such-and-such goes without the chiseled holds, nobody cared. I was filled with anger and negativity and depression at the fact that the sport would sag so low and nobody gave a shit.

These days I don't take the chiseling personally. I don't think anybody was whipping out a chisel and thinking, "Boy, this will sure piss Sherman off. Cool." Rather, I realize that the chiselers only wanted to do what I and others before them had done, but they lacked the ability or the patience to climb said problems without modifying the holds. I guess I should be flattered that people would so badly want to repeat my problems that they would go to such lengths. It's sad that their actions ruin it for everyone who comes along later, and that's the part I have trouble forgiving. So rather than feeling anger these days, I'm more likely to pity those who climb in bad style.

FB You got to climb those problems before they were altered. Why should you care what happens?

V I'd like others to be able to get out of the sport what I have. You can't do that if you bolt or chip every climb down to the lowest common denominator. When I started climbing, the sport was in great shape. At least I thought so. Dealing with risk and rising to meet a challenge were important facets of the game. We're in danger of losing that. That's why I'm resistant to change.

FB Speaking of risk, you seem to own a disproportionately large number of books featuring the Eiger. I even see a video copy of *The Eiger Sanction* here. Have you climbed the Mordwand?

V Urrgh. It tried to kill me. (Verm puts on his Clint Eastwood impersonation.) But I want another crack at that hill.

FB Is it worth dying for?

V Several times while climbing, I've come very close to dying. In some ways maybe it will be the Eiger that kills me, even if I get the chop somewhere else. I can live with that.

FB I don't follow.

V I started climbing when I was fifteen. I'd been bouldering a few times and I was hungry to learn more about the sport. I went down to the Berkeley library and checked out the climbing books. The first one I read was *The White Spider*. It made a huge impression on me. I was lost in high school. I didn't play enough sports to hang with the jocks, didn't smoke enough dope to hang with the stoners, and didn't own a muscle car to hang with the greasers. I detested the drama nerds and dropped out of Fortran class the first day. Furthermore, I was a minority. High school was definitely not showing me the way. Sneaking beers was my biggest passion. Then I read *The White Spider*. It was full of men's men dying glorious deaths in pursuit of a noble goal. I bought every sentence of it. I wanted to be like those men, or die like Tony Kurz trying.

FB I think we're getting somewhere here. So why did you end up pursuing bouldering instead of mountaineering?

V The boulders were my mountains. I lived in Berkeley, not the Alps. In bouldering I found a pursuit that seemed just as noble, if not as dangerous. Part of engaging in a noble pursuit is holding oneself to a strict code of honor.

FB Hence your penchant for throwing cheater stones down the hill.

V That would be a function of it. I'm sure most of the things I've done to piss off other climbers have all been done in the name of upholding the honor of the sport. Well, maybe a few were done in the name of fun. But every cheater stone rolled away, every bolt excised, every . . .

FB Do I see a tear?

V No way.

FB You really love this sport.

V (Sniff)

FB You love this sport like you love your dog.

V (Small heave, whimper)

FB You love climbing like you love pilsner on a hot summer day or stout when it's chilly.

V (Starts blubbering)

FB You love climbing like you love a 500-foot grand slam to the upper deck, a perfectly executed option play, or a scantily clad cheerleader.

V (Full-blown crying)

FB You love climbing like you love the Stars and Stripes, hot dogs, and hot salsa.

V (Wailing)

FB You love it like you love La-Z-Boys, barbecues, Zapps jalapeño potato chips, and 32-inch-wide screen, Surround-Sound television.

V (Buckets of tears, gasping breaths, chest-clutching sighs to the heavens)

FB You love climbing as much as you love sheep.

V (Immediately stops crying) I wouldn't go that far. So tell me; do you know where they get virgin wool from?

FB Yes! From ug . . . (Verm cuts me off.)

V Not around here.

PART II

VERM'S WORLD

THE BIGGEST CURSE FOR ANY WRITER is to write something that garners no response. Fortunately, this has never been the case with my column Verm's World.

From 1995 to the present, with a hiatus in 1997, I wrote a column for *Climbing* called Verm's World. As the name implied, it presented my opinions on the climbing world. Verm's World preached having fun climbing, while respecting the environment, and the traditions and history of the sport. Or as one of my fans said in the letters to the editor, "Now we have to be tortured by Sherman's meaningless, rude, obnoxious, offensive, immature diatribes about his warped sense of reality." Another fan concurred, stating that "Sherman's column is the one bit of literature I genuinely look forward to reading." He then added, "I think it was Clint Eastwood who said, 'Opinions are like assholes, everybody's got one.' In my opinion, John Sherman is right on."

I sometimes wondered how much *Climbing* valued the column on its own merits, and how much they viewed it as a catalyst for juicy letters. Certainly, the published letters generated by the end of Verm's World's first year made for two more columns worth of fervent opinions they didn't have to pay for. With the exception of one piece ("Unsung Hero") that they rejected several times, and a few jokes cracked at the expense of untouchables like Bobbi Bensman and Duane Raleigh (don't make fun of Bobbi's biceps or Duane's chisel), they pretty much let me write what I wanted. Sometimes I wonder if they were giving me free rein or feeding me enough rope to hang myself.

Other than setting the stage with the first Verm's World, these are not in chronological order. Rather they are grouped roughly into sections on history, ethics and approaches to the sport, and general satire.

History is currently one of my favorite subjects, and one I think would have enriched my climbing career had I been exposed to it more early on. Much has been written about great moments and stirring tragedies. Instead of rehashing these stories, I like to dig up the obscure tidbits and the not-so-great moments.

Ethics are always a hot issue. I used to feel everybody would be better off climbing like me. Now I'm glad they aren't; otherwise I'd have to wait in line for every climb I want to do. Notwithstanding, it's fun to stir up the pot on occasion. Rarely do such columns convince someone to change his or her own opinion. They do, however, provide a chance for readers to experience burning, self-righteous indignation, and we all know how good that feels.

Lastly, I believe that the climbing world takes itself far too seriously. The general satire pieces poke fun at climbing and climbers (myself included) in the hope that we'll learn to laugh at ourselves. I find this material the hardest to come up with, but the easiest and most enjoyable to write. If the muses would visit more often, I would restrict myself to writing humor. I find it more rewarding to make readers laugh than to make them think. Compared to my other work, the humor pieces generate more phone calls, and less "fan mail."

Ah, the fan mail. I mention the letters column in several pieces. It constantly amazes me at how worked up people get over what I've written. The scathing responses are so detailed that it's obvious my detractors have read and reread the offending pieces many times. I'm sure the folks who write these letters are the ones who can't wait to read my next column. I affectionately refer to them as my "fans." If it weren't for me, my fans might be stuck whining about global warming, viral epidemics, or nuclear proliferation. If it weren't for my fans, I'd have to find another job.

Laughing Matters

ELEVEN YEARS AGO I EXPERIENCED a turning point in my life. I was in Eldorado Canyon climbing with a British expatriate named Strappo. Strappo was an uninhibited fellow, fond of stripping off his clothes in pubs and cavorting around naked doing party tricks. Two of the tricks have become legend. The first consisted of wedging a rolled newspaper in his fundament, lighting it on fire, and dancing on top of the tables. The second, his hammerhead shark imitation, was accomplished with the creative use of a matchstick. Anyway, Strappo was leading the first pitch, fingers numbing on the frigid stone, while I jumped up and down at the base trying to stay warm. It wasn't long before Strappo said, "Stuff this, let's get out of here." I was all for leaving too, but what to do with the rest of the day?

"Let's go see *The Terminator*," offered Strappo.

Handicapped by my liberal Berkeley upbringing, I vetoed the idea. "A Schwarzenegger film? It's going to suck." I had never seen a Schwarzenegger film, but was pretty sure they didn't have subtitles and therefore lacked any redeeming social value. Strappo, however, would have none of my staidness. Soon I was doubled over laughing as Arnold uttered, "Fuck yoo, ahhshole."

How much fun had I cheated myself out of in life before that day? I shudder.

Coming back from the Banff Mountain Book and Film Festival last November, I was struck by the following truth: climbers in the United States, on average, have less fun than their Canadian brethren. The Canadians laughed at every joke in my slide show. The audiences south of the border were more reserved (or they don't know a good sheep joke when they hear one). At first I passed this off as a by-product of weak American beer, but soon the realization came to me that Americans were afraid to laugh.

What hideous disease, what foul malady, has destroyed our sense of humor? Nothing less than the greatest oxymoron since sport climbing—Political Correctness. If ever there was a humorless doctrine it is this one (unless you see the greater humor of a movement based on intolerance of intolerant people). In college, I took a course in Greek and Roman comedy. The one thing the entire class agreed upon was that the jokes that were still funny over 2,000 years later were the dirty ones. The PC Nazis want to sever this timeless thread of humor. Heaven forbid anyone be less miserable than they. Let's ban Aristophanes's *Lysistrata* lest somebody chuckle at the priapism jokes. Let's be nothing more than skidmarks in the briefs of depression.

The humorous spirit lies within everyone; we need but to be brave and let it out. Heck, I'll bet that even Marc Twight's charcoal soul has a soft chewy center. Had it not been for Strappo, mine may never have been released. Now I hope you will join me in releasing yours. To help in this release I have listed some climbers who have inspired me to have fun, either in person or through legend. The following people have proven that having fun and climbing hard are not mutually exclusive. I present, in no particular order, the charter members of the All-Vermin Team.

The Vulgarians—proof that a preoccupation with women, booze, and sheep doesn't hold you back on the rock. They infected an otherwise sterile early 1960s Gunks scene with their own brand of humor, best chronicled in *Vulgarian Digest*. Had I not been exposed to the *VD* early in my climbing career, I might now be stuck in some poser ad reefing on some silly 5.14 monodoigt, hating my way up the rock. The Vulgarians have often been ridiculed for their loutish behavior. Isn't it terrible when somebody is having more fun than you *and* climbing harder?

Tom Patey—Scotland's famous ice pioneer, but more importantly the writer who set the standard for climbing humor. *One Man's Mountains,* a collection of Patey's prose and verse, is must reading. In it he describes his climbing exploits, but just as important, he satirizes all aspects of climbing and takes the piss out of professional climbers. Chris Bonington was a favorite target: "He has climbed the Eigerwand, he has climbed the Dru—for a mere 10,000 francs, he will climb with you."

TM Herbert—back when Yosemite climbers were tops, TM was the strong man, able to bend 20-penny nails in his bare hands. TM was also climbing's foremost practical joker. He partook in many historic ascents, including the second ascent of the Totem Pole, a 400-foot sandstone pencil protruding from the sands of Monument Valley. While his partners celebrated on the tiny, airy summit, he tied the ropes around his ankles, let them slither over the edge where they couldn't be seen, then cried, "Oh no, the ropes!"

Gary Neptune—a shining beacon of sanity standing strong above the black PC seas inundating Boulder. Snap-On Tools designed their calendars with Gary's office—in his shop Neptune Mountaineering—in mind. Neptune was the first person to carry a golf club to the summit of Everest, a feat that appears to be unrepeated.

Derek Hersey—one of the coolest heads for soloing there ever was and always happy to make fun of sport climbers and their "rinky-dink" routes. One of the only times he was seen to panic was during an informal driving lesson (he never did acquire a license), when he came charging toward a toll booth from the wrong direction, much to the horror of the attendant. A standard gag in all his slide shows was to project a sequence of himself soloing Eldorado Canyon's overhanging and exposed *Vertigo Direct*. The shots were all taken from the same vantage point, but during different ascents and in a different pair of shorts each time. The climb was so scary, he would say, that he had to change his shorts multiple times en route. When news of Derek's tragic death reached Boulder, every liquor store in town sold out of Sheaf Stout, Derek's libation of choice, as legions of admirers paid tribute to his memory.

Catherine Freer—alpine hardwoman extraordinaire, also unfortunately deceased. Years ago I drew up a climbers' crossword puzzle. While others thought five letters for "climber's best friend" was "chalk," she knew better. On other clues, she provided answers that made even me blush.

Tom Cosgriff—the perfect blend of top-notch climbing ability, healthy perversity, and an indestructible liver. His Clark Kent looks and quick thinking have bailed him out of several jams. When rangers caught him approaching the Diamond on Longs Peak for an unregistered bivy, he took a quick look over his shoulder, hoped the rangers wouldn't notice the lack of a moon that night, then claimed that climbing the Diamond by moonlight was his party's goal. As long as they kept moving, no matter how slow, they couldn't be cited for an illegal bivy. The rangers knew they were being snowed, but had to concede to Cosgriff's logic. Numerous broken bones and near-death experiences add to the Cosgriff mystique.

Mark Wilford—perhaps America's best all-around climber. As college freshman roommates we didn't get along at all. "Clean them off yourself if they bug you," he said when I demanded he chip his frozen beer chunks off our windowsill. Fortunately, his stubbornness has preserved his traditional ethic. Furthermore, Mark has survived five (at time of this writing) vehicle rollovers. Canadian Alpine Club president Mike Mortimer notes Mark's inconsistency in the drinking department, yet he still makes the team, due in part to his skill with a crowbar.

Annie Whitehouse—a solid climber with a seedy sense of humor. Her inclusion here should move me up on her dating service priority list. Currently recovering from a back injury sustained in a mating posture favored by lower mammals and lawyers.

Rob Slater—doesn't drink, hates bouldering. How did he make the list? Sheerly on the strength of his ovine lust. He beat Greg Child to an El Cap route Child wanted to dramatically name *Heart of Darkness*. Slater named it *Wyoming Sheep Ranch* and came up with pitch names like *High Boots on a Full Moon Night*. Every team needs a designated driver.

Don Whillans—a classic Brit known for his acerbic wit and ability to down the suds. When retreating from the North Face of the Eiger in a storm he and Tom Patey ran across two Japanese climbers. Patey tells of the classic encounter in "A Short Walk with Whillans":

"You Japs?" grunted Don. It seemed an unnecessary question.

"Yes, yes," they grinned happily, displaying full sets of teeth. "We are Japanese."

"Going up?" queried Whillans. He pointed meaningfully at the gray holocaust sweeping down from the White Spider.

"Yes, yes," they chorused in unison. "Up. Always upwards. First Japanese Ascent."

"You . . . may . . . be . . . going . . . up . . . Mate," said Whillans, giving every syllable unnecessary emphasis, "but . . . a . . . lot . . . 'igher . . . than . . . you . . . think!"

They did not know what to make of this, so they wrung his hand several times, and thanked him profusely for the advice.

"'Appy little pair!" said Don. "I don't imagine we'll ever see them again."

Camp Hog's Chogderks—the Vulgarians of New Zealand, two decades later. They possess the all-important disrespect for any climber who takes himself too seriously. During my visit to Australia's Mount Arapiles in 1985, they ruled the coveted Top Camp. I'll never forget the Hogmobile drifting into camp and suddenly seeing both left tires pop off the rims. The Chogderks piled out in fits of laughter. Various campfire bombs livened up evenings. (Who would be last to leave their seat after an aerosol was tossed in the flames?) Possum tossin' was also good sport. Aussie possums are kind of a cross between an American opossum and a raccoon, and far more obnoxious than either. Their constant raids on food supplies and dry-heave utterances right outside your tent door negate any sympathy their cute looks might engender. Virtually indestructible, they'd go on hammer throw tosses of great distances only to come back for more minutes later. Camp Hog's underground publications are some of the funniest climbing rags ever. *Penthog* and other incarnations ripped on the antipodean climbing scene and everyone in it, especially the Chogderks themselves. Nevertheless, some of the pieces were scholarly essays, such as *BIG HOG—A connoisseur's guide to Instant Derrolistics, relativity, fireside ratiocination, and megabulkadvanced alpine polemics. And bullshit.*

And what about the Canadians? How about the renowned cartoonist **Tami Knight**? Perhaps her climbing record takes a backseat to her naked trampoline antics, but nobody else has as successfully exposed the foibles of the '90s climbing world in print. Were I to make the same rude, crude, and 100-percent-accurate observations I would be burned at the stake in Berkeley. Thank god it's politically incorrect to accuse a woman of being sexist. Write on, Tami!

Climbing, February 1995

The Verm's World History Aptitude Test

(or, If you know the answer raise your hand, or what's left of it)

EVERY FOURTH OR FIFTH TIME I introduce my dog to a climber and tell him her name is Thimble, they say "Cymbal?" thinking I have a lisp. Then I have to explain that her name starts with a T-H. The last climber to realize that I named her after what was, in pre–*Midnight Lightning* days, the most famous boulder problem in America, was British. Precious few American climbers have been able to figure this out. Is all that hype about SAT scores plummeting for real?

Maybe not. When I was a young climbing bum, I had only a passing knowledge of the Thimble, *The Nose*, the Eiger, and the Vulgarians. My buddies and I were more concerned with what we and the members of our generation were doing than what had gone on before. I suppose this is still a common phenomenon among young climbers, but now I feel like kicking myself with Laurent Grivel's revolutionary twelve-point crampons (1932) when I think of how long I moldered with no knowledge of climbing history. Neal Kaptain was the only person who told me history was cool, but at that time he was a Communist and macrobiotic prone to deep thoughts. As a twisted little climbing brat who was still in the pick-the-gobies-and-toss-them-in-the-crushed-red-pepper-shaker-at-the-pizza-parlor phase, I was happier to boulder with him than to look at his Comici and Gervasutti books. Now I wish I owned those books.

History *is* cool. About a year ago, I went to book pusher Michael Chessler and bought *Conquistadors of the Useless, The Hard Years, On the Heights, Starlight and Storm, The White Spider,* and dozens of other classics from him. The more I read, the more I thirsted—even after Chessler told me it's a sure sign a climber's washed up when they come to him to buy books. I hope he's wrong about the washed up bit, but if not, in the interest that others should not deprive themselves of our rich lore as I did, I present the Verm's World History Aptitude Test, or VWHAT for short.

1. Speaking of being washed up, who wrote the following? "This second defeat led to a great spiritual depression which was the fateful last drop which made my cup of delusion and bitterness."
    a) Marc Twight
    b) Walter Bonatti
    c) Michael Kennedy
    d) The Verm

If you said a or b, you're probably right, but Bonatti wrote that in 1964, when Marc was first autographing diapers, so we'll credit Walter. Bonatti, widely considered to be the greatest alpinist ever, had twice attempted the southwest pillar of the Dru with strong partners. Both times the Dru beat him back. Combined with his epic shortly before on K2, Bonatti was starting to doubt himself. In *On the Heights* he wrote, " . . . I no longer believed in anything or anyone. I was nervous and irascible with everyone, sick of everyone, bewildered, without ideals, sometimes even desperate without any apparent reason. . . . when someone suggested that K2 had done for me, I was seized with a paroxysm of weeping and what I suffered in silence no one could imagine. Then at last came the resurrection. One day, unexpectedly, a mad idea created by my spiritual depression occurred to me. I would return to the Dru and conquer it unaided and alone, and prove to myself that it was true that I was not finished."

At the time (1955), the southwest pillar of the Dru was *the* last great problem of the Alps. To attempt it solo was unthinkable. Bonatti succeeded in a five-day effort, one of the greatest feats in climbing history, but only after a terrific struggle and a series of terrible mishaps.

2. Which of the following accidents occurred on the third day of Bonatti's successful attempt?
    a) He smashed his ring finger while hammering in a pin, slicing off the tip and one third of the nail.
    b) Inside his pack a bottle of cooking spirits was punctured by a piton, contaminating half of his food.
    c) He dropped his bolt kit.
    d) He spilled a beer.

If you answered d, you're a winner. Having mastered the "exasperating" difficulties of *The Lizard* pitch, Bonatti kicked back for a beer before tackling the Red Slabs. There were no pop tops back then, so Bonatti poked a hole in the can with his ice hammer. The pick of the hammer stuck fast in the can, while beer foam jetted out of the hole stinging Bonatti's wounded hands and chapped face. This would be enough to send weaker climbers down, but, experienced alpinist that he was, Bonatti had packed *two* beers, as well as a small flask of cognac. By the way, if you answered a or b you were only off by a few days; both of these incidents happened on the first day of the climb. If you answered c, you're a loser and Bonatti would doubtless tell you so. He was adamantly against the use of bolts. "With the use of expansion bolts . . . conditions are greatly changed," he wrote. "The sense of the unforeseen almost entirely disappears and so too the challenge of the climb itself and the meaning of the word 'impossible.' . . . I would even go so far as to say that such sterile results are attained not only by the use of such climbing aids, but even by the fact of carrying them during the ascent, perhaps at the bottom of the rucksack, without any intention of using them, since the very knowledge that one can make use of them at any moment destroys the spiritual value of the climb."

While we're on the subject of bolts, let's talk about the most famous bolter of them all—Warren "Batso" Harding. Though both Bonatti and Harding had reputations for being tough as nails, they don't share the same climbing ethics. Harding likened the phobia concerning bolts as "almost comparable to the Puritans' aversion to and fear of sex." Harding's all-night drillathon up the final headwall pitch of *The Nose* is one of the most famous of Yosemite tales. His ascent of *The Wall of the Early Morning Light* is one of the most infamous.

3. Which of the following companies sponsored Harding and Dean Caldwell on this latter climb?

a) Rawl
b) Bosch
c) BlueWater
d) Christian Brothers

Let's look up the answer in Batso's book *Downward Bound*. "Now, as we waited out the bad weather, the excitement of the impending climb precipitated almost constant partying. Dave Hanna had lined up some sort of business relationship with Christian Bros. winery. It seemed C.B. might be interested in some action photos for advertising. How exciting! Now we're getting somewhere! Grandes professionales!"

The first photo shoot took place on a small ledge atop the first pitch. A tip for all you sponsor hunters out there—red wine photographs better than white, so do like the pros and fill those crystal wine glasses with cabernet sauvignon. Pity the fool who answered a or b. Despite the fact that Harding drilled 330 holes on this route (not all used for bolts; some he drilled for his invention, the bathook), he doubtless saved more money by having his wine supplied for him than his bolts. So nix a. Also nix b as cordless rotary hammers were still over a decade away. Give yourself half credit if you answered c, because Warren was retro-sponsored by BlueWater when he did a cameo appearance in one of their ads in 1988.

Climbers have long been known to celebrate their successes with a nip off the old bottle. Doubtless, alcohol is poor fuel for climbing, but in a roundabout way it has helped many a climber's career maintain momentum. Nothing makes you forget that hangover like a good 40-foot runout the morning after.

4. *Match the following climbers with their quotes:*
   Adrian Burgess
   Warren Harding
   Anderl Heckmair
   John Sherman
   Joe Simpson
   Don Whillans
   Bugs McKeith
   a) "(My partner) who was an absolute teetotaler, refused to touch a drop of this agreeably burning and warming energy-food. For my part I felt a pleasant warmth diffuse through my stomach and was glad that I had often trained on alcohol."
   b) "It was one of those brilliant ideas that tend to occur soon after you've eaten the worm at the bottom of the tequila bottle."
   c) In response to an Outward Bound type who has said, "I personally believe in attacking a hard climb as if it were a military problem—prepare for battle!" this climber said, "Oh well, (my partner) and I were not all that aggressive or well organized—it was more like preparing by bottle. Hiking to and from the liquor store, lifting all those heavy wine jugs around—great training!"
   d) "I started to climb, the sweat squirting out. It was hard,

no doubt about it. I was overweight, full of beer and not at all fit . . . "

e) "Last night's Cooper Stout was front-pointing up my forehead."

f) "Certainly for two months of the winter it had been the bane of my life and although my tactics might seem questionable to some, I for one have enjoyed every minute of it, from the red wine and dope nights in the cave to the neckiest moments on the climb . . . "

g) "In the space of two minutes, the entire bar was wrecked. It had been a good night. And not one climber was hurt."

The answers are as follows:

a) Anderl Heckmair, who did the majority of leading on the first ascent of the North Face of the Eiger. This passage, from My Life as a Mountaineer, refers to his ascent of the north face of Grandes Jorasses, in which he attributed his lack of frostbite to nipping off the bottle. His partner suffered frostbite.

b) Joe Simpson in *This Game of Ghosts*. He and a pal had just decided to ride a children's sled off a ski jump. In midair they realized it was a bad idea.

c) Warren Harding talking about *The Wall of the Early Morning Light* in *Downward Bound*.

d) Ha, you thought that was me. It was Don Whillans in *Portrait of a Mountaineer*. Upon first reaching Yosemite, Chuck Pratt insisted they party a bit, then he said it was time to go climbing. Whillans: "I squinted at the bearded, tanned face. Surely he couldn't be serious. Even though I was accustomed to drinking much stronger brews than the rather watery canned beer we were then downing, I was none too sober and neither, as far as I could see, was Chuck."

e) Yours Truly.

f) Bugs McKeith, pioneer of waterfall ice climbing in Canada, writing about the first ascent of Nemesis in the *Canadian Alpine Journal*.

g) Adrian Burgess from *The Burgess Book of Lies*. In this story a group of English-speaking climbers have just trashed the Alpenstock Drugstore, a bar in Chamonix, in retaliation for the waiters having beat up a Brit the night before for shoplifting a candy bar.

Hangovers, rockfall, storms, crevasse plunges—all have long been recognized as potentially career-shortening hazards. Back when climbing was what Hemingway would call a sport, there was another hazard considered just as threatening and even more insidious.

5. *Who said this of women?* *"It's true that these charming creatures constitute a serious menace for many a mountaineer, often diverting him from his ideals and aims."*

    a) Al Burgess
    b) Hermann Buhl
    c) Aleister Crowley
    d) Anderl Heckmair

The correct answer is b. Buhl was best known for his amphetamine-driven solo first ascent of Nanga Parbat. Thirty-one climbers had died attempting this mountain before Buhl climbed it (not counting Rand Herron, who survived the mountain only to die falling off the Second Pyramid in Cairo on the way back from Kashmir). Nevertheless, Buhl succumbed to temptation. In his autobiography, *Nanga Parbat Pilgrimage* (also published as *Lonely Challenge*), he recalls his friends saying, "We can see Hermann's finished, now that he's started with the girls!" Buhl was confident, though, and wrote, "But I understand myself well enough. . . . " Or did he? Later he got married and on the day of his wedding the sight of his bride in her gown was too much for him. He admits that "in that instant I forgot all my worries and cares and—I humbly beg their forgiveness—the Mountains too."

Heckmair was tougher. In *My Life as a Mountaineer*, he wrote, "Occasionally in my life I have come to places where the way divided. Always I have chosen the one that led back into the mountains, even when a woman stood in the other road." Al Burgess wrote in *The Burgess Book of Lies*, "The girls saw that we obviously were far more interested in climbing than in spending time with them." What were you thinking, Al? In 1902 Crowley was deputy leader of the first expedition to K2. He set the then-recognized altitude record of approximately 22,000 feet. He said, "No man who allows a woman to take any place in his life is capable of doing good work. . . . A man who is strong enough to use women as slaves and playthings is all right." Hmmm, and they call me a sexist. (PC types rejoice: Crowley probably only tied a record set 400 years earlier—Incas left ruins at 22,055 feet on the summit of Llullaillaco in the Andes.) Before I get into more trouble, I'd better change the subject. Let's talk about amputations.

6. *Who wrote the following passage?* *"They opened the door wide and with a sort of old broom made of twigs, they pushed everything onto the floor. In the midst of a whole heap of rubbish rolled an amazing number of toes of all sizes which were then swept onto the platform before the startled eyes of the natives."*

a) Ed Webster
b) Barry Bishop
c) Maurice Herzog
d) Reinhold Messner
e) Mike O'Donnell

Ah, yes, a giveaway. This was Herzog, who lost all his fingers and toes after the 1950 first ascent of Annapurna (the first of an 8000-meter peak). Herzog dropped his gloves on the descent. His mind was dulled by lack of oxygen—"Never for a minute did it occur to me to use as gloves the socks which I always carry in reserve for just such a mishap as this." All of his amputations took place in the open and without anesthetics. Many of his (and fellow summiteer Louis Lachenal's) toes were cut off during a train ride and swept out the door when the train stopped at the next station. Read the classic *Annapurna* for the whole story.

For extra credit: between all of the above climbers, could you come up with a complete set of digits?

The answer is no. You would still be missing the two biggest toes on the left foot (the left foot, due to poorer circulation, is more prone to frostbite than the right foot). Bishop suffered his frostbite on the first American ascent of Everest in 1963. He was also on the first ascent of Ama Dablam in 1961. He refused morphine for the amputation of all his toes and the tips of several fingers; instead, he relied on self-hypnosis to vanquish the pain. Messner is the greatest high-altitude mountaineer of all time. He lost six toes on Nanga Parbat. Webster lost eight fingertips and three toes on the first ascent of the Kangschung Face of Everest, earning him a spot in the Best of the 1980s edition of *Trivial Pursuit*. Upon meeting Messner in a Lhasa hotel after climbing Everest, Webster said to him, "A lot of people tell me we look kinda similar." (Because of their identical hair and beard styles, Webster's friends dubbed him Tiny Rheini.) Messner looked at Webster's injuries and said, "Oh no. First I must lose some more fingers, and you must lose some more toes." (By that time, 1988, Messner was down to just two toes left.) The Himalaya isn't the only place to get frostbite—O'Donnell, after surviving multiple trips to the Himalaya, lost parts of three toes from his left foot in a storm on Longs Peak in Colorado.

Many of us go to the mountains to escape life in the city. Frostbite is one of the risks we take. But what about bullets?

7. *Who claimed to have pulled a gun on his partner while on the mountain and forced him to continue climbing?*

a) Marc Twight to Scott Backes on Mount Hunter
b) Henry Barber to Rob Taylor on Kilimanjaro
c) Aleister Crowley to Guy Knowles on K2
d) John Sherman to Scott Franklin on Teewinot

It was Aleister Crowley, the self-proclaimed Beast 666, a master of the occult who filed his teeth to points, engaged in sexual excesses with freaks, and was dubbed "the wickedest man in the world" by the British press. Crowley's version of the gun-pulling incident on K2 is different from the generally recognized version in which Crowley, delirious with malaria, pointed the pistol at Knowles. Instead of continuing up, Knowles slugged Crowley in the gut, disarmed him, and started down the mountain.

So much for escaping the city. Maybe just ditching school is the key to climbing success.

8. *Who was the following said of?*

"Leaving school was no sad wrench for _____. He left and that was all there was to it. No doubt a lot of the staff were relieved to see him go, and no doubt the residents along _____'s route from home to school breathed a sigh of relief when they noticed how peaceful things had suddenly become; but they weren't any more relieved than _____ was.

a) Joe Brown
b) Don Whillans
c) Royal Robbins
d) Ron Kauk

This is a tough one as all of the outstanding climbers above were high-school dropouts. The answer is Don Whillans. He and Joe Brown were the famous "climbing plumbers" who made up the core of the Rock and Ice club, a group instrumental in the development of modern free climbing. The quote above came from *Portrait of a Mountaineer,* the biography of Whillans. For more on the Rock and Ice club, see also Joe Brown's *The Hard Years.*

Well, that's it. Had history tests been that much fun in high school, maybe those guys would have stayed in. Now for the scoring.

If you scored 90–100 percent on this test, you are obviously a washed-up climbing junkie desperate to find your own niche in climbing history. Michael Chessler and his accountants like you.

If you scored 50–90 percent, you have doubtless learned how much more fun climbs are when you know something of their history. Whoa, this must be where Verm hurled on the second ascent.

If you scored 30–50 percent, you need to take some rest days and pick up a good book; otherwise, your elbows will be history.

If you scored 1–30 percent, you're average. How does that feel?

If you scored 0 percent, you have more in common with me than you probably care to. That's right where I was when I started climbing. If this scares you, make your next approach to the library.

Climbing, June 1996

The Eleventh Commandment

THE LETTER CAME TO ME WITH no return address, just a Canadian stamp and a Canmore postmark. Despite its amusing historic content, it was still just chain mail, promising riches if I forwarded it, and tragedy if I didn't. As I balled it up, I wondered why anyone would want to burden me with such bullshit and responsibility. It rimmed off the lip of the trash pail, a shot I usually drill, and dropped into the shadowy corner behind to keep company with the spiders, bottle caps, and dust bunnies.

Five days later I was sipping beers with a friend on an Estes Park porch. We were watching an incredible lightning display over Lumpy Ridge and one-upping each other with the usual hair-on-end-buzzing-rack-Saint-Elmo's-fire stories. Just then, a tremendous flash and crackling roar came from the parking lot 15 yards away. Kids screamed, dogs barked, and there was an eerie hissing of air escaping from exploded tires. My friend's car was killed instantly—back window shattered, tires flat, engine dead. Three feet away, my van had apparently survived unscathed, an illusion I held until the storm had passed by and I slid open the side door and saw the smoldering hole in the roof.

Throughout history, people have viewed bolts of lightning as portents. I viewed it as an unnecessary hassle and a $250 deductible on my comprehensive coverage. I gave no thought to the letter.

That is until four weeks later. Bad decisions and bad luck had me stranded 1,000 feet up the Eigerwand suspended by three steel teeth in a rotten curtain of verglas, a bunting glove frozen to the rock, and a crumbling dollop of snow beneath my crampons. Between curses

I begged for forgiveness from my friends, my family, and my dog. I promised that if I lived through this one, I would forward the letter 50,000 times over. It's time to live up to that promise.

What follows is that letter. Be warned, you may stop reading now, or you can go on. Should you continue past this paragraph you will be rewarded for your actions, and held liable for any inaction.

Dear Friend,

Fame and fortune are being passed to you with this letter. Your dreams will come true, your wishes granted. Within four days of receiving this letter good luck will come your way— hidden holds, magic route finding, hitherto unknown stamina, bon temps.

This letter is over 3000 years old. It is a gift from the gods. Good luck to those who would ascend as near to heaven as they could reach on earth. It has been translated into 100 languages and added to weekly. The first copy was addressed to a Hebrew mountaineer who bore a strange resemblance to Charleton Heston. Upon bagging a new directissima on Mount Sinai he found three stone tablets on top. Two were to become the property of Christian mythology. The third would become the property of the family of mountaineering. Upon that tablet it stated "Thou Shalt Be Lucky and Live Long, but only if you pass this tablet on within four days and make beaucoup sacrifices to God." The adventurer safely descended only to discover some hanky-panky going on with a golden calf. In a fit of pique, he smashed two of the three tablets, and forgot to pass along the third tablet to his climbing buddies. For the next 40 years, he and his people wandered the desert suffering from earthquakes, plagues, fires, thirst, and war. Only then did he remember the third tablet. He passed it off to his bros at the local boulders, then, at age 120, made a stunning ascent of Mount Pisgah from whose summit he viewed the Promised Land.

Such phenomenal luck can be yours, and cheap too. Twenty copies forwarded, and $20 to the person who passed this luck to you. Given three millennia of inflation, this is the bargain of a lifetime. Need proof, read on.

In May of 1492, Antoine de Ville received the letter and promptly passed it on to another adventurer named Columbus. Soon thereafter, de Ville was awarded with a healthy sponsorship from the king of France, and on June 28th of that year he stood atop Mont Aiguille, having bagged the first recorded technical ascent in the history of mountaineering. Furthermore, his feat was not repeated for 342 years. Columbus on the other hand laughed at the letter and tossed his copy out. Needless to say, he was a failure as a mountaineer. While seeking a direct passage to India and the virgin peaks of the Himalaya, bad luck assaulted him. He was stopped by an entire continent, and had the additional misfortune to land upon an island with nary a boulder to pump out on.

In 1865 the letter was first translated into in English. Seven copies arrived in Zermatt on July 10th. Meticulous Swiss postal records indicate that only three copies were forwarded. On the 14th, four bodies plunged 4000 feet to end up on the Matterhorngletscher.

More than one copy of the letter has been found at the base of the Eiger. The first, dated 1935, read "My dear Max and Karl, whatever you do please forward this before you go up." Another, dated 1966, said, "John—I know you don't believe in superstition, but it couldn't hurt to forward this."

Hindsight is 20/$20.

On Chogolisa a memorable exchange took place on the descent. "I tell you Hermann, if you had forwarded that letter we wouldn't be in this whiteout now." "Don't be a fool Kurt. It didn't stop us on Broad Peak. Now you just lead on and I'll be right behind you."

At the advent of World Cup climbing competition the coach of the French national team passed out copies of the letters and stamped envelopes to each of its stars. In the next several years French climbers disqualified in early rounds were routinely given free passes to the finals.

Twenty copies and 20 dollars are all it takes. Send them today. Don't risk another torn tendon. Don't tempt that serac.

This letter has been around the world 40 times and atop all the 8000-meter peaks.

The luck will come to you in unexpected ways. In the 1960s a Californian surfer of French Canadian descent was munching cat food burritos to pursue his climbing dreams. One day he went hungry, so he could buy 20 stamps. He mailed his jumars to the person who sent him the letter. He wished to become tall. He became a multimillionaire clothing magnate instead. His joking, dour-faced sidekick failed to forward his copy. Nevertheless, he wished for a real first name. Everyone calls him by his last name. He is now a substitute teacher.

Going to the Alps? Britain? Scared you'll waste your whole vacation climbing plastic and watching it rain outside? 20 copies. 20 bucks.

In the late 1970s, a young punk mountaineer from Seattle broke the chain—despite numerous climbing successes, sponsors shun him—and has been miserable ever since. His column in Climbing lasted one issue.

However another northwestern climber passed on the letter 50 years ago. Since then his fecundity of first ascents, as well as his luck with the ladies has made him a legend. He was not the only mountaineer to experience sexual rewards from passing on the letter. From the Canadian Rockies comes this report: "My husband had an old copy of the letter he had kept. It wasn't until he inadvertently threw his ropes off of Nanga Parbat that he made the pledge to forward the mail. Hours later they discovered a fixed duffel bag left on the mountain with enough food, fuel, and rope to get the team down safely. But I'm getting off the subject. It used to be that he could please me but six times in a day. Our marriage was in peril. But since he passed on the letter I'm proud to say he's up to ten times a day and we're shooting for the dirty dozen. Not bad for a pudgy 39-year old."

Meanwhile, across town another married couple received the letter. The wife forwarded copies and was rewarded with copious quantities of strong tasty beer. Her husband poohpoohed the letter. His pride-and-joy testpiece ice climb was flooded by a sea of posers and down-rated drastically. The subsequent angst he experienced caused his hemorrhoids to flare repeatedly. Later, he forwarded the letter, and he is now happily divorced.

Bad luck is free. Good luck however, has a price. Believe it, you must not retain this letter. You must pass the magic on within 96 hours. Secondly you must send a check or money order for $20 (US funds or the equivalent in Swiss francs) to the person who sent this luck to you. Do not ignore this letter. It works.

So there you have it. No literary masterpiece, but try buying a letter grade anywhere else for less. Make checks payable to John Sherman and send them to Verm, c/o *Climbing* magazine. Thou shalt make me rich.

(I got some "funny money" sent to me c/o Climbing, *but nothing negotiable. Several people did tell me they quit reading after the warning.)*

Climbing, May 1998

Night Climbers Versus the Gym Dandies

Why buildering is better

IN THE NEVER-ENDING PURSUIt of beefier forearms and bigger numbers, climbers created the artificial climbing wall. I'm told the first such wall was built in England at Leeds University in 1964. Their artificial wall lies in a bleak, narrow hallway. Dark bricks make up the two-story vertical walls and every once in a while a brick is inset, outset, or chipped away a bit to create holds. None of the holds move, yet people still go there to climb year after year, wiring every conceivable variation in the hopes that some Yank like myself might happen by for a sandbag.

On current artificial walls the surfaces are textured, the holds are changeable, and angles and curves replace the two-dimensionality of their predecessors. Drawing from the well of existing climbing technique, hold designers and wall architects create structures to be climbed. Routesetters follow suit and in the end climbers aren't forced to adapt themselves to meet a challenge. In this respect gyms suck. "Unclimbable" terrain is the forge from which new technique emerges. Still, gyms are businesses and no gym owner can be expected to devote expensive wall space to routes nobody can presently climb. Beginners may learn technique in a gym, but for experienced climbers, gyms offer little more than a social setting in which to get pumped. However, not all artificial surfaces suffer from this malady.

Just the other day, John Gill showed me one of his many buildering routes on the University of Southern Colorado campus in Pueblo. A horizontal pillar of pebbly concrete supports an overhang just at arm's reach above one's head. The idea is to leap up and clutch the 2-foot-wide, holdless support beam between your arms, squeezing so hard that you remain suspended and can swing your foot above your hands

49

into a neighboring crack. I had never seen a move like this in any gym, nor on any rock for that matter, and if I ever hope to do this problem I'll have to learn a new technique and develop new strength. Gill last did this problem when he was forty-eight, so I figure I have thirteen years to get that good; and who knows, maybe I'll find a problem that requires such a move on the rock someday.

Buildering has been an integral part of many climbers' training regimens since the inception of the sport of climbing. Why buildering is so great for one's climbing is that architects, like nature, do not design their walls to be climbed. Therefore the climber must face an unforgiving geometry. Adjusting to meet a challenge was always one of the fundamental premises behind climbing, but is in danger of becoming extinct in this chisel-happy, "create-your-own-challenge" age. Buildering encourages one to better one's self. And besides, it's fun.

As far back as 1937, buildering was the subject of a substantial (183-page) guidebook called *The Night Climbers of Cambridge*. Buildering has a long and healthy tradition at Cambridge, England. Students there lived inside walled campuses and were held to a strict curfew. Those students who gallivanted around town past the curfew had to climb over the walls to sneak back in. Some students took the skills thus acquired and continued upward to explore the rooftops and bag the many ornate spires bristling from the Cambridge skyline. Some of these "roof-climbers" were rock climbers as well, but most were into buildering for the sake of buildering alone.

Buildering, of course, is usually illegal, and therein lies some of its attractiveness. Whipplesnaith (the nom de plume of *Night Climbers's* author) puts it thusly: "The college authorities, acting presumably on purely humanitarian motives, have set their official faces against roof-climbing, and no one would have it otherwise. . . . this official disapproval is the sap which gives roof-climbing its sweetness."

In *Night Climbers,* Whipplesnaith describes the various skills developed for roof-climbing, including chimneying, drain-pipe technique, choice of shoes, concealment of ropes under academic gowns, and proper blood-alcohol content. He also stresses the code that one leave no trace of his ascent—avoidance of the authorities being the key to the health of the sport. Nevertheless, the students pulled a few pranks, such as strapping umbrellas to the top of the cathedral spires. These were shotgunned off by the authorities, only to be replaced with Union Jacks, upon which the patriotic sharpshooter refused to fire.

Whipplesnaith's crew was on good terms with the bobbies; it was the dons, porters, and proctors of the college who represented the greatest threat. Interestingly, a number of dons were once roof-climbers themselves, many brought into the sport for the sake of climbing King's Chapel.

"There is probably no building in the world which has aroused such interest among climbers as King's Chapel," writes Whipplesnaith. "Many men, not otherwise interested in night climbing, make it their ambition to climb it, and all save the very few are disappointed." The ornate twin spires of King's Chapel were for over a century the highest points in Cambridge, stretching 160 feet above the ground. Whipplesnaith suspects the first ascent to be as long ago as 1760, a coin with that date on it being found on a ledge 20 feet shy of the top. This coincides well with the invention of the lightning rod in 1752. King's Chapel had been fitted with such rods, and the thick metal conducting cable running from the top of King's Chapel to the ground provided the key to hoisting oneself up.

Night Climbers is a guidebook and heavy on move-by-move beta, some borrowed from buildering guides dating back to 1901. The beta is far more poetic than today's. For example: "Get a knee on to the lower cross-bar, using half a pull-up and half a press-up on the bar above, avoiding the slippery dust with the fingers by gripping as close to the edge as possible. Your hair is now standing on end. With a forearm on the upper bar and a hand on the crest, things become easier, although the last bit is fairly difficult, the height and the stone pavement below making it unpleasant—or, in technical parlance, 'interesting.'"

Dozens of photos complement the text, many showing certain crux moves and dashed lines of ascent. Obtaining these photos was tough work for both the cameraman, lining up and focusing his bulky camera in the dark, and the flashman, who lugged about a primitive flash the size of a wok. The explosion of the flash was sure to attract attention, lending considerable risk to the recording of these climbs.

My own buildering career started on the University of California's Berkeley campus in the mid-1970s. Berkeley has a glut of climbers and a dearth of rock, so it was only natural that climbers would seek out other things to climb. My first building climb was the classic 20-foot handcrack on Hildebrand Hall, moderate until you tried to do it in as few moves as possible, or as many moves as possible. Just around the corner was a brick wall dubbed the Penny Wall. At the time nobody had been to its top. The high point was marked by a penny sitting atop the last brick reached. The edges of the bricks were so shallow that a quarter would have fallen off. The half-digit crimps were hideous enough, but the real trick was trying to stuff your feet in the grooves. Roseanne would have better luck cramming into a size 6. We didn't have sketchpads in those days so the concrete slab at the base presented a real danger. The last time I saw the Penny Wall, there was a line of change on the top row of bricks.

One buildering technique I cared not to perfect was the belly flop I took out of a 7-foot-wide chimney near Worster Hall. Nevertheless, the full-body-stemming practice prior to the plunge came in handy years later on The Priest in Utah. The real prize on Worster Hall was not the chimney, but the Worster Liebacks. These lie in a small concrete dihedral buffed to a dull gloss. A narrow gap in the back housed a drain chute that could be laybacked facing either wall. To stay attached, one's feet had to be close to one's hands, which were on just a single-digit edge. The left side was a strength problem and the right side was a Nat problem. We could do the left side; Nat could do the right. Nat Smale was a natural-born powerhouse. He was also the only person who could squeeze the vertical walls of the smooth concrete support pillar under the Bear's Lair stairway and pull up on it.

I badly wanted to do the right side, but possessed neither the skill nor strength, so I resorted to shenanigans. I took a pair of Chuck Taylors and painted the soles with liquid neoprene. Then, to prevent the coating from oxidizing, I wrapped the shoes in Baggies. That night I pulled on my shoes, heel-walked to the base, laid my Baggies down to keep the soles clean, and chalked my fingertips. I pasted one foot to the wall; it stuck like a limpet. I pulled up easily. This was going to be casual. I pasted my other foot on the wall; it skidded like a roller skate. Somewhere along the way I had gotten dust on that shoe. My cockiness went limp. Nevertheless, I learned a good lesson—technique is preferable to trickery. I eventually struggled up it by fair means.

Man-made structures are generally less permanent than nature's constructions and the buildering at Berkeley evolved through the years. Dirt shoved under the balconies on Evan's Hall covered up one of the coolest underclings in the world. We were all pretty sad about this, except Nat, who had the balls to go to the neighboring balcony we couldn't reach from the ground, downclimb a 2-foot-deep arm-bar slot, hang off a kneebar, reach under the balcony for the inch-deep undercling slot, slap a foot against the wall, drop the knee out of the bombay slot, then shuffle across the dusty rail and back up the chimney on the other side. The rest of us mourned the loss of Evan's, but not for long. Soon the Optometry Building went up.

Cataract Corner, Optic Nerve, Poke in the Eye—the Optometry Building was a bonanza for Berkeley builderers. The concrete-form walls were pocked at roughly 2-foot centers and every 10 feet or so a flared, inch-and-a-half-deep groove shot up vertically. The walls were raw, stark, and possessed a harsh geometric beauty. The boxy toes of our EBs (they seemed slim then) barely dented into the insubstantial pockets. Our fingertips strained on the slopers, shoulders wrenching our noses deep into corners capping roofs. The moves were like nothing else on campus.

Like our Cambridge brethren before us, we were constantly on the lookout for police. Having been caught, warned, and lectured to numerous times, we knew it was better not to run when a cop came up—unless we had been warned within the previous six months. Two warnings in six months equaled handcuffs, so when the math added up against us we ran, toes smashed into undersized EBs, sprinting down pathways the cruisers couldn't follow.

The one time the cops did catch up with us was at the University of Colorado. In cold weather, students in upper-story dorm rooms would chill six-packs on their windowsills. The buildings were faced with natural rock—inch-wide gaps between flagstones provided hearty handholds, and the jagged edges of the rocks left ample room for the feet. It was about as easy as vertical face climbing gets. One day Harrison Dekker and I spotted some tasty imports only a few stories up on a neighboring dorm. Doubtless the owner was too young to legally drink so we quickly pirated the swill, but not before some Goody Two-Shoes finked on us. The cops found us in Harrison's room consuming the evidence. Just like in the TV shows, they split us up and questioned us separately.

Throughout climbing history there have been great partnerships—Shipton and Tilman, Boardman and Tasker, Chouinard and Herbert. Much is said of these teammates' abilities to communicate wordlessly. So it was that day for Dekker and Sherman. We both conjured up identical alibis and the fuzz had no choice but to let us go back to our beers.

Since the advent of local rock gyms, American buildering has been in decline. What if gyms were designed differently, or by non-climbers? Would they produce better climbers?

Perhaps the closest man has come to intentionally mimicking nature is a wall I saw in a gymnasium in Australia. Like the Leeds wall, it's vertical and composed of inset and offset bricks. Which bricks were knocked out of alignment and the amount of inset or offset was determined by a computer programmed to give a random distribution. To this extent it was designed not to be climbed, but to imitate real rock. The wall itself looked staid and boring, but the opportunity to leave the horizontal beckoned. I pulled out my shoes and prepared to mount the wall when an employee accosted me.

"You've got to pay to climb this wall," he told me.
So much for simulating nature. We turned around and left.

(Rereading this piece filled me with nostalgia. Not so much for buildering, but for the days of a young body that decried rest. I haven't buildered for years, because nowadays I save every cell of connective tissue for real rock.)

Climbing, June 1995

It's Big, It's Bad, It's Retro-Trad

Verm proposes a solution to all ethical squabbling, and a new game for climbers to play

IF THERE IS ONE THING CLIMBERS love as much as ticking off a hard-fought goal, it's a good old-fashioned ethical pissing match. Bickering is perhaps the one aspect of climbing that hasn't changed in the last 500 years. Naturally, the existence of ethical controversies requires differences in style, but there needs to be more: a willingness to disrespect others.

Back in Basic Rockcraft (1971), Royal Robbins offered up a solution to climbers' ethical squabbling. He called it the First Ascent Principle. It suggested that if all climbers respected the style of the first-ascent party, then people wouldn't get pissed off because their routes were retro-bolted or chopped or whatever. His was the old live-and-let-live philosophy.

Close on the heels of the First Ascent Principle was the philosophy that a climber repeating an established route should climb in as good a style or better than that of the first ascent. If the climber wasn't ready, he waited until his skills improved. Success was then accompanied by a tremendous feeling of accomplishment, intensified by bringing oneself up to the level of a climb, instead of bringing the climb down to one's level. For me, these rewards have led to a life-long passion for the sport. When it comes time for me to get in the coffin, I'll climb in, and I won't pull on any gear.

It's hard for me to imagine approaching the sport in any other way, but plenty of climbers do. In the last decade, style of ascent has taken a nosedive, which is most obvious in the sport-climbing arena. Leading with all gear preplaced caters to the lowest common denominator. My 200-plus-pound cholesteroloholic nonclimber landlord could safely try *To Bolt or Not to Be* (5.14) at Smith Rock, but I'd never let him take the sharp end on the *First Flatiron* (5.4) near Boulder. Of course, if people want to spend their climbing careers clipping bolts and not enjoying the greater thrills offered by clean gear leads, that's their prerogative. At times, however, sport climbing and clean climbing come into conflict, breaking down the First Ascent Principle.

Sport climbs can infringe upon other climbs in three ways. Retro-bolted routes are the most obvious example. Short of adding more holds, slapping bolts into a climb previously done without them is the ultimate in bringing a climb down to one's own level. Take Eldorado Canyon's *Guenese*—it used to really mean something when you led that route. A couple of quarter-inchers and a questionable pin led to the section below the roof, where, if you bothered, you could stuff a wired Stopper behind a flexing flake. It was just psychological pro, because everyone who fell on those moves ripped the nut out, hurtled down the face, then stopped 5 feet off the deck. Embarking on that runout, you wondered if the aging upside-down pin would hold another fall. If you led that route you belonged to an exclusive club. Now there's a bolt there and a few more above. Today, if someone says he did *Guenese*, chances are he hasn't shared the experience of those who put it on the line.

I could fill this column (and several more) with a list of other such emasculated routes, but let's get on to a more insidious form of contempt: establishing new bolted lines close enough to existing routes to alter their character. The best example is a line Richard Rossiter bolted next to *Perilous Journey* on Eldorado's Mickey Mouse Wall. *Perilous Journey* is another of the routes where a lead or solo (the rope being excess weight on this one) puts you in a very exclusive club. If you get in trouble on *Perilous Journey,* you either have to climb through, downclimb, or deck out. With the new bolts nearby, you could weenie off to the side. When I heard about these bolts I was foaming at the mouth to chop them, though it would mean departing from my long-standing policy of only removing bolts added to routes on which I participated in the first ascent. The debate as to whether I should change policy was moot. I was told I'd have to get in line to chop them.

That atrocity is gone, but not so another route from the same drill—*Bird of Fire* on Chiefshead in Rocky Mountain National Park. Here the line is removed enough from the adjacent gear-protected lines that their feeling of commitment is still pretty much intact. However, the overall experience of the wall is diminished. It used to be a major accomplishment to do a route on the big, brooding northwest face of Chiefshead. Now anyone can join the Chiefshead Club if they can hike 5 miles and clip a rope through a carabiner. Again we have disregard for the first ascents of others.

Another prime example of such disrespect occurred on Chinamans Peak in the Canadian Rockies last year. The route *Sisyphus Summits* recently reduced that face from a serious balls-out undertaking to a single-rope, eleven-draw sport route. Blob Wyville, a Canmore local of umpteen years who lives in the shadow of Chinamans Peak, was so disgusted he penned an opinion piece entitled "Sissys on Sisyphus" in the Calgary Mountain Club's newsletter. In it he reminded us that the history of climbing has been one of striving to improve upon the style of climbs done before. He also informed us that local tradition has supported the removal of fixed protection when a route has been climbed without it, resulting in the cleaning up of many fixed pins.

Wyville's opinion piece led me to an interesting thought. Sport climbing has been dying a natural death lately. The fast-food nature of sport climbing provides only fleeting satisfaction; hence, guys like Jim Karn and Ben Moon have been seen swinging ice axes lately. Karn even asked me for a "Sport Climbing is Neither" bumper sticker. Take a gander at the Who's Cool column and you'll see more and more climbers labeling themselves as "all-arounders." The sport-climber label, now so intimately associated with Mountain Dew ads and MTV, has become stale. The young climbers of today are no more interested in mimicking Watts's and Karn's style than Watts and Karn were in emulating Barber and Bachar. So what direction can the sport head now? Retro-Trad ascents.

Retro-Trad is of course a misnomer. I'm not talking about going back to traditional style. My God, that would mean climbing like Robbins. That would mean respecting others' first ascents. (OK, so Robbins slipped on the Dawn Wall; he admitted it, though.) The new school of Retro-Trads, call them Rads, will attack the bolted climbs of the world with a rack of gear around their broad bronzed shoulders. They'll clip as few bolts as possible, protecting themselves with clean gear, and they'll remove the bolts they don't use. This will benefit the climbing world in many ways.

First off, it won't be an embarrassment to be a climber anymore. My friend Rufus teaches high school. He has also taken a 150-foot fall on El Cap *without* leg loops, then gone back a week later and finished the route. When he told his students he was a rock climber they instantly labeled him a wimp, associating him with all those guys out there climbing in those cute little Lycra tights. Rad ascents will put adventure back into climbing. Climbers will bring themselves up to new levels of strength, boldness, and commitment.

Secondly, Retro-Trad ascents will benefit access. By removing bolts from the crags, climbers will be seen as environmentally friendly. Anyone who has dealt with land managers knows that bolting is one of their biggest concerns about climbers' impacts. Many land managers view bolts as a symbol of climbers imposing their will upon Mother Nature without regard for environmental concerns or other user groups. They don't buy the line that bolts are just cigarette-sized chunks of steel in the rock. Less bolts, fewer problems.

What about climbers' egos? How will we keep them intact? Once again Rad ascents come to the rescue. As the amount of unclimbed rock diminishes and the climbing population soars (one estimate has it doubling in the next three years) there will be fewer first ascents per capita to do. Nevertheless, one line can have numerous Retro-Trad ascents. Joe Blow can get his name in *Hot Flashes* for bypassing half the bolts on *Scarface*. Then Jane Blow gets a contract extension for eliminating three more via some strategic clean gear in pockets. Finally Joe Jr. makes the cover of *Climbing* for doing it all clean. More glory per square inch of rock; this trend could last for decades.

What about the climbing industry? Can they cash in on Retro-Trad ascents? Big time, baby—Big time cha ching. Hangers and quickdraws don't cost much; technologically advanced gear does. The Retro-Trad revolution will pump up sales quicker than Congress fattening the defense budget. Rad ascents will encourage the development of new gear, stuff that will put SLCDs on the mantel shelves next to ring angles and ten-point crampons. As the manufacturers get fat on sales, more sponsorship dollars will come available, and they'll go to those using the new clean gear.

How about national pride? I constantly hear how we have to catch up with the Euros, that they are the superior climbers. How did they get that way? By changing the rules. By missing out on the free-climbing revolution in the 1960s and '70s (free climbing in its original form, not hanging on gear) and going straight from "French Free" ascents to hangdogging, the French got the jump on everyone. It's easier to be "superior" if you play by a different set of rules. By embracing the Retro-Trad ethic now, North Americans can once again be on top where we like to be.

What about the sport climbers who will lose their precious fixed pro? How will they continue to pursue maximum gymnastic difficulty on the rock? By bouldering and toproping. It doesn't take an Einstein to figure out that you can do harder gymnastic climbs if you don't have to let go to clip gear. Imagine how lame the level of Olympic gymnastic competition would be if the contestants stopped after each tumbling move to clip a bolt. Someday some badass will toprope the world's hardest climb, then move on to a harder toprope project instead of bolting and "leading" the last one for the photographers. At that time, gymnastic climbing standards will soar. For those sport climbers who still need to clip bolts we have no shortage of gyms, plus the continent of Europe.

More adventure, more access, more glory, more pride, more money: the Retro-Trad juggernaut is rumbling our way. Is it unstoppable? There is one alternative. Those climbers who plugged all the retro-bolts in the old trad routes or bolted new lines on traditional crags could quickly remove all their bolts and send them to me at *Climbing* magazine with a signed note apologizing to those climbers, past, present, and future, whose climbing experience they've diminished. At the same time, those folks who have chopped bolts from routes first done as sport climbs can replace the bolts and send in their apologies as well. This would mean subscribing to the First Ascent Principle and treating other climbers with the respect we all desire.

Naaahhh, forget I even mentioned it. Before that happens, we'll all be front-pointing in Hell.

(Needless to say, nobody mailed in any bolts, but one letter-writer did accuse me of promoting "excessive maiming and dying." Retro-Trad ascents remain a fantasy and access problems are worse than ever. Nevertheless, bickering is thriving, thanks in large part to the Internet. Alas, this invention removes some of the thrill of argument, as climbers can piss each other off without risking fisticuffs. Call it Sportwhining.)

Climbing, December 1995

Boulevard of the Behemoths

BUSCH AIN'T BAD ON A HUMID JUNE day in Virginia. I know, I just slammed a quart for lunch. It seemed the right thing to do after spending the morning on a successful trophy hunt. No, not turkeys or whitetail; we were after elusive quarry, the *Scotchgard immobilius,* better known as the shag-topped solescrubber, or to the layperson, the fixed rug.

For years fixed rugs were an endangered species, just clinging on in a few areas best suited to their needs—urban boulder fields rife with spray paint, broken glass, and soft, lazy climbers. But in the '90s the population has exploded, creating a heyday for the modern hunter.

I'd been to the famous holes in the west: Indian Rock near Berkeley, with its thin, but feisty towels; Ilium Boulders near Telluride, a hidden gem where the soft, drippy rugs stand out in front of a background of harsh and inhospitable mountains; and of course Morrison, where the Black Hole has set records for trophy hauls for years. I've even pulled a few lunkers out from Hueco Tanks, though the dry climate and slabby landings don't generally favor this otherwise hardy species. As far as the East goes, I hadn't been there for a couple of years. I surely wasn't prepared for what I'd find there in the '95 season.

I was traveling with D. Changeling, a cagey newcomer skilled in ferreting out fixies in the overhunted canyons of Stoney Point. We had two months to scour the Midwest and East. I suspected this is where the truly big brutes resided, the grandaddies that took hours to haul in. I first got a notion of how big rugs grew east of the Rockies when I visited Chandler Park in Tulsa, Oklahoma. There my local guide took me to a little-known pocket where I reeled in the heftiest single specimen in my career, a plump deep shag buck with a mature growth of moss and microorganisms. I struggled with it throughout the descent, its slime-infested haunches and fifty-pound heft proving a true test for my oaken arms. But like Tracy hugging Hepburn, Fields gripping a gimlet, Butkus clenching a quarterback, I hung on. At long last, stumbling through the poison ivy, tripping over the thorny vines, and slipping through the mire, I broke its will. By the time I reached the road we were both exhausted, but I proved stronger and the final quarter mile back to the van was as much victory parade as work.

D. and I cruised the Midwest north of Oklahoma with only limited success. It appeared that Chandler was an anomaly, one of those rare days when you pull in a legend that the oldtimers call The General. I was beginning to get depressed and suspected that all the litterbugs had moved into the gyms. Fortunately, I was wrong: New England proved more fertile. Only at the most obscure areas were we skunked. Nevertheless, I suspect we could have done just as well out West. A month had gone by and we'd only pulled in nine keepers.

Finally our luck changed on the banks of the Potomac, just a bent page and a scandal west of D.C. There the rocks were formed ideally for rapid growth of carpets. Planes of schist slice into the mud at a 60-degree angle, forcing sheets of water from the frequent rains to form long bogs at the base. The carpets residing in this muck quickly become fat. These were tricky son-of-a-guns and hard to track down— sometimes you'd only see a palm-sized patch of pile breaking the surface. We found the best way to sneak up on these was to imitate climbers. The rugs seem to have no fear of being picked up by them. First we'd crank up the boom box really loud, then with chalk on hands and sneer on lips we'd nonchalantly flick a tape wad or cigarette butt onto the ground. When the rug least expected it, we'd grab a corner and heave mightily.

We tugged sixteen chartbusters out of the muck, but at the same time some real beauts got away. The rapid growth rate of Carderock rugs is offset by a short life cycle. Some folks blame it on the acid rain. Whatever the cause, in just a few seasons even the proudest nineteen-dollar-per-square-yard tight loop bull rug will lose its weave and become just another twirly, spineless pile of slop. More than once we were fooled by these cagey codgers. Spilling a ten-dollar pitcher doesn't compare to the disappointment that comes from stalking a 20-square-footer, clutching it by the short curlies, jerking like a titan, and only coming up with a handful of rug ramen.

With a few weeks of vacation left, we bid Carderock adieu and headed south into Virginia. Virginia isn't known for its rug hunting, but for years I'd heard of a small area called Moorman's Boulders located five leagues northwest of Charlottesville. I was warned that there wasn't a whole lot there, just a pair of dinky yet delightful bouldering walls hiding in the hardwoods next to the tranquil Moorman River. Usually you don't see much climber trash in such an idyllic setting, but this place was a gold mine. The first wall, a scant 15 yards from the car, yielded four fair-sized specimens right off the bat. The real treasure, however, lay a hundred yards farther downstream. Imagine my glee when I emerged from the tunnel through the bushes to see a 50-foot-wide wall, overhanging, thick with chalk, and the entire base covered in carpets. We're talking everything from small carpet store samples to 30-square-foot remnants. Thirty square feet! Layer upon layer they were stacked: level loops, plushes, sculptures, even a Berber or two and in all the fashion shades—red and brown, yellow and brown, orange and brown, brown and brown. Not only that, there was indoor/outdoor too. The not-quite-natural Astroturf green brought tears to my eyes I tell you. This was it—Home of the Hogs, The Honey Hole, Boulevard of the Behemoths.

D. and I had already hauled three loads out when a local arrived. I'm sure he thought nobody knew of this place because you should have seen his jaw drop when he saw our remaining catch. It's a good thing there are no limits on rugs, otherwise the warden would have had us in for a good decade. I couldn't help showing off one rug to the kid. Only three by three, but eighteen pounds if it was an ounce—astonishing for a low-pile plush. The mud clung thick to both sides (Lucky Pierre from a three stack) and earthworms slithered in and out of the mesh. There was even a cute little centipede all yellow and squinting in the newfound daylight. The kid was speechless. Jealousy can do that. Fearful that we'd be back again, he told us "It wasn't this way two days ago. This is really rare." Typical local talk; they'll say anything to keep you away. I've got news, pal—your secret's out. You had your chance to clean up and you blew it. Nevertheless, I felt charitable and offered the kid a chance to get in on the action. I have to applaud his nobility as he declined, knowing the catch was not his doing, and let us have all the fun. He did offer that "there's a dumpster a mile down the road." There wasn't. Oh, those crazy locals.

Before we could get the haul loaded in the van we had to take hero shots. Before we could get the squabs lined up, another local arrived. Younger than the first, he was a slight boy just coming into some peach fuzz. He was heartbroken to see the pros had come in and scored huge. This was worse than the time his school's homecoming queen was caught running deep patterns with the rival school's halfback. He pleaded with me, "Can't you leave just a few back there for us?" His droopy basset hound eyes touched me. I felt cruel, like I'd yanked a pacifier away from a six-year-old, but I held firm. The kid had to grow up sometime.

I did what I could to console the boy. I talked about game management. How we had to take out the trophy specimens so that the young rugs to come could have a chance to get just as plump and juicy. I explained to him how hard climbing and an environmental ethic couldn't mesh. How there is no shortage of insecure, self-centered climbers desperate to ascertain their dominance over the rocks, to piss on the fire hydrant of nature. How these climbers would quickly reseed the areas. How climbers were dumb as dog chow; they still hadn't clued in to carrying their own compact, lightweight strip of carpet with them to and from the crags. How carpets carried home after each bouldering session stay clean and dry and always clean shoes better than dirt-choked fixed rugs. How cleaner shoes equate to highest level performance on the rock.

It was no use. The boy was crestfallen. He looked longingly at our booty. Thirty-two rugs in all. Over 200 glorious pounds of fiber and filth. He shuffled away with his head hung low. The young fellow was obviously in a tizzy, desperately clutching to the shreds of his rent-apart worldview and wondering if there was anything he could do about such injustice. The urge to catch up to him, clap him on the shoulder, and say "fret not" was great, but I checked myself. I knew this wouldn't be the last such haul from Moorman's Boulders.

(I feel this is my most successful piece. It combined a strong ethical stance with a hearty dose of satire and succeeded on both counts. After it ran, I received several calls from climbers who told me they laughed out loud reading it. The same callers told me that the next time they went bouldering, they couldn't leave without picking up the fixed rugs. I did receive one angry letter from a Moorman's local who felt that my article would endanger access if the landowner read it and found out that climbers were trashing his land.)

Climbing, August 1995

To V or Not to V

The sordid tale of the rating system every bit as open-ended as the egos that use it

WELCOME TO THE SMORGASBORD that is bouldering. The boulderer picks a problem from the menu, tastes the moves, digests the sequence, then kicks back on the summit with a pleasant fullness. Shortly thereafter, out plops a V-grade, and not surprisingly, the bigger the grade, the more stink it causes. Strangely, at this buffet, most climbers act like flies, preferring to buzz around the grade, rather than the entrée.

When it comes to stirring debate, no subject beats up a bigger froth amongst climbers than ratings. For decades bouldering was spared due to the simplistic, close-ended B-system: B1 equaled hard, B2 equaled stinkin' desperate, and B3 equaled unrepeated. There were relatively few boulderers to argue ratings and a problem's reputation rested more on its merits than on its rating. Problems were referred to by name, not as "the V11 2 feet left of Joe Hardboy's project." All this changed in the late 1980s with the birth of the V-system.

Hueco Tanks in the 1980s had a Wild West flair: lots of territory, not many climbers, and plenty of seedy diversions. There was so much unclimbed rock to go around that competition was mild at best. It was Fat City. Day after day, problem after problem went up. The majority of problems at Hueco were unrated, but a handful were labeled B1, and the odd desperate, B2. These grades were assigned in relation to the standard problems in Colorado: *Right Eliminator* and *The Standard Route* on the Mental Block being B1, *Left Eliminator* and the *Pinch Route* being the start of B2.

It was obvious that Hueco had many problems as hard as the *Pinch,* and quite a few harder. The B2 standard was getting clogged, and by definition one could not rate a repeated problem B3. As envisioned by John Gill in the 1960s, the B-system would be a sliding scale. By definition, B1 is as hard as the hardest roped climbs of the day. Hence, in the 1960s B1 would roughly equate to 5.10; in 1998 it should equal 5.14. Being close-ended, the B-system requires frequent downgrading. At some point in the 1970s, though, the scale got stuck. After awhile, the B2 rating given the *Pinch* and its peers was so hallowed that downrating it would be the action of an infidel. No one dared take that step, and eventually it was forgotten by most boulderers that B-grades were supposed to fluctuate. Thus, V-grades were born.

Originally V-grades were called H-grades, for Hueco grades. It turned out, however, that there was already an H-system of climbing grades developed by Henry Barber to denote seriousness. A, B, C, D, E, and down the line were all used in other systems as well. Not until J could we come up with a letter not yet used in some system (and since then, J has been used in Joshua Tree for jump problems). As all my shoes and other gear were marked with a V for Verm, and as this new Hueco system was as much my idea as my cohorts, one of my buds suggested we change H-grades to V-grades. I didn't argue.

V-grades were designed to unclog the B2 category, so originally V1 stood for bottom-end B2. The *Pinch Route* in Colorado and routes in Hueco as hard as the *Pinch* were assigned V1. Consequently, *Center El Murray* became the standard V1. The *Right El Murray* was called V2 or V3, as was *Mushroom Roof.* As originally conceived, the V-system was of no use to the majority of climbers in America. Most would never even break into V1.

Bucking tradition, the V-system popped out of the womb sporting a full head of hair and thick beard. Fully mature, it was nothing more than a macho pair of fists to beat one's chest with—none of that immature stuff, when a system tries to helpfully direct climbers toward routes of a given difficulty. This was all in good fun, as there were only about half-a-dozen of us using the system, and we never saw it going beyond our little clique—at least I didn't. That soon changed. Sick of being Hueco's walking, talking bouldering guidebook, I decided to set my knowledge of the park down on paper. That way people could get their answers from the book and I wouldn't have to spend each evening at the salad bar scribbling the same old topos on everyone's napkins.

Compiling the first Hueco bouldering guide was a much bigger task than I'd anticipated. Boulders were stacked upon boulders and each gully looked the same. As long as I was going to the effort to get everybody to the right holds on the right side of the right boulder,

I figured I'd go one step further, and give them grades for each problem as well. This is when V1 tumbled down to its current level. I figured bouldering was all about challenge. I wanted V1 to be a standard that would require effort from a fit novice. I reckoned a novice climber who could do ten pull-ups could do a safe V1, but only after a few tries. The original V1s now became V6s.

Often, I'm asked why I didn't use YDS grades. I feel YDS grades are best used to rate accumulated difficulty, not single moves or short sequences. In the case of continuous boulder problems over 20 feet long—problems which depend more on stamina than power—I think YDS grades are more suitable than V-grades. After all, quite a few boulder problems are longer than some sport climbs. The French have recognized this difference as well. They have two grades for bouldering: a regular bouldering grade, and a "traverse" grade for longer problems. I once suggested grading longer problems with YDS grades (e.g., V5.13+), but this never caught on. Just as few people were willing to downrate their favorite B2 when standards increased, nobody wanted V-grades stripped from a cherished endurance problem.

Being the ego-bloated radsters we were, we hadn't bothered rating any problems below original V1. For that matter, nobody had. It was up to me to climb or reclimb the 900+ problems in the guide to assign them ratings. This led to the definition of a problem's V-grade being how hard John Sherman says it is. You might imagine it quite handy to have your very own rating system, but it comes with a heavy responsibility. For instance, I could downrate Fred Nicole's *Slash* from V14 to V2 if I wanted, and by definition, that would be its appropriate V-grade. But this could wreak havoc on his career and his sponsors' gear sales, thereby dangerously tipping the economy of the climbing industry. So unless Fred sends me a late or underfed royalty check, I'll let the V14 stand for now.

As we've seen, I shoved V-grades back into rating system adolescence in an effort to help out visitors to Hueco Tanks. How long would it take then, for this system to remature into an ego-yardstick? Mere months. When the first Hueco bouldering guide hit the stands in 1991, the biggest V-grade listed in it was V9. Instantly the race was on to be the first to climb V10. Climbers would stop at nothing to win this race. Case in point: the earliest "first V10" claim sent to the mags was for a chiseled problem on an access-denied wall put up by a climber who had told me weeks before that a problem already published in the guide was definitely V10.

This could only lead to one thing—the race to put up the first V11. Currently, the race is on to climb the first V15. At the current rate of roughly one sponsor-stroking, contract-fulfilling breakthrough per year, we should get to V26 by the year 2010.

By bringing the joy of number chasing to bouldering, the V-system introduced legions to a sport they would otherwise dismiss. Why has the V-system become more popular than other bouldering rating systems? Because the numbers are bigger. Face it, B2 was a puny number. Who wants to chase that? Similarly, A5 is too small a number to get that scared for. Open the top end of the A-system and aid climbing would become hugely popular. That some piton or haulbag manufacturer hasn't popped the lid on A-grades yet is beyond me. That all the crash pad manufacturers don't send me a case of beer every Christmas is beyond me too.

Sometimes I think the V in V-system should stand for Virus, because of the speed with which it spreads. V-grades quickly radiated from Hueco throughout the country and even overseas. It has become the most prevalent bouldering rating system in the world. Australia, New Zealand, South Africa, Canada, and several other countries have all tested V-grade-positive. And even though we tossed their tea into Boston Harbor, the Brits have gobbled it up as well, swapping out the V-prefix for a B, and expanding the bottom end to assuage the lesser egos. Continental Europe is the last holdout, but for how long?

Most European areas use Fontainebleau grades, but some are already embracing V-grades. Given that the French have yet to win a war this century without our help, they seem bound to lose as always. Just as nine out of ten Frenchman understand English, but refuse to speak it, so too will V-grades flood their minds, yet never pass their lips. Fight as they may, Fontainebleau grades seem fated to succumb to superior numbers—who will want to climb 8a when for the same effort they could score a V11?

Much as I love to poke fun at the French, the above scenario brings me no joy. What started as a secret handshake in the cult of Hueco's hardcores turned into a monster. Every time I see a chiseled hold on a boulder, I know the demon has passed that way. The beast is a farce, possessing the trappings of bouldering, but none of the soul. Like Victor Frankenstein, I tried in vain to control and even to kill my unruly creation. Failing that, I disavowed it, and haven't rated a problem in years.

For years, I hated V-grades. Some sport climbers, knowing my hardcore traditional stance on roped climbing, took glee in calling me "The Father of American Sport Bouldering." They credited the current popularity of bouldering to my introduction of V-grades. In large part, I believe they're right. I imagine I know how devastated a father might feel when his son takes up figure skating instead of hockey. Later, the father comes to terms with it, accepts it as the way it is, and maybe that kid wins an Olympic medal. So what solace is there in all this? Besides seeing the V-system so rapidly evolve back into the joke it started as? I see three positives.

First, bouldering is bolt free and in that sense more acceptable to land managers. By enticing rock gymnasts to the short stones, it has spared some walls the agony of being drilled to death.

Second, some climbers hooked on bouldering via number chasing will mature and accept the bouldering experience as an end in its own, sans ratings. Bouldering then becomes a fulfilling, lifelong part of their lives.

And lastly, there is the grade-inflation aspect. Just recently I saw an Internet guide to a batch of boulders I'd been keeping mum about for years. Sure enough, the rediscovered problems all had V-grades. Nostalgically, I dug out the notebook topos I drew in 1991. Everything was now a grade or two higher.

There I was with my arm in a cast, climbing harder than before and all I had to do was log on. Without my topos, I couldn't remember 95 percent of the names or numbers I gave the problems, but I remembered the problems themselves. I remember the hard slick quartzite that would turn to sugar in places. I remembered sloping topouts, and desperate pock-marked slabs. I remember one problem that looked easy from the ground, even after spending an hour trying to leave said surface. I remember wondering if the wind would ever pile another foot of sand under one problem so that I could reach the first holds. I remember sheep bones under problems, eagles' nests on top, and ten-pound-test spider webs. I remember finding mining claims in a Mason jar, and a crayon drawing underneath one enormous boulder dubbing it the "Priceless Mansion." When the wind died it was so quiet one could imagine hearing mud cracks form in the nearby playa. Years from now, when today's developers of these boulderers stiffly sink into their La-Z-Boys, I hope they have similar memories. As with all climbing ratings, the true value of V-grades is in their ability to be forgotten.

BONUS:
A PRACTICAL GUIDE TO APPLYING THE V-SYSTEM

As mentioned above, having one's own rating system can be very handy. Case in point—those two V17s I put up yesterday didn't feel very hard. Any climber can enjoy equal success simply by creating his or her own rating system. Nevertheless, most climbers seem content to stick with V-grades. This being the case, I'm often asked what is the proper way to employ this system. I hope the following chart clears up any confusion.

V0: A problem you wouldn't admit to doing no matter how cool it was.

V1: A problem you would admit to doing, if it had loose holds, a death landing, and your partner backed off of it.

V2: A problem, if cool enough, that you would recommend to others to prove you're not a ratings snob.

V3: A problem you ruthlessly wire and incorporate into your warm-up routine, in the hopes that visiting partners will struggle on it.

V4: A problem that might give you trouble, but, "Hey, anything below V5 is so easy I can't tell the difference."

V5: A problem, if you were to live in Boulder, Colorado, that you might actually flash.

V6: A problem, if you were to live in Boulder, Colorado, that you would expect your girlfriend to flash.

V7: A problem you fell on repeatedly, but really, you could have flashed it.

V8: A problem you religiously avoid, because you're "saving it for the flash."

V9: A problem you have no chance of flashing.

V10: A problem you knew you could have done, even though your spotter took thirty pounds off for you, so you counted it anyway.

V11: A problem, if flashed, that you might get free shoes for, but only if you fax the mags this month.

V12: A problem you would do if only your fingers were a bit smaller, your reach a bit longer, your spotter more attentive, the weather more amenable, your shoes not blown out, your elbow not so sore from training, the sun not in your eyes, and you hadn't eaten that funky take-out Chinese the night before.

V13: A problem commensurate with your well-published abilities, that you deserve credit for, even though you didn't do it, because as the mags reported, "It was too humid."

V14: A problem only Fred Nicole could do, after you gave him the beta.

Climbing, March 1999

Training with the Verm

IN THE LAST COUPLE OF ISSUES of *Climbing* we've had Training with Ben Moon, Training with Bobbi Bensman, and Training with Geoff Weigand. I ask you, have any of these climbers done the Eiger? Summitted K2? Kissed the benchmark atop Mount Owen? No way. Which puts me one up on them already. I've done the Koven Route on Owen. Okay, so it took five tries, but it was awesome, and the survey marker was nice and clean against my lips.

Now I bet you're wondering how I train to pull off feats such as the Koven (III 5.2). About fifteen years ago I rigorously did weighted chin-ups for about two months. Then, in 1983, while on crutches recovering from a hip operation, I worked out on Nautilus machines for three months. Other than that my training has involved playing with plastic-handled squeeze grips and twirling a Dynabee for enough minutes to blow out the bearing. I haven't touched either in over ten years, so how do I muddle up anything harder than the Koven? It's all mental.

In a thousand-word column I could never describe all the mental-preparation tricks I've learned in the last twenty years, but I can give you one I picked up a couple years ago. One that is so simple and so effective you can treat yourself to Cheetos and malt balls for the rest of your life. You can cancel the rock gym membership and subscribe to HBO instead. You can rent a cart the next time you play eighteen holes. You'll climb better than ever and be happier about yourself. The trick: divorce yourself from ratings.

Most climbers would give up breathing before they give up their fixation with numbers. Why do numbers hold you back? Because they demand so much attention. Ratings are held up as the measure of climbing success, not how good you feel on top, or how hard you pushed your body, or what mental barriers you overcame. Many people get into climbing to escape the dollars-as-a-yardstick-of-success syndrome. But too often the intangible joy we feel when we first flow over the stone is supplanted by the same old value system, only here the currency is YDS-grades or V-grades or WI-grades. Soon, we pour energy into comparing ourselves with others, not with actually doing the moves.

I believe ratings systems hold the climbing world back. The professional climbing game lures many of the most gifted climbers. Sponsors demand column inches and column inches demand big numbers, hence number-chasing becomes rampant. Talent is spent competing at the sport, not mastering it. I've heard of climbers breaking holds off their own routes because somebody else downrated it. Was the feeling of success upon doing the route so fleeting that the number was all that counted? It's all going to look pretty silly in a decade or two when climbers are warming up on 5.14. People can always take your numbers away from you. If your pride is based on ratings then it will be stripped too.

The boulders have always been the traditional venue for breakthroughs in technical difficulty, and two boulderers in particular blew away the standards of their eras—John Gill and Jim Holloway. Their harder problems weren't repeated for decades, if at all. I'm hard pressed to think of any well-known climbs put up in the last decade that have gone more than five years without being repeated. Why did Gill and Holloway climb so hard? Because they were focused on climbing, not competition. Gill preferred bouldering in solitude. "I've always detested the extra energy you get by having spectators," he says. Early on, ratings preoccupied Holloway. He wanted to do B2 and put up B3s. "Later on I didn't care about the ratings at all," Holloway says. "I wanted to work on things that were hard for me." Indeed, Holloway's best efforts came after he dissed the ratings.

You could argue that Gill and Holloway, both noted physical-training fanatics, were stronger than the current crop of climbers and that's the real reason they blew away the standards. Nevertheless, there are a dozen active climbers as strong as these two, so why aren't they forging new levels of difficulty? I'm not talking a piddly letter grade or two. I'm talking routes so hard the climbing community won't assign a number to them for twenty years because the grades haven't caught up. (Take Gill's Thimble route, a 30-foot climb with a high crux, now rated 5.12a. In 1961 he free-soloed the first ascent in kletterschues, with a menacing guardrail at the base. A 5.11 wasn't claimed in the climbing community until 1967, and then on well-protected crack climbs. A 5.12 not until 1975, ditto with the good pro. If you want a non-bouldering example, look at Oliver Perry Smith, an American who put up 5.10s in Germany in the early 1900s, over half a century before the grade was proposed here.)

Ratings are an anchor: attach yourself to them and you'll never drift far from the climbing community. You can hug them, kiss them, embrace them with every gram of strength, but they'll never kiss you back. To break free from the numbers try the following:

1. The easy step. Go somewhere where you don't know the routes or ratings, find a climb or boulder problem you like, and without looking it up in a guidebook, just do it. You'll be amazed at what you can pull off if nobody has told you you can't do it.

2. The tough step. After you do the climb, resist the urge to tack a number on it. Fortunately, ratings are not a physical addiction; you can kick them quicker than cigarettes.

I know the tricks, so how come I'm not the world's best climber? Because I eat pizza. I drink beer. I watch cable TV sports. I'm pushing the fun envelope. Giving up on ratings has dismayed those who feel I should have a V-grade ready for every problem I try. But by letting moves and aesthetics arouse me, not numbers, I pick climbs I really want to do, not to have done. This leads to an incredible feeling of focus. My experiences are more memorable, and dare I say it, more pure. And yes, I do moves I never thought I would, especially at this body-fat percentage.

Now if I could only forget about *that* number.

Climbing, March 1995

The Dog Ate My Belay Plate

When training fails, it's time to whine. This following piece is by no means original—climbers have suffered from Chronic Excuse Syndrome since the inception of the sport, giving ample fodder for satirists. Shortly before his death in 1970, Tom Patey, Scottish ice pioneer and humorist, compiled an extensive excuse list in "The Art of Climbing Down Gracefully— A Symposium of Commonly Used Ploys. . . . " Two and a half decades later, I felt it was time to update that list for the climber of the '90s, as well as add tips for its use. This piece was not actually a Verm's World column; it appeared in the Black Diamond catalog. Sometimes the best gear for a climb is a good excuse.

ABOUT A YEAR AGO I HAD a great stroke of luck. I participated in some medical research pertaining to climbing injuries. The doc took my history, x-rayed my hands and feet, then declared that I was one of his most outstanding subjects yet—I'd had nearly every hand, finger, and foot injury he'd seen in his entire climbing study group. I left the medical center beaming. It's not every day that a barrel full of prime excuses falls into your lap. If milked properly, this cow would last for years. I could fail on any climb I wanted and walk away proudly.

My joy was short-lived. I made one critical mistake and I have only myself to blame. I told the doctor to look at Maria Cranor's hands if he had a strong stomach. Maria has the hands of a spastic carpenter—her thin fingers take numerous dog legs and the knuckles are swollen like grapes. Little did I suspect the doctor would actually go out of his way to check out this former Black Diamond bigwig. A few radiograms later and he declared that she had three finger fractures she hadn't known about previously, including one where the tendon had torn out a chunk of the bone it was attached to. A tactical blunder such as mine would cause most climbers to wallow in self-pity. Not me—I was too damn busy being jealous.

Excuse-making is one of the most fundamental and important of climbing techniques, but also one of the least mastered. Most climbers think that if they just practice a lot that their partners will buy their alibis each time out. Wrong-o. Unless you know the rules, chronic excuse-making can actually hurt your climbing. I know this from experience. So others won't have to suffer as I have, I'm setting down a few rules for making excuses right here. After those, we'll go over some examples and examine their effectiveness.

RULE 1

Always make your excuse beforehand: the earlier, the better. Post-failure excuses have all the impact of a the-dog-ate-my-homework ploy. Seed your field early. Don't wait until the climb is in sight; drop hints the day or even the week before. Early excuses also reap benefits when you succeed "against all odds."

RULE 2

Be subtle. Instead of saying, "You ever get the feeling that your elbow is part of a shish kabob?" bring along a 100-count bottle containing a single ibuprofen. Shake it about, the lone pill rattling pitifully, then gently mutter, "Darn bottles don't go as far as they used to."

RULE 3

Work in pairs. Whining about your own problems is in bad taste, but if an "unwitting" accomplice should prompt you in front of others, it's acceptable and expected for you to discuss your troubles. Make them draw it out of you. After grudgingly giving up the details, repay the favor and say, "But I'm sure it's nothing like pain you had in your shoulder last week . . . "

RULE 4

Don't forget mental anguish. If partners think you're keeping something hidden—say a failed kidney, a malignant tumor, an impending divorce, or a blown tendon pulley—then it's obvious that the stress of keeping it secret is eating at you as well. Never underestimate this implied mental stress factor; it's worth up to three letter grades.

RULE 5

Know your partners. Your excuse must be better than theirs. If you've had five surgeries, don't team up with somebody who has had eight. If you've had ten, avoid someone who has had twenty. If you've had forty, don't tie in with Kim Schmitz.

RULE 6

Counterpunch when necessary. If you have violated rules one and/or five and your partner scoops you on your planned excuse it's time to stick a needle in his or her balloon. For example, let's say Boone (not his real name) looks up at his project and remarks, "I'm not sure about the crimpers on this 14d, I lost all my calluses when I bleached my hair the other day." You fire back, "You'll do just fine. It never stopped Ben Moon." Now if Boone fails, it can only be for one reason: he's weak.

RULE 7

Props are fine. A pink slip on the dashboard, an inhaler falling out of your pack, three empty Jägermeister bottles on the kitchen counter . . . all speak loudly so you don't have to. If you have scars, let them be seen. If you don't, get some.

RULE 8

A true craftsman doesn't blame his tools. He blames someone else's. If success is the least bit in doubt, be sure to use your partner's rack. Eyeball said rack with curiosity. If necessary, establish unfamiliarity with mundane questions such as "Who makes this nut?" If stuck with your own rack, salt it with some brand new gear. Say, "I've been meaning to try out these new biners (cams) (nuts)."

RULE 9

Wear a shirt. If you are buffed, ripped, or shredded and people know it, nobody will be impressed when you succeed and everyone will snicker when you fail. Furthermore, wearing a shirt helps keep you pale so you have that pencil-pushing office lackey appearance. You'll look so geeky, they'll never suspect you train. Note: the only exceptions to the shirt rule are if you have scars (see above) or a good beer gut to show off. Second note: women who climb topless need no excuses. Nobody will notice if they're getting bouted or not.

RULE 10

Nurture any popping joints. Body parts that announce themselves always engender a "doesn't that hurt" query. Grimace when you say "No."

RULE 11

For heaven's sake don't use a real excuse. No one will believe you.

Now that you know the rules, let's examine some common and uncommon excuses and their potency.

TENDINITIS

Don't try this one on me. I've had it in three tendons in the left elbow, two in the right, and in all eight fingers. I've had it in both wrists and in one shoulder. I've had it so bad I couldn't pick up a twelve-pack. Right now it even hurts to pick my nose. Let me tell you, nobody's buying it. Your only hope with this excuse is to pick a really obscure body part upon which an injury will reflect an unheard of dedication to the sport. Nothing says "heel-hooking roof god" like tendinitis in the backs of the knees. As well, if you're one of those twisted types who *likes* training and takes pride in their immense power, toss them this line: "Do you know anything about tendinitis of the lats? Should I ice them or keep them warm?"

HANGOVER

Again, don't try this one on me; I've had one since 1976. Too often this excuse violates rule five. If you complain of front points to the forehead, your partner will claim he's running jackhammers. Bitching about "acute toxic encephalopathy" sometimes makes this ruse work, but unless you actually vomit, preferably in your partner's car or on his or her gear, this puppy ain't going far. And if you do hurl, look out, your partner might just outdo you. This is no fun when you're following a pitch.

ILLNESS

This is the time-honored classic and usually quite effectual when accompanied by visual or olfactory symptoms such as oozing welts, scarlet rashes, or giardic gas. It works best if your malady is contagious—your partner will keep his or her distance and you can then work the "I thought we were in this together/this would be easy if I got a little support" angle.

WORK-RELATED STRESS

Tread lightly with this one. If you're a climber, odds are all your friends know you work as little as possible. You can turn this around however, by being stressed out by the prospect of possibly having to get a job.

THE ONE SUREFIRE EXCUSE

In a word—hemorrhoids. Long approaches, hanging belays, stemming corners: you name it and hemorrhoids will make it miserable. Like tendinitis, hemorrhoids can flare up at any time, making them convenient. Unlike tendinitis, not everybody has or will admit to having 'roids, though I have several friends who use this excuse regularly. The beauty of this stratagem is nobody will ever check to see if it's true.

So there you have it, the keys to successful climbing. Now that you know the rules, it's time to practice, practice, practice. By the way, I was at the doctor's a little while back. Physical work made me gasp and wheeze. I was so short of breath that my lungs felt like two peanuts. They ran some tests on me and said I had airway hypersensitivity to methacholine—in layman's terms, asthma. What can I say? I haven't felt this great in years.

Black Diamond catalog, Spring 1997

Solving the
Everest Problem

*The juiciest climbing story of the '90s was the debacle on
Everest in 1996. It had all the elements of a Greek tragedy and
the popular press glommed on big time. Climbers and non-
climbers alike were eager to point fingers. "Something needs
to be done," the pundits cried. But what? The simple way to
eliminate deaths on Everest would be not to set foot
on the mountain in the first place. This solution is obviously
unacceptable; we can't take away every millionaire's God-
given right to stand atop the world. Hence, I put on my thinking cap and came up with the following game plan.*

*Some people may find making light of tragic circumstances
to be harsh—à la space shuttle jokes. In no way is this meant
to be disrespectful of those who died.*

MUCH HAS BEEN WRITTEN, AND EVEN more said, about the "Everest
Problem" in the last several years. The big problem is that everyone
wants to climb Everest, but only doctors, lawyers, socialites, and lot-
tery winners can afford to. This had led to several "Everest Tragedies."
These tragedies fall into three groups: climbers dying trying to save
incompetents, the noble peak being downsized to a chintzy trophy,
and the lack of any insurance company CEO casualties. Below, I
present two easy steps toward eliminating these tragedies.

First: outlaw "executive teamwork challenges." You know, the
week-long ropes courses culminating in a day solo in the wilderness
without an espresso machine. The idea being that if you push a bunch
of office lackeys to rappel off a cliff when they don't want to, then
they'll go back and tackle that K2 of paperwork on their desk and

humble it in a two-day alpine style tour de force. Get real; taking these chumps out into the wilderness makes about as much sense as putting me in the Oval Office for a week and saying "have at it." A couple of interns later, and I'd be ready dispense a little Mideast Policy.

The big problem with these challenges is they are calculated to culminate in success. I say chain the office lackey to an ice chest full of bacon sandwiches and see if he can outrun a hungry black bear. The last thing we want is these people leaving the executive challenge feeling good about themselves. All this does is make them think they can do anything, like climb Everest. This is counterproductive and bad for the economy. Far better they slink back past their secretary to the friendly confines of a leather desk chair and do what they're really good at: i.e., push pencils, fire employees, and raise your and my premiums.

Second: demote Everest. Two summers ago, I was on the volunteer rescue patrol on Denali (aka Mount McKinley, or the Poor Man's Everest). Some 500 climbers dotted the mountain at one time, many that couldn't put on crampons without help. Much of the talk at the 14,000-foot rescue camp had to do with the "Denali Problem," which is identical to the Everest Problem. Towering dramatically beside Denali is Mount Foraker, by most anyone's estimate a far more comely mountain. There were zero climbers on it. I had no doubt that if people were told Foraker were the highest peak in North America that 500 climbers would be over there, not on Denali.

So if not Everest as the top of the world, then which mountain? Certainly, some hint of adventure must be retained for this crowning achievement in one's life, and by definition, an adventure should have an uncertain outcome. Furthermore, the mountain should look good in postcards. Hence, I suggest Pikes Peak. If your car has not had a recent tune-up, there's a chance you won't reach the summit on your first attempt. As well, Pikes has a majestic countenance and thin enough air to make you breathe hard at the summit. While the millionaires take turns tagging Pikes Peak's summit, Everest could play host to teams of climbers pushing routes up ever-harder lines.

These two easy steps should eliminate all type one and type two Everest tragedies. As for the insurance company CEOs, I suggest the reader temporarily put down this reading material and pick up *Guns and Ammo*.

previously unpublished

Will the Real Doctor Doom Please Stand Up?

(or, "I Am Marc Twight, Yank My Chain")

While the following piece may appear to be purely for yucks, it does touch on the subject of selling one's image to the media. Few professional climbers have established an image as strong as Marc Twight's Doctor Doom. This was bolstered by Marc's writings, as well as a profile in Outside *magazine entitled "I Am Marc Twight, Feel My Pain." In print, Marc comes off all gloom and doom, but in person he seems bright, energetic, and wickedly quick-witted.*

The idea for this article came about after I went on record saying Tami Knight and Marc Twight were the two funniest climbing writers out there. I imagined how bummed Marc would be if people didn't think he was depressed. This was the easiest interview I ever did. That was because I never actually talked to Twight for this article. Sometimes I think I should do all my interviews the same way.

BY NOW, MOST READERS will have heard of Doctor Doom, if not through his titillating articles in *Climbing*, then through the responses they generate in the letters column. Doom, if not the best alpinist in the country, is certainly the happiest and is perhaps best known for his ability to share that joy through his sunny prose and persisting ad presence. As so often happens to such happy-go-lucky folks, the Doc has been the butt of numerous jokes and parodies. It's gotten to the point where it's hard to tell where Doctor Doom the Caricature ends and Doctor Doom the Person begins.

To clear up this confusion, I flew up to Jackson, donned fatigues, rented a Hummer, then drove over the pass into Victor, Idaho. I hung a left at the mailbox with the smiley face on it, praised the Hummer's clearance as I drove over a pair of frolicking poodles, and pulled up to the front door of Doctor Doom's new bunker home.

When I arrived, Doc was just finishing a rigorous five-hour aerobic workout. Not only had he completed the entire Jane Fonda series including the pregnancy workout, but he'd whipped through the Kathy Smith tape twice, cranked *Buns of Steel* on fast forward, and was topping it off by sweating to the oldies with Richard Simmons. Littered about the floor were Gu wrappers, miscellaneous climbing gear, a stack of letters to the editor forwarded to him, and a concealed-weapons permit. Nothing unusual. I stepped over a few teddy bears, then plopped down into the La-Z-Boy beneath the Barney poster while Doc put on some music. A smile washed over his face as he heard Bobby McFerrin croon "Don't worry . . . be happy." It seemed like a good time to turn on the tape recorder. Soon, however, I realized that the smile was forced . . .

V Marc, how's it going?

DD Fine, great, swell. (DD bursts into tears.) I'd be happier doing lines of Drano, pulling the pin on a hand-grenade enema, soloing *Bridalveil Falls* in summer . . .

V What happened? Did some Frenchie repeat one of your psycho Cham routes?

DD Get real. Pigs will fly, the Cubs will win the World Series, you'll get laid before that happens.

V So you're saying the French don't have what it takes? That they're a bunch of two-bit glory hounds sitting on the laurels of Terray and Rebuffat?

DD At the minimum.

V So it's more like they're just posing weenie fluffboys not worth the glossy pages they're hyped on?

DD You're getting close.

V Nothing but a horde of limp-wristed girly men who couldn't sink a Pulsar in a lukewarm Slurpee with both hands if their contracts depended on it?

DD Exactly.

V But the French women—tight pants, lacy tops, a distinct joie de fella . . .

DD Whoa, buddy—leave my wife out of this; I prefer to keep my sex life to myself.

V You and a lot of climbers.

DD I noticed you do have a firm grip.

V Back to the tears. What's got you down? You're usually such a happy guy.

DD It's your fault. Everybody laughs at me now.

V 'Cause you're hilarious. The way you lead people about on a leash of penumbral prose and pitch-black posturing. I love it when you write, "My life is full of shit and blood and pain . . . " When I read that I laughed so hard the beer rushed out my nose. You can't help it if you're the funniest writer out there.

DD You didn't have to tell everybody. They were taking it seriously.

V Gee, I'm sorry. I'm such an asshole.

DD Hey, that's my line, don't be stealing it. It's no bed of roses marketing an image these days.

V Tell me about it; despite ten years of pimping myself, the best I get accused of is being a "creeping self-promoter." You'd think they could say "galloping."

DD See what I mean?

V So how did you choose the tortured angst-child image?

DD By default. I really wanted to be a cowboy climber—you know, ride up to the crag on my horse, then drop my chaps to show off my Lycra—but the market was maxed. Ditto with the vulgar-but-lovable drunk image. Of course, the clean-living, serious climber devoted to the sport is too boring to sell, even when you toss in a side dish of evangelical Christianity. So, seeing as I didn't have enough money for a sex change, there wasn't much choice left. I had to invite the nasty dark demons to torture my soul, or at least my readers. The easiest way to do this was to go punk, and just borrow lyrics for the articles. Do you think I liked running a purple mohawk?

V At least it paid the bills.

DD Think so? Take a look at this. (DD hands over his latest bank statement.) Feel my pain.

V Ouch.

(At this point DD pulls out a pistol, racks the slide, and gently nudges his camo headband up with the muzzle.)

V Whoa, wait one minute.

DD Don't try to talk me out . . .

V Isn't that a Witness .38 super auto?

DD Why, yes. It is.

V With the 5-inch barrel and red-dot scope?

DD You got it.

V Is it comped?

DD No recoil on this baby.

V Cool. What kind of load are you running?

DD 125-grain, jacketed hollow-points with five grains of bull's-eye powder.

V Really? At this close a range, wouldn't you prefer something with a heavier bullet and bigger diameter, say a .45?

DD Hmmm, you're right. The slower velocity would be way more satisfying; so would the greater knock-down power. (DD lays down gun.)

(By this point in the interview, I realized that Doc was truly a troubled man. The teddy bears, the Barney poster, the smiley-face mailbox: they were all just sad attempts to capture that lighthearted-ness and joy that characterized him in the past. I felt bad about my part in all this so I tried to offer up a solution.)

V Have you thought about a new image? I see you have some weights here. How about doing the macho burlmeister thing? Largo's been out of the rags for years. You could cash in easy.

DD *Au contraire.*

V What do you mean?

DD Bobbi.

V Silly me. How about your own line of clothing?

DD Know Fear?

V You could market Reality Bath burlap boxers.

DD Hmmm . . . (DD heads into kitchen for food and drink.) Care for some raw chicken?

V Thanks.

DD Prozac?

V After you.

DD Ethanol?

V Mmmm.

DD Zoloft, Wellbutrin, Prime Quest?

V Certainly. (Gulps pills.)

DD Did I tell you about the time I was soloing Le Grand Poubah? I was but a hundred feet from the summit when the lightning strikes began. The only escape was up, but that year the verglas pitch hadn't formed. Luckily I had a lip full of Copenhagen. I hocked up thick quarter-sized patches of spittle onto the rock, laid the flat edge of my tools in the goo and waited for it to freeze. Thirty moves like this later and I was five feet from the top. By that time the storm was right on top of me and my hairs were standing straight up, poking out of the vent holes in my helmet like antennae. I remember seeing the blue sparks race along my tools and the brown-flecked placements sputtering. I was sweating wadcutters, but I was out of Cope and my mouth had turned into an empty chalkbag. In desperation I reached down for my third tool and started swinging . . .

V C'mon, Doc, I can't get these boring hero stories past my editors. They want something captivating—some insight into Doctor Doom the Person. Here, I've got a list of questions they wanted me to ask. First, what kind of toothpaste do you use?

DD None. I find my teeth sparkle more on photo shoots if I floss first with razor wire, then buff the surface with a half-round mill bastard. Which reminds me of the time I learned it was best always to sharpen tools by hand, not on a grinder. I was on this incredible unclimbed pillar in Canada. It looked like a hundred-meter soda straw, water pouring down the middle and everything. Halfway up I broke one pick. Overheating on the grinder had given it distemper. No sweat—I went on with my third tool. Twenty feet higher I placed my next-to-last screw. As I torqued it in, the pillar snapped at my waist. Ten tons of blocks tumbled down and water was gushing everywhere. Alas, my partner became a cockroach, squashed under the jackboot of fate.

Anyway, there I was, dangling off one tool. The rope was pinned under the ice blocks and tugging hard at my waist. I couldn't let go with either tool to cut the rope, so I ran the cord along the inside of my left boot and gave a mighty mono-point kick with the right. The rope exploded and I instantly sprang upward. Unfortunately, I couldn't pull my right crampon out of my left boot. The teeth were too deeply seated in my metatarsals. My other two picks snapped a move later and I was left pinching a rapidly melting rib with my left hand as I drilled out a shallow mono-doigt with my remaining screw. Seventy feet higher, I started to get pumped from the feet together hop-kicking and alternating one-finger pull-ups. By this time the screw was dull and useless. There was only one way out, and that was to dyno for the sloping top . . .

V We're getting off the subject. My editors want to know if you wear boxers or tighty whities.

DD Tell 'em I'm in the pouch. Speaking of which, I needed every cotton-stretching cell when we were descending from the first ascent of Pik of Glorious Leader of the Current Ruling Party.

V Wasn't that formerly called Pik of Celebration of Downfall of the Corrupt Regime?

DD Only until we reached Camp II. Between Camp II and Camp V it was Pik of the People's Popular Coup. Then from Camp V to the summit it was Pik of Everlasting Tribute to Our All-Mighty General. Only when we returned to basecamp was it Pik of Glorious Leader of the Current Ruling Party.

V I take it this was a long climb.

DD Four weeks. Anyway we were coming back down the Pachinko Couloir after sitting out a storm for five days with only our sweaty mildewed insoles to eat. It was 90 degrees below zero, with 100 mph winds. We were weak, and my partner Q.D. Kirtins's feet had frozen into black lumps of coal. The descent was slow going and it was starting to get dark. We were only two raps from easy ground when a whirling discus of rock struck Q.D. in the shoulder, slicing through the gear sling and sending our rack three hundred feet down into the bergschrund. We had no anchors and Q.D.'s arm was dangling by a few tendons. I plugged the exposed arteries with my remaining Camel squares. I told Q.D. to calm down, that I'd get us down alive. The only hope for an anchor was to wedge something in the chimney behind us. The packs weren't wide enough so I had no choice. With the adze of my ax, I hacked through the remaining tendons on Kirtins's arm. The limb was still pliable enough that I could wedge it into the crack like a three-foot Big Bro. I wrapped the fingers and thumb into a circle and threaded the rope through. Five minutes later the arm was frozen solid. I draped Kirtins over my shoulder and rapped down to the next ledge, where lo and behold, there just happened to be a perfect foot-sized crack . . .

V Pardon me for interrupting, but we're drifting off the subject again. Let's talk about you. You've been called an arrogant brat, psychotic, tortured, dark, juvenile, haughty, without class, self-serving, egotistical, neurotic, overrated, overstated, overexposed, overpaid, over serious, underhanded, and under the influence. And that was just in the last letters column. How do you respond to these comments?

DD (For the first time in the interview, a genuine smile bursts forth on DD's lips.) Thank god someone is listening to me. Michael Kennedy, how 'bout a column of my own?

(At this point DD's phone rings and the answering machine shrieks out his prerecorded message: "Hellfires are burning, my soul's charring black. Leave me a message, I might call you back." I listen in as DD screens the call. At first we just hear chuckling then a voice says, "That's cute, Marc. This is Michael Kennedy. I've reviewed your proposal for your own Misery Loves Company column and I feel that it does not meet our editorial needs at this time. Thank you for your interest in *Climbing* magazine and please feel free to query us in the future." Click. The smile tumbles off DD's face like a calving serac. DD's lovely photojournalist wife comes home at that moment and tells DD that it is time for his photo shoot. DD leaves the room to change.

When he emerges, DD is clad in a white robe covered with

sponsors' emblems. He kneels on a Gore-Tex-shrouded pallet, butt to heels, and ponders the ice ax laid in front of him. A shaft of sunlight beams through the front door gun port, highlighting the ax, sparkling off the freshly honed tip. His wife takes a few quick meter readings, then settles in behind her camera. DD parts his gi to the waist, exposing a rippling torso tattooed with two dashed lines forming a crucifix on his abdomen. Next to the lines it says, "Cut here." DD leans forward, picks up the ax and places the tip at the end of the horizontal line. Like out of a movie, or the first Snowbird competition, the beam of light follows the pick to his skin. The reflections from the lettering on the pick dance about his chin as he stares at the entry point. "Ze light, it eez so beauteeful," exclaims his wife. "Now, Marc, now!" He raises his head, closes his eyes, and is about to shove the blade home when I think of one last question to ask him.)

V So after you kill yourself, do you have any big plans?

DD (Relaxing his grip on the ax.) Well, there's this route on the north face of Latapountang. A thin runnel of ice drips down from the corniced seracs like an unrolled intestine spilling from a gored matador . . .

Climbing, March 1996

Pushing the Limits

90 min/some French company/coming soon to a video store near you

As the previous piece illustrates, Marc Twight is a godsend to any climbing satirist. I'm not sure if the film he starred in, Pushing the Limits, *ever got released in the U.S. Perhaps had* Climbing *printed this rave review . . .*

FIRST OFF, THIS B-GRADE, stunt-filled French feature film has less than two minutes of climbing in it. So why is it being reviewed in *Climbing*? Because it stars our beloved Doctor Doom. Yes, after spending the last decade ducking behind a wall of soul-searching prose, Marc Twight has finally dared to bare it all—in front of the cameras no less. The rumors that Twight makes love to another person, or at least pretends to, are true. More about the sex scenes later.

Twight stars as Xigor Copeland, the male lead in *Pushing the Limits*. Xigor leads a tribe of daring young men who can't seem to attract women so they spend their days BASE jumping, extreme skiing, snowboarding 50-degree slopes, and sky surfing near their secluded hideaway in the Alps. At night they male bond over arm-wrestling matches and shots of formaldehyde from a bottle with a pickled snake in it. Pretty idyllic, but as none of them has a job, it's getting kinda hard to keep the chopper gassed up. Hence Xigor approaches TV extreme sport hostess/exploited babe Fiona Damon to get stunt gigs for his boys. The ploy works, and soon Fiona's boss, the evil Nick Phar-Jones has the boys taking greater and greater risks to keep his show's ratings skyrocketing. The plot is so simple, even I followed it until the final Eurobabble soliloquy.

As an aficionado of cheesy action films, I was disappointed by *Pushing the Limits*. There are no car chases, no explosions, no fistfights, and no gunplay. None of that man's man kind of stuff that is the staple of American action films. Instead, Xigor and his band could be described as Frenchmen's men, pretty boys in headbands who pack their testosterone into parachute bags instead of holsters. Which leads us to the good point of *Pushing the Limits*—the stunts. There is some radical extreme sports footage in this flick. Speed skiing off the edge of cliffs and flying your canopy down sort of stuff. The climbing scenes, however, are lame, the big scare coming when Xigor's Walkman goes silent and he nearly peels off an ice solo. Hanging on with one arm, he manages to flip the cassette and keep going. *Pushing the Limits*'s big attraction is the aerial stunts. The sky surfing footage is beautiful and exciting. Perhaps it's a little overplayed, but if you're the kind of viewer who can watch the Reebok sky surf ad thirty times in a day and still get psyched, then this is the movie for you. If that's not the case, then you can still find amusement in the doltish dialog, lips-are-moving-but-nothing-comes-out dubbing, and mediocre acting.

Pushing the Limits is more than just an action flick, it's a love story as well. Everyone in the film is madly in love with themselves. This works out well for the actors, as little more is asked of them than to display a Chamonixan smugness. Things get sticky though, when Fiona and Xigor get together. Fiona's charms are irresistible, or so she tells Xigor, but in the edited-for-Americans version we don't get to see them. Unless you get a hold of the director's cut, there is even less sex than climbing in this film. This may be fortunate, because Twight has confessed that he didn't feel up for those scenes. There is an inkling of this, when Xigor first kisses Fiona. After a suavely roguish wink (answered by Fiona's dumbfounded stare), Xigor steps forward to plant the buss. When he gets about a foot away his expression changes. His lips refuse to pucker, his face turns to stone, and he ends up giving the Vanna White of French tabloid sports shows the kind of kiss you would give your mom.

That scene aside, Twight's acting isn't nearly as bad as a critic could hope for. He holds his own with his costars, and at one point, throws a pretty convincing kelp-heaving rage. Given how poorly the movie is dubbed, it would be unfair to criticize any of the actors. So self-promoters take heart—if you keep at it long enough, you might land your own starring role in a forgettable movie.

previously unpublished

Unsung Hero

During the editing of "The Wilford Case" in 1991, I got so exasperated at being asked for boring details about the subject that I sat down and cranked out a parody profile. I followed what I felt was Climbing magazine's profile formula; "Unsung Hero" was the result. It was soundly rejected, not because it made fun of Climbing magazine, but because it ridiculed a number of climbers who admitted they were chiseling holds. These climbers were big names seen in big ads and apparently above the law. The media had spent a lot of time promoting these individuals and it wasn't about to admit they were doing wrong. I reworked "Unsung Hero" a couple of times, and tried to get it into Verm's World, but never with any luck.

Often I hear climbers cry "we have to police ourselves, or else the land managers will." When I wrote this, I still believed the climbing community could police itself, as long as the media cooperated. Chiselers I felt were fair game for public ridicule. Give them credit for their actions. If they are proud of their chiseling, they have nothing to fear from the press. If ashamed, then let them take their lumps. Climbing felt I could make my point without naming names. I disagreed. Anonymity equals protection. I have yet to soften my stance on chiseling. I think the climbing media really dropped the ball on this issue. As to self-policing, I believe the climbing community is too big to do this now. Peer group pressure is ineffective unless everyone knows everyone else. Ten years ago, this could have worked. Now I think it's a pipe dream.

IT'S NOT EVERY MORNING that a climbing legend comes into my office in a wheelchair. I'd never met him, but I knew right away it was Ozzie Sheppard. That would make the redhead rolling him in his wife, Adeline.

Ozzie looked a mess. His hair was slicked back with some sort of foul-smelling pomade and his lips were chapped worse than Reinhold Messner's. He handed me a battered manila envelope; label atop label adorned the front. *Quickdraw, Bosch Boy, Pumpfest* . . . this envelope had traversed the desks of every major climbing mag out there. This is how it usually happened; they try the big mags, then they end up at my desk begging me to slip their rejected drivel into *Climbing*.

I told him "I'll see what I can do," shook his hand, and watched Adeline's derriere sashay out the door. Then I slipped the envelope into the out file—standard procedure.

Later that afternoon, Michael Kennedy poked his head in the office. I'd heard his cane thunking down the hall, so I had ample warning to try to look busy. The Big Cheese was getting crotchety since he turned fifty. I stuffed *Golf Digest* into a drawer, extracted Ozzie's envelope from the wastebasket, tore it open, and started scanning the pages.

No wonder the big media rejected him. This was taboo stuff—nobody mentions Chip Holdz's name anymore. Sure, the climbing industry tolerated him when he was putting up the big numbers, but he ended up poking fun at the other big names they'd worked so hard to build up. This was bad for business so it was see ya, Chip, gaze at some new Cover Boy.

Somewhere there was a lesson to be learned in all of this, so I'm slipping in Ozzie's encomium right before the deadline. They won't know it's in print until it reaches the stands. It might embarrass some folks, and maybe it will cost me my job, but we mustn't forget the past, lest we be doomed to repeat it.

The contents of the envelope, please.

THE UNBELIEVABLE CHIP HOLDZ
By Oscar Sheppard

Mention the name Chip Holdz and most people think of cover photos, media entourages, and autograph model harnesses. But Chip boasts a lot more than a chiseled pair of tan deltoids and half a dozen full page ad photos each month—when it comes to the big numbers, he claims more ticks than you can shake a Hartz ninety-day collar at.

Not a climber in the world has claimed more 5.15 first ascents than Chip, and even fewer have risen to super-stardom so fast. After Chip did his first 5.13 redpoint (*Hell* 5.13a, six days), he brashly ignored the 5.14 range and immediately became the first person to break the 5.15 barrier with *Money for Nothing* (still unrepeated since crucial holds broke when Chip lowered from his successful ascent). Rich N. Unskrupulos, publisher of *Bolt and Tick*, calls Chip "the hottest media property in the sport today. Finally a climber to make Americans proud. One who can take those wanking Euros on at their own game and come out first . . . in the rankings that is."

Chip grew up in Longmont, Colorado, right next to the turkey processing plant. His initial interest in climbing was sparked by a family vacation to Mount Rushmore when he was fourteen. His mom, mother of two and local PTA chairperson in 1994–95, recalls the moment. "Chester, that's Chippy's real name, saw the carvings in the rock, the displays at the visitor center, then these oddly dressed guys grinding up the nearby rock with power drills. He was never into boy things, you know, BB guns and such; in fact he preferred dolls, but he took an interest in those climbers immediately. Ralph, my hubby, figured Chester was finally showing an interest in power tools and he swelled with pride when Chester said he wanted to be a climber. Poor Ralph, when he found out it was the opportunity to wear girl's underwear in public that drew Chester to climbing, he couldn't take it. He switched from Lite to Wild Irish Rose to Everclear within the month. Funny, they never noticed at work. Anyway, when Chester got home from vacation he spent his entire allowance on gear and several new outfits."

Chip had an immediate impact on the climbing scene. After failing to tie in properly, he was 10 feet up his first 5.6 when he seemed confused and at the advice of his belayer, famed old-timer Ozzie Sheppard, leaned back on the toprope to survey the holds. It was a quick glimpse. The rope parted from the harness and Chip landed on Ozzie, snapping the belayer's back. Paralyzed from the waist down, Ozzie's climbing days were over and he was forced into a demeaning career as a climbing journalist.

Grieved at the loss of Sheppard, the local scene turned its eyes toward Chip. Within a year, Chip had done a greenpoint yo-yo beta-flash of Eldorado's *God's Golden Hour of Power* (aka *Genesis*—Chip prefers to call it by the first free ascensionist's tag) and at Horsetooth bagged the first lead of the *Standard Route* on the Mental Block (after adding three bolts), which he opted to rename *No Holdz Barred*. A year later he soloed it and renamed it yet again—this time *Holdz of Glory*. It was obvious that Colorado was too small for a climber of

Chip's stature. There were worlds out there to conquer. Climbing worlds. Chip Holdz, still lanky and baby-faced, dropped out of high school and went on a pilgrimage.

He moved out of his parent's house, taking only his shoes, harness, and his sister's airline ticket to her exchange student program in France. While this move was to help Chip's career immensely, it proved disastrous for his sister Minnie, who was moved down the exchange program priority list. Anorexic to begin with, Minnie fared poorly at her new high school in Southern Sudan. Chip's father, a Denver attorney, has refused comment on his son's actions pending the results of the lawsuit.

In Europe, Chip met the two people who more than any others, would help him carve his place in climbing history: French women's champion Anna Ballic and Brit new route guru Jack Hammer.

"Anna showed me how to sculpt my body into an ultimate climbing machine," Chip says. "She also helped land me my first endorsement contract with Stridex." Ballic set a tough regimen for Chip to follow. Chip wasn't seen at the crags for six months. He spent the entire time in the gym, doing a secret regimen of upper-body workouts. When he finally emerged, they cut the casts off his legs. He was built like a golf tee. His detractors will add that the size of his head matched the picture, but this is just figurative speech from people jealous that they didn't flash *Le Tedium,* 9b+.

From Hammer, Chip learned the fine points of modern technique. "I thought I'd learned all there was to know about chiseling holds from *Goat's Notes* magazine," Chip says, "but Jack taught me stuff that makes Mount Charleston look like a primitive area." *Chip, Chip, Hooray!* was the most remarkable of Holdz's first ascents in the UK, not just for its difficulty, E10/8c/RIP/QED, but for the way it broke new ground in gritstone ethics. "It seemed such a shame seeing all that unclimbed rock go to waste," Chip says. "It was obviously impossible to climb in its natural state, but [Chip grins as he says this] nothing's impossible when you team up with the proper tools."

"Nothing's impossible when you team up with proper fools," retorts I. B. Bitter, a famous British has-been. Chip took the criticism in stride. "They just resent me because they're afraid to strive for excellence and they don't have a girlfriend as gorgeous as me," says Chip. "Did I say that right? Yeah, I guess I did."

Yes, Chip did have a girlfriend, his first ever, an Irish-American lass by the name of Adeline O'Juggs. On vacation from the States, Adeline had already established quite a reputation overseas. The UK locals called her "Gogarth," until complaints came in that the infamous seacliff "wasn't that loose." When asked to recount their (three) days together, Adeline had this to say:

"I was initially attracted by the bulge between his leg loops. I guess I should have been tipped off that it wasn't there before he stepped above that bolt. Anyway, Chip looked easier than a *Shelf Road* 5.11, so I took him. You think he's quick to hang? He came off faster than Ron Kauk in the finals at Snowbird in 1988."

His European education over with, Chip returned to the States. Heartbroken by his breakup with Adeline, Chip took his frustrations out on the crags. In Oklahoma, he completed the unfinished late 1980s route *Raleigh Round the Crag, Boys* after removing the only natural hold. Originally touted as 5.15, it has subsequently been down-rated to 5.14a/13b (WDS—Wyoming Decimal System). In Idaho, he scooped the locals with the 5.14d *Ya Narrow Minded People,* a varnish-smearing testpiece that hasn't been repeated since it dried. He further cemented his reputation with *Leavitt, or Leave It Alone* (5.15b) at Joshua Tree. Perched on an enormous boulder that catches late afternoon sun twelve hours a day, this route is a photographer's wet dream. Indeed, its crux move has already appeared on five straight covers of *Monodoigt* magazine. Paparazzo Neg Effstopperson has bought all rights to photos of the route for a rumored six figures. Neg has this to say: "It's the essence of climbing, that crux. Locked off low at the chest, crossing through high with the other hand, eyeballs lasering in on the next hold, bolt way below the chin. And the lighting—if any move cries out to be underexposed two stops on Baileychrome, this is it."

Chip's latest coup is the first brownring ascent of Clear Creek Canyon's *Trad Gone Bad.* The reigning local hardboy had tried it for years but had repeatedly come up short, a fact not lost on Chip who renamed the route *Squirt's Myth.* Checking in at a cool 5.15e, this is no doubt the "ultimate route in the universe" according to Chip's belayer, Hyme Affluff.

What routine does Chip follow to climb at such unbelievable levels? Here's his schedule for a typical day:

7:00–7:30 A.M.	Wake up and devour breakfast of ½ cup wheat germ and 1 cup uncooked rice doused with 8 oz. diluted prune juice followed by a Metamucil chaser.
7:30–8:30 A.M.	On toilet.
8:30 A.M.–Noon	On phone with sponsors and agents.
Noon–1:00 P.M.	At tanning salon.
1:00–2:00 P.M.	Do hair, pull Lycra on.

2:00–4:00 P.M.	Publicly chide fluffboys for carelessly snapping flakes to larger sizes, kicking footholds in bigger, and otherwise altering rock on his latest project because "I detest such tactics, but it's too late to do anything about it now so I'll just have to use the holds as they stand." Shakes head.
4:00–6:00 P.M.	Do posedown session with photo and/or video crew.
6:00–6:30 P.M.	Purchase clean needles at pharmacy.
6:30–10:30 P.M.	In gym.
10:30–11:00 P.M.	Scarf.
11:00–11:15 P.M.	Barf.
11:15 P.M.	Sleep.

Very few climbers have the dedication to follow such a strict regimen. Asked if there's a climber of his caliber that he respects, Chip says, "No, none of my caliber, however I do respect W. O. Ethicks for his skill in route reporting. His routes are always published as soon as they go out of condition, allowing for maximum sponsor strokage before second ascent downrating. He's one of the few climbers out there who understands what the sport is all about."

What does the future hold for Chip? More glory, more money, more column inches, and of course his own line of clothing featuring Chip's Ticks T-shirts. And all well deserved, for who but Chip Holdz and his sponsors have ever rewritten climbing history like this? From now on all previous accomplishments, if they even deserve recognition, are simply prehistory and will be duly labeled B.C.—Before Chip.

previously unpublished

No GUTs, No Glory

Relativity and quantum mechanics as they apply to the climbing universe and the search for the Grand Unified Theory

By John Sherman, B.A.

When published in Climbing, *this piece was cut drastically for space reasons. I feel this may have cheated me out of a Nobel Prize. Below is the full report.*

JUST RECENTLY I TRAVELED OUTSIDE the realm of the known climbing universe. All the way to Louisiana in fact. During the long and tedious drive across East Texas, I listened to a tape of Stephen Hawking's *A Brief History of Time*. In *A Brief History of Time,* Hawking lays out the current scientific theories surrounding the evolution of the universe, the beginning of time, the existence of black holes, antimatter, and the such, all in layman's terms. Ordinarily, I wouldn't concern myself with thoughts more esoteric than Monday Night's point spread, but I experienced an epiphany while listening to Hawking and staring out the windshield at the unattainable horizon. The scene in the rearview mirror was no different. Hawking was right; the universe was not a flat plate supported on the back of a giant tortoise—it was indeed a curved four-dimensional sheet with no beginning or end. The proof was right in front of my eyes.

Hawking's conclusions were based on the theories of relativity and quantum mechanics. These theories don't always agree. Hence, as we nudge into the twenty-first century, the current great quest of science is to come up with a single Grand Unified Theory (GUT) that would explain how everything in the universe works, from supernovas to hockey pucks. As you read this, the search for the GUT is ongoing and the world's greatest brains are busy at this task. In the name of science, I felt it was the least I could do to add my observations to the pool.

Hawking's IQ is roughly equal to Avogadro's number (6.023 x 10^{23}), while mine more closely approximates Planck's constant (6.626 x 10^{-34}), therefore I shall restrict my observations to the relatively simple world of the climbing universe. Nevertheless, my work will perhaps be the key to unlock the door to the GUT. How so you ask? Current work centers around two fields: relativity, which primarily concerns itself with the big picture, how planets, stars, and galaxies relate to and affect each other; and quantum mechanics, which deals with matter on a subatomic level. While today's scientists are fooling around with Hubble telescopes and particle accelerators, they are completely dismissing the middle ground and what that can teach them. The climbing universe, as we know it, exists only on land masses of the planet Earth, is readily visible, and is easily observable. As well, it is highly self-contained, as any universe must be. For the price of one government toilet seat, scientists could road trip to Hueco Tanks and end up with enough data to keep them busy until they get tenure. I will save them the trouble.

HOW THEORIES WORK

Before we go further, let's introduce Hawking's definition of a scientific theory. He states, "a theory is just a model of the universe, or a restricted part of it, and a set of rules that relates quantities in the model to observations that we make."

Here are two examples. Relativity predicts that time moves slower for a person who is close to a massive object, such as a planet, than for a person who is farther away. In 1962, scientists proved this with a pair of very accurate clocks, one positioned atop a water tower, and one at the base. The clock on top did indeed run faster. What practical implications does this have for the, ahem, layperson? Let's go to the bedroom for example two. When a man is on top during lovemaking, he is farther from the center of the earth. Consequently, his clock is ticking faster. Relativity predicts that he will climax before the woman beneath him. Field observations prove this to be the case.

Now let's see how physicists' predictions agree with our observations in the climbing world.

THE SECOND LAW OF THERMODYNAMICS

This is not to be confused with Gill's first law of highly dynamics. The second law of thermodynamics states that in any reaction, energy is always lost. This lost energy is called entropy. Entropy is always increasing in the universe, because all things want to go toward a more disordered state. Hawking gives the example of a cup of water on a table. This cup of water is in a highly ordered state. If it falls off the table, it will break and the cup and water will reach a more disordered state.

One would think we could easily refute the second law of thermodynamics with a quick trip to any sport crag. What initially started as a random set of natural holds on a rock wall is soon scrubbed, chipped, and glued into very distinct bolted pathways, and a hierarchy established with the assignment of Yosemite Decimal System (YDS) grades. Clearly, the climbing universe is becoming more ordered every day. Or is it? Much of entropy is in the form of heat or energy released in reactions. The second law states that any action designed to create order, say the bolting of a crag, will release more energy to the universe than it will organize. In fact, in the case of the bolted crag, we can easily measure this lost energy by adding up the caloric values listed on the PowerBar wrappers discarded at the base of each climb. In those rare cases when climbers pick up their trash and put it in order, say in a trash can, additional physical effort is required, which produces entropy in the form of heat, sweat, and body odor. Hence, within the climbing universe, the second law holds up as true.

BLACK HOLES

In space there are spots where matter has accumulated so densely that not even light can escape the matter's gravitational pull. Because no light escapes, we cannot see a black hole itself. Clever scientists, however, got funding for research into this theoretical possibility. Billions of dollars and a Hubble telescope later, they had proven the existence of black holes by watching the stars around them dance to their gravitational pull.

Had they just looked at the climbing universe, they could have saved a lot of money. I personally have climbed with several black holes, partners so dense that no intelligent thought could escape their mind. In space, the boundary around a black hole at which light cannot escape is called the event horizon; in climbers it is known simply as the skull.

Further research into black holes showed that although no light escapes (and by the laws of physics, nothing can travel faster than light) certain kinds of radiation emanate from black holes. In climbers this is seen as a constant dribble of numbers escaping their lips. Once again, I could have saved the scientific community tons of money and wasted thought time. This money and thought could then be directed toward more burning questions, like "Why can't any company make a decent headlamp that doesn't switch itself on inside your pack?"

THE LIFE OF STARS

Stars are huge balls of hot gas that spit out light and heat as the gas burns in a nuclear reaction. The energy released in this reaction causes the star to expand, while the gravitational forces caused by its own mass make it contract. These forces hold each other in check. The sun is one such star, and a quick look at the clear night sky will assure you that there are millions more. Small, relatively inert bodies called planets revolve around the stars.

Climbing stars are also full of hot gas, and surrounded by other bodies. Because these other bodies follow the star about, each star is convinced that he or she is the center of the climbing universe. As there can only be one center of the universe, or possibly none, this frame of reference, in which hundreds of climbing stars all see the world as revolving around themselves, proves part of the theory of relativity. This states that it is just as likely that your car remains still, and the ground under it is moving at 70 miles per hour, as is the reverse. It all just depends how you look at it.

Each star has a limited amount of gas to burn. Paradoxically, the bigger the star, the quicker it burns its gas, and the shorter its life span. In the climbing world, such stars are known as Himalayan climbers. Other celestial stars continue to age and burn up their hydrogen fuel. Eventually, the expansion caused by nuclear reaction can't compete with the contraction of gravity and these stars end up as burnt-out cinders, or black dwarves. Some completely collapse into black holes. As climbing stars age, they burn up their column inches. As pats on the back become fewer, their sagging egos collapse and they end up either as mountain bikers, golfers, or gear reps.

In the extreme case a star will be so big that it will consume its fuel, contract quickly, then explode as a supernova. The resultant matter sprays all about, some of it contributing to the formation of new stars. Such a supernova is seen in the Crab Nebula. This happens too in the climbing universe, when enormous egos collapse at the end of a vibrant climbing career. This rapid collapse increases the subject's density so much that the subject explodes and sprays all about ethics. Often the subject will reinvent itself as a clothing magnate. One need look no further than the Chouinard and Robbins Nebulas for proof of this.

Some celestial stars avoid total collapse and continue to shine, although dimly, as white dwarves. At this point they are low in brightness, small, and extremely dense. Such climbing stars are known as senior contributing editors.

THE EXPANDING UNIVERSE AND RED SHIFT

Scientists believe the universe is currently expanding. Everything is moving away from everything else, much like dots on a balloon all move away from each other as the balloon is inflated. Their proof for this lies in the Doppler effect. Imagine your partner zippering an A5 pitch as you belay. His screams sound higher pitched as he falls toward you than after his body flies past. This is due to his screams being compressed to a higher frequency as he approaches you, and expanded to a lower frequency as his body soars past. The same thing happens to light from distant galaxies. Galaxies moving away from us will appear redder, and those moving toward us should appear bluer. Cosmological observations show an abundance of "red shift" of the light, indicating that the universe is expanding.

But what about the climbing universe? Is it expanding as well? Any gear rep will tell you yes. Any Access Fund member will say no. Is there scientific evidence to support these conclusions? I regret to say the jury is still out. Studies of light coming from aging climbing stars shows neither a red shift, nor a blue shift. Instead a distinct green shift is observed. My own theory is that as the climbing universe expands, stars try desperately to stay as close to the center as possible. Their rush toward the center is counteracted by the expansion of the whole; hence they do nothing but orbit about helplessly at a safe, but frustrating distance, giving off a neutral or green shift. Others believe the green tint is the reflection of the "limelight" (so called for its hue) in their receding visages, and use this to support an expanding universe theory. (One study reported a distinct red shift primarily amongst trad climbers. Further investigation showed that these were just exploded nose capillaries.)

MATTER AND ANTIMATTER

The discovery of the positron in 1932 proved the existence of antimatter. When a particle and antiparticle, say a positron and an electron, collide, they annihilate each other. Nothing in physics denies the possibility of antiworlds or antipeople (the latter often refer to me in letters to the editor). The implications are staggering. Did Mallory and Irvine summit Everest only to shake hands with their antipartners who had climbed the opposite side of the mountain? This would explain them disappearing without a trace. It would also mean four climbers had summited prior to Hillary and Tenzing. Will people rush to claim the first antiascent of routes? How many anti-8000 meter peaks await first ascents?

FORCES

There are four forces in the universe: electromagnetic forces, weak nuclear forces, strong nuclear forces, and gravity. Electromagnetic forces are positive or negative. Quantum mechanics states that positive and negative forces attract each other. This explains why Marc Twight has been married twice. Weak nuclear forces cause radiation and strong nuclear forces hold atoms together. Gravity is the weakest force of all, but it is cumulative with increases in mass. This proves what I've maintained all along—that there is more gravity pulling on a lardass like myself than on some snotty-nosed anorexic sportpup. If we factor gravitational forces into climbing ratings as follows:

Overall Rating = YDS grade x mass x acceleration of gravity

. . . we discover that I have climbed harder than any climber ever. This corresponds quite accurately to my own observations once we take into account the uncertainty principle.

THE UNCERTAINTY PRINCIPLE

The uncertainty principle is the backbone of quantum physics. It states simply that when we try to measure things on a subatomic level, we don't have a good enough ruler to get accurate results. To measure the position and velocity of very small things, like electrons, scientists bounce light rays off of them. They can measure nothing shorter than a single wavelength, which is longer than the particle itself. One could measure with wavelengths shorter than visible light, but the shorter the wavelength the more energy these contain. This energy will knock about the particle being measured, giving poor results. Thus, the finer physicists try to measure things, the sloppier the results. An exact parallel is seen in the climbing world when we try to measure the petty differences between climbers. Rating systems are constantly tweaked finer and finer to where climbers claim they can tell the difference between "soft touch 5.13a" and a "stiff 5.12d." Of course differences in weight, strength, foot size, climatic conditions, reach, flatulence, and even fingernail length all affect relative difficulty, thus making the division of difficulty a fruitless endeavor. As with quantum physicists, the finer climbers try to measure things, the sloppier the results.

THE FIFTH DIMENSION

There are four generally accepted dimensions of space-time. These are basically up/down, left/right, back/forth, and past/future. But if there are four dimensions, why not five or ten or more? Indeed certain modern theories of the universe call for twenty-six dimensions. After toying with these theories of four-plus dimensions, Hawking seems to prefer to stick with the four mentioned. If Hawking were a climber, he'd clearly see that there is a distinct fifth dimension. Under the big picture, relativity, this dimension would best be described as us/them. On the subatomic quantum level it becomes me/you. The evidence supporting the fifth climbing dimension is so overwhelming that it need not be cataloged here. Those who doubt it are obviously black holes. I suggest they go back to solving their move sequences with Euclidian geometry (which we know is invalid due to the curved nature of space-time), the most common cause of sloppy footwork.

TIME

We've already seen how time moves faster the farther you get from the planet and how this relates to sex. As sex is a rarity in the climbing universe, we must look elsewhere to test this theory. Indeed, we find confirmation in the example of the belayer and leader. The belayer, being below the leader (i.e., closer to the earth's center), senses time passing very slowly and yawns repeatedly. The leader, being higher, senses time rushing by rapidly. The farther up he gets, the quicker his strength ebbs, and the more likely he is to feel his next bowel movement coming in ahead of schedule.

According to Hawking, time has three directions which can be described by arrows. There is the thermodynamic time arrow, which points in the direction of increasing entropy. There is the cosmological time arrow, which points in the direction the universe is expanding. And finally there is the psychological time arrow, which points in the direction humans perceive it, that is from past to future. The laws of physics don't really care which way the arrows point, because the laws remain the same no matter what.

Physicists however, do care. Now this, I'm afraid, is where I have bad news for Hawking and his colleagues. By sticking to the very big or very small picture, they have concluded that the arrows all have one head pointing the same way. When we examine climbers, though, it is apparent that the psychological arrow often has two heads. I know one climber all too well who habitually gives accounts of his future ascents. These recollections are so vivid that they often appear in *Hot*

Flashes. That nobody else has witnessed these ascents, which have yet to occur, proves that the arrow of psychological time can have two heads for some people, but only one head for most. This may run contrary to physicists, but not to physics.

CONCLUSION

The great goal of scientists as they approach the twenty-first century is to bring together relativity and quantum mechanics into a single GUT. Perhaps this is a needless endeavor. If they'd take their noses out of their microscopes and telescopes and spend a day at the local rock gym listening to climbers babble about sequences, grades, and whatnot, they'd see that relativity and quantum mechanics are already unified. Both theories hold up, because no matter what the scale—subatomic, universal, boulder, or big wall—it holds to nature's laws that climbers will never agree on anything.

(After this column ran, I received a call from an astro-physicist who had attended one of Hawking's famous lectures. He was impressed by this piece. Hmmm, no wonder they haven't come up with a GUT yet.)

Climbing, August 1998

Should You Go Nuts? Or Bolts? Or Just Screw It All?

A handy psychological profile test for climbers

DECIDING WHICH OF THE MANY subdisciplines of climbing to pursue is a perplexing task. Should you swing axes? Pound pitons? Clip bolts? Solo naked? Until now, the only proven method was to dabble in each area, a trial-and-error process that necessitated a time-consuming and expensive series of ascents and epics. By the time you discovered your climbing identity, you were too old to crank anything anyhow.

Fortunately things have changed, and we can now present this quick psychological profile test. For decades, such tests have been used to determine whether individuals might make good police officers, lion tamers, rocket scientists, or whatever. Your answers to the following questions will determine your personality type and which line of climbing you should pursue. There are routes to do, so let's not dawdle; here are the questions. Remember, there are no right or wrong answers. The important thing is to be honest and to answer each question before moving to the next.

1. *Are you recording your answers with:*
   a) a pencil?
   b) a pen?
   c) in your head?
   d) sneaking a peek at the scoring scheme so you know how to skew your response?

If you said pencil, you show the courage to be on record, but also a willingness to change your opinion if appropriate: your forte is routefinding. Heavily crevassed glaciers and tortured icefalls are begging for your presence—you belong in the Northwest, Alaska, or the Himalayas. Those of you who answered pen are confident, have strong opinions, and will be damned if you're going to change them. You'd make an ideal traditionalist. If you're keeping score in your head, you're probably scared to dirty this magazine, and prefer your life to be as ordered and sterile as possible. Alternatively, you may be embarrassed to let others know you read Verm's World. This preoccupation with what others think of you and the desire for sanitary experience will make you a terrific gym climber. If you've already read this before committing to an answer, you're obviously willing to cheat. You'll want tension from above, and lots of it. Find yourself a like-minded belayer and head to some obscure over-bolted crag with no witnesses. Don't forget to fax your achievements to *Hot Flashes*.

2. You are beating your hand with a rock hammer. Does it feel better to stop after ten blows or 100?

Ten blows says you are impatient and have a relentless desire for immediate gratification. Go bouldering. If you said 100 blows, you show the capacity to withstand monotonous suffering: pick a sport route that is way over your head and spend the next year working it. If you answered, "Why stop?" don't even think of climbing anything that doesn't require a portaledge.

3. Would you rather make out with a sheep or a goat?

Answer "Which one is male and which female?" and you show a strong bias toward traditional mores (well, maybe); buy an alpenstock (or a Bosch). If you said, "Which one has the nose ring?" you are a slave to fashion; move to Bend. If you immediately answered "sheep and goat," you show great self-confidence and an adventuresome spirit—you will make a great solo alpinist. If you said neither, you will never be a climber; give up.

4. You are at a climber's barbecue, it's dark near the grill, and nobody is looking. Do you:
   a) "accidentally" grab the grease-splattering hamburger instead of your One World Irieburger?
   b) sprinkle your last few grams of late-1970s "Spanish Fly" rubber onto the burger of the babe you plan to hit on, but not until your forearms get colossally pumped from "casually" pinching your paper plate like it was a Ten Commandments tablet?
   c) yell, "Hey, Dale, you want me to turn your rice grain over?"

If you answered "a," you're normal—renew your subscription to *Climbing* and buy all the stuff in the advertisements. If you answered "b," you're dreaming, not to mention washed up—renew your AAC membership and hope you don't end up in *Accidents in North American Mountaineering*. If you answered "c," you have a helpful, even self-sacrificial nature. With a bachelor's degree, you could become an expedition doctor; without, you can still become a belay bunny at Rifle.

5. *Which rope is stronger? The green or the blue one?*

Those of you who answered this question doubtless know something the rest of us don't. You might enjoy ice climbing.

6. *You are stuck in the woods without any toilet paper. Do you wipe with:*
   a) a snowball?
   b) a smooth rock?
   c) a pinecone?
   d) a *Rock & Ice* mini-guide?

You don't have to be the sharpest knife in the drawer to figure this one out: a = alpinist, b = sport climber, c = crack climber, d = Nobel laureate.

7. *Would you rather climb a wall with:*
   a) Charles Barkley?
   b) Hillary Clinton?
   c) Richard Simmons?

Answer this one and you are obviously nuts. Guiding is the profession for you.

8. *You've just met a young girl named Dorothy who flashes the project you've been working on for the last six months. You ask where she got her phenomenal finger strength, and she says a wizard granted her one wish and will grant you one, too. She takes you to a wizened old man with a squeaky voice who bears a strange resemblance to Warren Harding. What do you wish for?*

If you asked for courage, you probably think you are the alpine-climber type. Wrong-o; an authentic alpinist would ask for regularity, preferably once a day at 3:30 A.M. If you asked for a brain, perhaps you're a wannabe who craves the extreme mental control required for soloing hard mixed routes. At any rate, if you're in that game you come back in tatters from each climb (if at all) and imbibe accordingly—you'd actually ask for a new liver. If you asked for a heart, you probably dream of monstrous feats of cardiovascular endurance. Alas, you are but an armchair mountaineer; any bona fide expedition climber knows the proper response is to click the heels of the ole double boots together and chant: "There's no place like home. There's no place like home." If you answered, "I can't think of anything you can give me that I don't already have," you obviously feel superior to others. You demand respect you don't deserve and believe you are underpaid. You balk at calling those you answer to "superiors," and make no secret of the fact that if you were in charge, the world would be a better place. There's no doubt about it, you're better at spraying than actually doing anything. You should be a columnist for *Climbing*.

Climbing, November 1996

PART III

PLACES

To a large extent, life has been one extended road trip for me. Many a climbing epic has taken place before or after the climbing shoes were donned. I remember one road trip where I fell in love, got the mumps, and broke my finger all in the course of a few weeks. Furthermore, on the same trip my car, passport, and credit cards were all stolen. To top it off, I was stung in the crotch by a Portuguese man-of-war. Still, I got in some good climbing. Surly locals, fickle transport, hostile rangers, language barriers, digestive fiascoes, lousy weather, fleeting romances: you name it, it can happen. For example, one friend of mine entered a "Tough Man" boxing smoker to continue financing a road trip. He beat up all comers on his way to winning $1,000. This would have gone a long way to propelling the road trip, had his dental bill not been $1,200. Somehow, it's all worth it.

Whenever a magazine promotes a certain area, that area sees a sudden influx of climbers. This isn't always healthy, but it seems a short-lived phenomenon; as soon as the next issue comes out, the sheep flock elsewhere. I have mixed feelings about promoting any given area. I've been bummed when the hordes descend somewhere I want to go, too; at the same time, much of my travel has been inspired by accounts I've read in books and magazines.

Often, I feel that too much emphasis is placed on climbers, and not enough on the climbs themselves. Until recently climbs shaped the climber, not the other way around. Rocks and mountains are works of art with Mother Nature being the artist. The first ascensionist, far from being the artist, is more akin to the employee in the frame shop. As climbers we just view these works of art from close range. When I read a travelogue or area survey, I want to know what it's like to climb in that area. I want to hear good stories, not "50 yards downhill of Snoozefest is the exciting Sominex, also 5.15j." Ratings take a reader out of the action, but feelings don't. "Lunging for a butter-smeared belly button, my last pro a wobbly nut out of sight beneath my feet . . . "says a lot more to me than "after eight V9 moves I hit the crux . . . " Therefore, I usually try to keep ratings out of my prose. This can be tough, because a glimpse at any climbing rag will show that big numbers sell magazines. They also date them.

Many of the articles in this section deal with bouldering. I came from a small group of fanatics that carried John Gill's biography, *Master of Rock,* about like a bible. We'd travel the country trying to find and climb the problems pictured in classic spots like the Black Hills Needles, or obscure areas like Shades Crest, Alabama. Those were good times for me, and through my articles on bouldering I hoped to encourage others to continue the tradition of nomadic bouldering.

Also in this chapter are articles on the Alaskan ice climbing Mecca of Valdez and the twistos-apply-here mud-nailing in Utah's Mystery Towers. Finishing it off is a piece on my attempt to climb in all fifty states of the nation, a strange quest at best.

Hit the road.

Pumping Syenite

The 1980s were virtually devoid of writing about bouldering. In 1981, Climbing published John "Largo" Long's classic "Pumping Granite," an ode to the great high bouldering around Idyllwild, California. They didn't print another bouldering feature until the last issue of the decade when this appeared under the title "Texas Tall Tales."

At times it was lonely being a boulderer in the 1980s. The sport-climbing boom lured most gymnastically inclined climbers away from the boulders and onto the bolts. The up side was having places like Hueco Tanks virtually to one's self to develop. I remember going weeks without seeing another climber there. I was outstandingly fortunate to be in the right place at the right time. At the time this was written, Hueco was quickly gaining in popularity. V-grades were still a season away and you could always find a spot in the campground. Bouldering felt like the purest pursuit life had to offer. It was really happy times for me.

I originally titled this "Pumping Syenite," in hopes of emulating Largo and inspiring other boulderers. I don't know how many times I read Largo's two bouldering features, "Pumping Sandstone" and "Pumping Granite" and stared at the pictures. They were right up there with Master of Rock *when it came to inspiration for me.*

HE ROCKETS HIS LEFT HAND UP as his right arm presses down, locking at mid-thigh. His hips swivel 90 degrees allowing the right hand to graze the glute before it makes a controlled journey upward tracing the lat, coming inside the shoulder, then stretching upward to cross the left hand at full extension. His footwork astounds—toe matches, cross throughs, en points. The crowd gasps. This is a master at work. A subtle wrist wave, then eyes pinch in a grimace while lips smirk. The crux is only a move away. The crowd starts chanting, "Splits, splits, splits." Legs fly wide at three and nine.

No, this isn't the beta for the latest Hueco Tanks desperate. It's Tim "TNT" Toula in Juarez, shredding the dance floor at the XO disco. The crowd parts. Tim hits the deck in full splits, rebounds instantly, and twirls a half pirouette. Is this rebound action magic? Can it be harnessed for use in climbing? Or does it depend on a sharp blow to the testes and is this why disco died?

On the boulders 30 miles northeast of the XO, the action is even more intense. After ticking the park's half dozen illegally bolted sport climbs, climbers have three choices. Summon the nerve to repeat the runout Mike Head testpieces, leave Hueco Tanks, or go bouldering. Few climbers are capable of the first and leaving Hueco means going somewhere colder. So bouldering it is. The climber soon discovers what an elite few have known for years. The bouldering at Hueco beats the tights off of the leading.

Climbing in its purest form, that's bouldering. The athlete alone with the rock, the single goal being the summit. No cheating—every fall is a ground fall.

I'm lying in the dust of a perfect landing, scoping the flake 10 feet above me. Sure enough, that's my fingertip stuck to it. I don't care if they all died 10,000 years ago, I curse the enormous greasy-haired sons of bitches anyway. Why blame myself when I can pin it on the mammoths? Seeking relief from itching hides, they rubbed against the base of the Mushroom Boulder removing a few lice and most of the footholds. The polish, or mammoth rub as it's called, only reaches 10 feet up the face, but that's high enough to have thwarted all attempts at one of Hueco's "last great problems." Were this painful line on any other boulder I would be less captivated by it. As it is, it runs straight up the middle of the widest unscaled patch of America's premier boulder. The Mushroom's North Face strikes again.

Just feet from the road, the Mushroom's 50-foot-wide by 12- to 20-foot-high North Face overhangs a perfect landing. The soundness of the microflakes, the utility of the huecos, and the strength of the lines are enough to make any boulderer's tips moist with desire. Given the difficulty of the problems, the landing sees a lot more action than the summit. Fortunately, topouts are a cinch. Jugs lace the summit, begging you to throw for them.

The steepest section of the wall is home to the *Left, Center,* and *Right El Murrays.* The *Center El Murray* has been justly dubbed Hueco's Greatest Problem. (This is only possible because the *45 Degree Wall* holds the title of World's Greatest Problem.) Many a tough guy has had fits at the *El Murrays,* knowing that if he doesn't tick all three he'll leave Hueco only half a hardman.

There are hundreds of legendary climbers, but only a handful of legendary boulderers. One can point at an impossible looking face and tell his partner, "It goes." The partner replies with incredulity. To make a believer out of him the next line always works. First it was "John Gill did it," then it was "Jim Holloway did it," now it's "Bob Murray did it."

I've just done a new problem and am quite pleased with myself. Eagerly, I approach Bob Murray and start raving about it. " . . . then you hook your right heel on this sloper and slap for a pinch. Right then your left foot comes off and you stab it in a tiny hueco." My arms and feet are waving about at imaginary holds in the air. Bob, usually shy, interjects, "Then you flip your left into an undercling and lunge up with your right, match hands then throw for the top." His beta is flawless. For me it's the story of Southwest bouldering. Yet again Murray was there first.

Bob Murray really does exist, though he's rarely seen. He seldom repeats problems because he'd rather work on something new. Many of his problems see one ascent—his—then after everyone else gives up on it the chalk disappears and the problem (Bob is neglectful about naming his climbs) is forgotten. Years later someone sees the line of vague features and starts working the rock, the thrill and glory of a first ascent driving him on. Meanwhile, Bob is out there somewhere cranking at a standard we can only imagine.

According to local legend, there's one striking face Murray hasn't climbed. The boulder is Texas-sized, the lip looming 20 feet up above an uneven rock slab. Fall from the last move and your legs will snap like matchsticks. I scramble over to the gymnasium, one of Hueco's favorite warm-up walls, to recruit a spot. I've got thirty pounds on the biggest climber there, so I lure the two least emaciated dudes away from the gym with the promise of spotting a major first ascent. On the way back to the problem the idea of two spotters sounds better and better. If I fall, it seems unlikely that both can get out of the way.

A couple of half-digit cranks, a first digit sloper, and a shallow scooped sidecling lead me halfway up the 30-degree overhang. So much for the technical stuff. I try to relax on a digit and a half "jug," the last hold I can drop from and still walk away.

The ironrock's soundness assures me, first ascent glory entices me, adrenaline powers me. Soon my hands are above the next bulge. The thought that my spots will get hurt worse than I drives me up another two moves. My tips dig into the last holds, save for the knob at the lip, a long way off in the worst direction. I huff a token "watch me."

Each move up has increased my fear exponentially. Suddenly the terror is gone. Thoughts of falling are replaced by extreme confidence. With my feet up I can't let go with either hand, but I know I'll stick the lunge.

From the ground it must look like a hurried desperation slap, filling the spotters' spandex. From my perspective it seems an eternity, sinking down, pushing up, choosing which hand to stab with, flying for so long, the lip coming closer and closer, all the while my focus so intent on 2 square inches of summit knob my hand feels like it's being yanked to it by a giant rubber band. I descend with the best case of adrenaline shakes I've ever had. The spots haven't budged—they're in shock. My complexion is bleached and the trembling won't cease. The buzz lasts for hours. The next time I go climbing I want more.

I get it. *Flat As a Pancake, Midnight Express, Do Fries Go with That Shake:* all feature career-ending landings. My confidence soars. I happily cross the line between the daring and the foolish. Some say I'm approaching the next line, the one between the foolish and suicidal. By the time I start working on the Kiva Cave Wall, spots are hard to come by. Five days and several pinball plunges later, *Splatter High* is ticked. It's time to double the anti-inflammatory dosage. My joints and tendons feel fine, but my head is swelling something awful.

Four years ago, you could take every climber at Hueco Tanks to the same problem and on a busy day, form a line of three people. Now it's 1989, and I'm looking at Hueco's first lines ever. Over a hundred climbers are competing in the first annual Hueco Tanks Rock Rodeo. Nevertheless, one very unique problem has no line.

Laguna Prieta, the Black Lagoon, is a stagnant sump, some years several feet deep, other years bone dry. The lagoon, full last fall, is slowly shrinking in the dry winter. As the still water evaporates, a huge populace of insalubrious organisms crowds into a concentrated murk, the sort of water even the dumbest kid wouldn't retrieve an errant softball from. Tempting the competitors is a ten-foot roof crack jutting over the lagoon, approachable only by canoe. The crack is 5.11 in difficulty, but boasts 5.12 scoring, a "give" problem whose completion is essential to anyone with aspirations of victory.

I've viewed the crack only once, on a dry year when I could walk to the base. A severe case of Arapiles elbow grounded me that year.

In the years between then and now, my memory kept pace with my brain cells, both diminishing greatly. I recall a short jam through the roof. It's over a body length. I'm floating above my previous viewpoint and still it looks higher off the deck than I recall. The captain pushes his paddle down to give me a depth reading. It sinks three feet before he pulls it out, black goo clinging to the blade.

After my umpteenth nervous chalkup, I gingerly stand up in the listing canoe and mount the rock. It's a one-way deal; no amount of begging can procure a return trip, so I plan to get it done with as quickly as possible.

In short order, I'm wrapped around the sawtooth lip. An attempt to finesse my legs over results in a snapped foothold and a belly scraping swing along the lip. A single handjam holds me, allowing a second chance. This time I grind both knees into the lip and crawl over. Later that day, two big-talent climbers take the plunge. I know your dying to read their names, but I'd be dying if I revealed them.

It's less than a week later when humans and the amoebic fluids of Laguna Prieta again meet. Europeans have a fascination with the American West, particularly Germans. As Hollywood or Sergio Leone have instructed them, the three Germans wear bandannas around their necks as they kneel along the shore of Laguna Prieta. Water is precious in the desert; they know that. And doubtless they know there is a drinking fountain 200 meters away at the toilet blocks. But in the desert there is only one proper way to drink water. In unison they bend over, wave the backs of their hands across the surface to part the scum, cup their hands full, and slowly let the nectar drain down their throats.

Just as a few drops of Laguna Prieta water will demolish the hardiest GI tract, a few solid days of Hueco bouldering will waste the burliest guns. Rest days are essential, but what's there to do in West Texas besides climb? Inside the park the potential for exploration is endless. There are always more Indian paintings to see or classic boulder problems to discover. Most climbers, however, prefer to spend their rest days outside the park. Below is a list of activities that have entertained climbers in the past.

Go desert driving. Unimproved roads abound. Catch some air. Flatten some rabbits. Terrify your passengers with your driving skill. Rent a car and *really* go desert driving. Break the frame. Blow the tires. Then take it back and ask for a refund.

Go to El Paso. Cruise the mall with a new-wave hairdo and watch white bread Americans cringe. Take in a dollar movie. Play golf. Go eat cheap food. Take in another dollar movie. Taste the abundance of natural lithium in the water. (This characteristic mellows El Paso's manic depressives and keeps the rape and murder statistics low.) Go to the Lamplighter Lounge and watch 6'2" Ashley dance.

Go to the Fiesta Drive-in. Watch XXX features from the comfort of your own car. Check out the bulletin board there—watch XXX features from the comfort of someone else's car.

Go to Juarez. Eat at the Crippled Coyote. Get sick. Buy a velvet Elvis painting. Drink cheap beer. Buy a Winking Jesus. Meet dozens of preteen pickpockets. Take in a donkey show (note: they don't use live donkeys anymore so don't get your hopes up). Hey, this is Mexico. You can do anything you want. Just remember, so can the Federales.

Of course, if you really need a rest, I suggest staying in camp and reading a book.

Camping in Hueco comes in two styles: luxury and Pete's. The affluent will plunk down nine bills a night for a site inside the park. Once there, they'll pitch the tent, plug in an electric blanket, then crank up the toaster oven. While the entrées are baking they'll enjoy a hot shower, or at least wait in line for one.

Poor climbers stay at Pete's, the Quonset hut just outside the park boundary. The downstairs houses Pete's family and a tidy little store that sells beer, foodstuffs, and sometimes chalk. The upstairs is a marked contrast. It houses the climbers.

Pete's upstairs is a veritable science fair project—the floor a petri dish covered with a nourishing medium of dirt and moldy food scraps. Above this lies a layer of sleeping bags filled with unwashed climbers. When not in their bags, the climbers cluster about the stove, breathing the smoke and any number of unhealthy airborne critters, wondering not if, but when they'll contract the "Quonset crud." At least the rats are gone now, thanks to Shithead the Cat, but he split when his menu was exhausted. Somehow, the love of the climbers who named him wasn't enough to keep him around.

Despite the unhealthy conditions, Pete's has a certain allure to climbers, especially young ones ("Mom would have a fit if she saw me here") and Europeans ("Ja, dis iz reely de Wild West"). The camaraderie is vividly apparent. Each climber shares the same goal: let someone else clean it up.

By now, most readers should be ready to quit their job, sell all their lead gear, blast down to Hueco, and live the romantic life of a bouldering nomad. Unfortunately, the transient climber's lifestyle is not as romantic as it seems. Romance and full-time climbing mix well for as long as oil and vinegar. Nevertheless, there is a fantasy shared by most male climbers in which an unattached woman climber of knee-weakening beauty appears at the boulders, is charmed by that climber, then travels around the world's climbing areas with him for the rest of his life. It is general knowledge that such women do not exist, or at least aren't single, but the fantasy remains. Four rent-free years had borne out the validity of these observations to me. Then one day she appeared. I'll call her Helga, not her real name. *Sports Illustrated* has featured uglier women on the cover of its swimsuit issue. Her stats are perfect: currently single, self-employed on extended climbing vacation, in need of partner, friendly.

At last, the dream is playing out in real life. I knew that just such a woman had been saved for me, being the nice, deserving guy I am. Enter Gomer, not his real name. Friend of over a decade who recently broke up with his climbing girlfriend of many years and still bears the gobies. As any good friend would do for a broken buddy, I tell him to get out of that lonely house, come check out the awesome bouldering I've been telling him about for seven years, and enjoy being single for a change. Gomer takes my advice, comes down to Hueco, and as any good friend would do, gloms onto Helga and leaves Hueco for a destination he regrettably can't reveal to me. Which leaves me 15 feet up a lichen-splattered overhang on sloping pinches, a back-breaking landing below, the fear pushing Helga out of my mind, then the overwhelming confidence shoving the fear out as my entire existence is focused on the next hold, a downsloping grease nipple so distant that the only choice is to lunge.

(Years after writing this, I found out that Murray had climbed the "problem Murray hadn't bagged," albeit on toprope. I don't know why I didn't include my name for this climb in the article, because it's one of my favorite high-ball boulder problem names of all time—See Spot Run.)

Climbing, October 1989

East Side Stories

In the 1980s the major climbing magazines all featured an info column in which correspondents would report the new routes established in their local areas. Several of the correspondents became household names, not so much for their own climbing achievements, but for their style of reporting said achievements in the third person. After listing newsworthy climbs established by their peers, their accounts would go something like this: "Undoubtedly the finest new route in the region was Me, Me, Beautiful Me, *put up by [correspondent's name]." The following travelogue was written as a parody of this style. When the "fan mail" arrived, it was apparent some people didn't realize this was a parody. Others were even further lost. One "fan," blinded by sobriety and his own glowing 5.12-leading ability, took umbrage when I mentioned Mammoth and drugs in the same paragraph. Geez, what was I thinking?*

THE EAST SIDE OF THE SIERRA NEVADAS, 1977. Our Hero, youthful, impressionable, and yet to gain his characteristic bitterness, gets his first taste of East Side excitement. It's a cool summer night and he's up to his neck in Hot Creek, the bathtub temperature stream soothing a pair of Tuolumne-cramped calves. A score of laughing heads and twice as many shoulders are visible through the moonlit steam. Our Hero's eyes fix on a brassiere hanging from the footbridge. Suspended in the cups are two bottles of Jack Daniels. Fifths. The eyes sweep the surface, searching for the buoys that minutes ago filled those cups. Healthy bobbers abound. It's one of those cosmic experiences that alter the course of a life. Our Hero is hooked on the East Side. He has yet to see the boulders.

It's not long before Our Hero is introduced to Deadman Summit. Located just a hundred yards from US 395, the main road between Tuolumne and Mammoth, Deadman Summit provides an irresistible bouldering challenge. Tall pocketed faces, deep pumice landings, thick pine forests: it's the sort of place you could lose your head over. In fact, the prospector it's named after did just that. Local legend says it wasn't the fantastic bouldering that caused him to lose his head, it was a dispute with his partner.

Our Hero lucks out and keeps his head, however his tips are soon turned into mincemeat by the zillions of little piranha teeth lining the rhyolite pockets. A two-hour session is long by Deadman's standards. Not only are the tips turned to mush, the brain usually is too. The problems tend to be high; 20-footers are commonplace. To conquer these, it helps for the boulderer to be higher. To quote sometimes local Bill Russell, "This kind of problem takes two Schlitz Bulls under the belt to do. They don't make you any bolder, but they take away the fear."

If you forgot the Bulls or the buds, don't despair—Deadman's crushed pumice landings are the best in the world. Imagine falling into several feet of fluffy popcorn. The only drawback is that your feet sink down so deep that the pebbles and dust fill your shoes. Not only do slippers fit the letter-slot pockets and thin cracks, they can be emptied out and put back on in seconds. Of course there's something to be said for lacing and unlacing boots. By the time you get them emptied and refitted, your forearms will have partially deflated. If you need more time to de-pump you can play treasure hunt. They never did find that prospector's head.

Many other good volcanic crags lie in the forests near Deadman Summit such as The Swiss Cheese, Rick's Rocks, and the Bachar Boulders. It is at the latter that we rejoin Our Hero, about to turn thirty, bitter at the changes in his sport, and more bitter that those changes have neglected to fatten his pocketbook. He's facing one last chance to grasp his share of fame before joining the Senior Tour. The face is beautiful, slightly overhung, 25 feet high, sparsely pocketed, but well defined by two bounding crack lines. Its reputation for difficulty is well established. Our Hero has heard from locals that "only Moffat has climbed it" and "only Kauk has climbed it." He can't shake the thought that if he pulls it off they'll say "only Sherman has climbed it." Visions of greatness clog his brain—groupies, sponsors, his own TV ad, a cover shot in *Climbing*, more groupies. He cranks. He pulls.

He throws. He shakes. He does it. Upon topping out he's greeted by a cool breeze, a mountain vista, a trembling pump, and a finger that feels half an inch longer than when he started. He realizes that he's all alone, Greg Epperson did not capture the ascent on film, and nobody has gotten famous on the East Side since Norman Clyde.

Fortunately, all is not lost for Our Hero. Mammoth is close by and contains all the support facilities he needs to buoy his spirits. Mammoth is actually a suburb of Los Angeles, where rich, trendy Angelinos live on winter weekends and employ a local populace of semi-indentured servants. Many of the Mammoth climbers work in the resort industry, thus having plenty of time in the summers to climb and collect unemployment checks. Surrounded by money, drugs, and prime recreation areas, and located above an occasionally rumbling magma chamber, it's little surprise Mammoth locals know how to party. Being at the crags is no excuse for not having a good time. The fresh pine scent is often mixed with the heady aroma of fine smokeables.

But what's it like farther south in the Owen's Valley? Let's rejoin Our Hero at the world-famous Buttermilks.

Uh oh. Our Hero looks in desperate shape. The combination of high desert sun, polished granite boulders, too much chalk in the sinuses, and twenty or so cold beer compresses on his swollen elbows has left him a bit peaked. The Bishop boys throwing this shoe demo have proved adept at partying as well as climbing. Now they're moving to Round Valley for barbeque action and more partying.

Our Hero, the once proud partier, has met his match. Like Tyson in the tenth against Buster Douglas, Our Hero fails to go the distance and collapses, before midnight, on the floor of the house. Or is he on the porch? No, it's half and half. A debate ensues; should Our Hero be denuded of his eyebrows?

Morning dawns. Our Hero's stomach feels like it's filled with battery acid and helium as it threatens to rise out of his throat. Nevertheless, he still has his eyebrows, thanks to the intervention of his buddy Mr. Big, who got him into this mess and is now driving him to Bishop for breakfast. Just when Our Hero's headache has decided to settle into position, iron maiden nails piercing the forehead, his cranium leaps for the windshield. Mr. Big has stomped the brake pedal to the floor, perceptibly slowing his loyally untrustworthy VW "Van Hosen."

Our Hero's precious brows stop just inches from the glass. "Holy shit," he exclaims. "Fuckin' A," agrees Mr. Big. Apparently neither of them has seen a mountain lion in the wild before, much less nearly wrap a big cat's head around one end of the bumper and its tail around the other. The lengthy catamount lopes quickly, gracefully across the road then hops a fence into a pasture of cows. The pair slap a high five. They're so excited they nearly forget their hangovers.

Dude, I thought the last two paragraphs were supposed to be about the Buttermilks, not drunken idiots and Ranger Rick nature thrills. Okay, here's the scoop on the boulders. They're big, they're round, they're surrounded by sage and coarse sand landings. They usually feature a glossy polished side and a lower-angled grainy side. Most of the classic problems are found on the polished faces. The holds range from plates and flakes, to incuts and huecos, and are either distressingly smooth or painfully rough. Many a smooth-looking dinnerplate hold features tiny crystals on the back side for lancing fingertips.

Like Deadman's, Buttermilk sessions are often ended when the tips cry "Uncle." Toprope anchors exist only on Grandma and Grandpa Peabody, the two 50-footers that dominate the hillside. Other bolts have appeared in the Buttermilks, but not for long. This is one area that refuses to be reduced to a playground for those whose egos exceed their ability and commitment. Come here expecting to climb at your limit, not above it.

What's this? Our Hero looks confused. He's just topped out on a 30-foot granite Buttermilk egg and now, after glorying in his achievement, not to mention the tremendous surroundings—the 13,000 footers towering to the west and the snow-shrouded White Mountains shimmering in the east—he takes a look down and can't find the descent. The solitude of climbing on the East Side is never so noticeable as when nobody's around to point out the descent on a boulder you neglected to walk around first. While Our Hero ponders his predicament, let us visit the nearby burg of Bishop.

The southern of the two towns that dominate East Side rock climbing, Bishop is sleepy and happy to stay that way.

Perhaps the biggest event of the 1980s was the opening of the K-Mart. Nevertheless, there are two big annual events deserving mention—the Memorial Day Weekend Mule Days and the Labor Day Rodeo. Bishop is the self-declared "mule capital of the world," a claim no other town seems to be challenging. The Mule Days parade is noteworthy for being America's largest non-motorized parade. And you thought car exhaust smelt bad. Besides the standard amenities of supermarkets, restaurants, and liquor stores, Bishop has the best climbing shop on the East Side: Wilson's Eastside Sports. Many of the local climbers can be found in the back, sniffing glue and repairing boots.

Low overhead and cheap, brain-dead labor has also attracted other climbing businesses to Bishop, namely chalkbag and T-shirt power-house Kinnaloa.

Just north of Bishop there's bouldering at Fish Slough, Chalk Bluff, and the Vatican. These areas are warm enough for winter climbing and feature soft volcanic rock marred with pockets. Sources who have never climbed in France claim the holds are "just like Buoux."

As we return to the Buttermilks, we find our hapless hero back on the ground, but by no means safe. He's involved in what appears to be some kind of religious self-flagellation, beating himself with his bouldering rug. On closer inspection, we see wallet-sized welts rising on his arms and legs. Not bothering to strip the size 8 Fires from his size 10½ feet, he runs downhill toward the car, fleeing from the invisible attackers. The no-see-ums are out and they make mosquitoes look friendly as butterflies. Silent and no bigger than a flea, no-see-ums administer instant pain, followed by days of burning itching akin to open poison oak blisters with Bengay rubbed in. They are unfortunately common throughout the East Side during prime bouldering weather. Our Hero will soon discover, however, that greater winged terror is in store for him.

Until recently, Aeolian Buttes, the oldest volcanic rocks north of Mammoth, were relatively undeveloped. Their gargoylish appearance and pink, unvarnished color suggest unsound conditions, but closer inspection reveals many faces to be solid. As with all East Side areas, the setting is striking. To the east lie the desolate Mono Craters, looking like Iwo Jima after John Wayne was through with it. To the west tower the mighty Sierras. Aeolian Buttes occupy a low ridge in between.

One boulder exerts a singular pull on Our Hero. It's called The Pit Bull due to its mean demeanor (even the descent is 5.10) and when viewed at a particular angle, its resemblance to Mt. Spuds in the Bud Light advertisements. Our Hero is attempting to climb the line between *Child Eater* and *Party Animal*. On a previous visit, he backed off his chosen line from great height, just one move from meeting up with the top section of *Party Animal*. He now refers to this problem as *Know When to Say When*. He'd be happy to forget about it and leave it for a better climber to tick the first. Alas, another climber, one stricken with incredible shrinking ball disease, has declared his intention to bolt it into a sport climb. Our Hero has something to say about that. He just says, "No." No to pansyass 30-foot leads. No to bolts on East Side boulders. No to degrading the efforts and visions of our predecessors. In a fit of traditionalist bitterness, he laces on his best boots, paws at his carpet patch, and mounts the rock. In no time he's reached his high point. He glances down. The landing is East Side standard issue—it could only be better if it were closer. Still, from this height, broken legs are a distinct possibility. He digs his fingers into a delicate thin-walled pocket, brings his feet up to smear two polished dents, and stretches out left to barely reach a tiny, flat shelf. He tries to weight it, but he's extended so far laterally he feels like he's stroking a Chihuahua's head, a mean Chihuahua. He can still back off and feel like a turd for returning just to fail again. He could go for it and blow it, slam into the deck, and feel like a foolish turd with two sore armpits hugging a pair of crutches. Or he could go for it, succeed, and feel like a genuine hero for getting away with something so foolish. Should he swing onto it?

While Our Hero ponders his fate and wastes valuable reserves of endurance, it's time for us to look into the winged terror we were earlier promised.

On an outcrop a couple hundred yards away is an unhappy creature. No, it's not a sport climber, nor is it his editor. It's a falcon, pissed off at Our Hero for climbing on a rock bearing its shit. The falcon draws its talons across the rock, putting an edge on the claws that would make Freddy Krueger proud. It takes to the air keeping a keen eye on Our Hero, watching for his next move.

Our Hero cuts loose onto the Chihuahua head. No going back now and the falcon knows it as well. Emitting a shrill throaty cry it dives. Swoosh, the soundwaves of a projectile beat Our Hero's eardrums. Recognizing the danger, Our Hero's spotter screams out the falcon's movements, "From your right. Thirty feet, 20 feet, 10. . . . " Our Hero digs into the holds with a double-adrenaline grip. Swoosh. . . . Our Hero hurries upwards. He grasps the top of the wall and peers Kilroy-like over the lip. "Twenty, 10. . . . " It's coming straight for him, black tears flanking the flesh-razoring beak. He ducks his head. Swoosh. . . . Hair freshly parted, Our Hero tops out. Ho man, no time for summit parties.

Back on the ground, shaking from the falcon-molested downclimb, but satisfied that justice has been done, Our Hero is left with one nagging question. What's happening at the hot springs tonight?

Climbing, June 1990

Nothing But Problems

Whether Alison Osius volunteered to edit my articles, or whether it was punishment for misdeeds against management is unclear to me. What is clear is that we both enjoy a good verbal tussle. Editing sessions with her were "enhanced" by her smug Eastern education butting into my don't-take-no-shit-off-no-one Western arrogance. One day I spotted a Sunday supplement to the Aspen Times *on her coffee table. The entire front page was devoted to her with big headlines gushing, "Author, Climber, Bride." To which I retorted, "How 'bout 'Hellcat, Bitch, Editor.'" We both had a good laugh over that. Alison loved her tough new nickname and even had Hellcat emblazoned on her nameplate at work. Feminists got their panties in a twist over this article, and several cried out "How could you let that pig call you that?" Easily. Alison edited this piece.*

"Hellcat Bitch Editor, I got your participle dangling right here." It was all I could do to keep the words in my mouth and prevent my hand from performing an obscene gesture. It was another editing session at *Climbing* magazine, and once again I was aghast at the changes I'd been asked to make. At least the editors were willing to work with me—unlike some magazines, which prefer to surprise an author in print. Finding it easier to argue my points face to face, I was in for numerous trips across the Colorado Rockies. This took me from Fort Collins to the mag's headquarters in Carbondale, and past numerous boulders in between.

After a while, the battles were getting to me: the revisions, the censorship, and particularly the grammar rules. It was even getting tough slipping subtle off–color jokes past the Hellcat. My one solace was the fantasy all writers harbor—that one day I'd present my editors with something they could never touch.

In print, my fantasy could never happen, but there was plenty of rock just up the road at Independence Pass. Several miles short of the pass, the road takes a tight turn to the left. Rounding this curve, the driver is confronted with a steep, scruffy 200-foot granite face that is the focal point of climbing on the pass—the Grotto Wall. A hundred yards below the Grotto Wall, in the crook of the hairpin next to the parking pullout, lies a gargantuan boulder. On the right side of the south face I found what I was looking for. A line that drew a parallel between fine writing and fine bouldering. A vigorous line, concise (all holds necessary), and with an emphatic ending (horror lunge).

At first I doubted it would go. The holds felt miserable. On the second day, I was getting high enough that the falls hurt, even though I was landing on my sketchpad (a foam-padded carpet swatch that takes three Advils' worth of cartilage shock out of each session). On day three the big grip came. When I looked down, my 2-by-3–foot sketchpad appeared no bigger than a postage stamp. The only way to ensure hitting it was to jump off on purpose. I knew I'd just licked the crux, and the dyno above looked easy. Nevertheless, it was a sloping diagonal crack I'd shoot for, I couldn't tell which hand to go with, and I was chicken. Time for The Scottrope.

Scott Blunk is The Scottrope. Six foot seven inches tall, 215 pounds—in a bar fight he'd make Jean Claude Van Damme look like Pee-wee Herman. I trust a spot from him more than a belay from any climber at Smith Rock. The only problem with bringing him up to my project is that he's good enough to snake it from me.

On the first attempt I had no regrets bringing The Scottrope. I sketchily gained my high point and, with the pad plus a 3-inch-thick foam sleeping mat below me, went for the dyno. My fingers nailed the slope, clamped down, and jetted off. I flew so far past my landing pads they might as well have been in the car. Scott strolled to his left and snagged me just before I impaled myself on some broken branches.

The next time up, I went with the opposite hand and squeaked through. A fine piece. I call it *The Ineditable.*

My interest in Independence Pass bouldering began months before, on the weekend Hellcat Bitch married my old funneling buddy, her boss, Mike. (They strategically left out the bit about "Does anyone know why these two shouldn't be wed?" Doubtless, they knew

I'd scream, "It's just a career move" or "She doesn't have the cajones to lower after each fall.") The day after the nuptials more climbers crawled over the Pass than ever before. I felt sorry for the bolts—they were taking a beating.

I was jawing with some old acquaintances, waiting for a tow up one of the Pass Wall's routes, when I decided to check out the boulder across the road. The top of this big block was even with the pavement. Down the embankment was a cavernous overhang reminiscent of Hueco's *45 Degree Wall*—good holds, well-spaced, with an intimidating lunge at the top. At the bottom was a jumble of rocks embedded in ice, which still hadn't thawed in June.

The ice, the hard cranks, the incredible release after the powerful lip moves: it all reminded me of a time long ago, when trips to Aspen demolished sinuses and livers, not skin and tendons. A friend of Mike's had set me up with a memorable date. She was a woman who, after draining her drink, knew what to do with the ice cubes. I promised to name a climb after the event. This was the one, *ICBJ*.

I reckoned that if such a classic as *ICBJ* existed on the pass, then certainly there must be other good problems. I had to look no farther than the undeveloped talus slope beneath the Grotto Wall—a place that one day will live up to its name, the World of Hurt.

The finest challenge in this land of worst landings is *Deep Six Holiday*. Beneath *Deep Six* is a pit of angular blocks, any of which would make a fine tombstone. Above is a mantel not unlike the topout on The Mental Block's notorious *Pinch Overhang*, seriously sloping, with nary a dime-edge overhead for help. Between is a fin of granite, a crucial foothold that flexes an inch when weighted during the power undercling to the lip. Some day the fin will burst. My former girlfriend used to tell me, "God looks after the stupid." He did his bit that day. It's the only boulder problem I've given an X rating to—a fall would likely end one's career. This is in contrast to other World of Hurt problems, most of which deserve a capital R (bone fractures likely) as opposed to a lowercase r (probable deep contusions).

Independence Pass had me psyched for high-mountain bouldering. As long as I was west of the Continental Divide, a climbing trip with Craig Hazelton seemed in order. Craig is the "Trainer of Champions," a title he earned from teaching the now-North Carolinian honedaddy Harrison Dekker how to climb. He's also to blame for teaching me to climb sixteen years ago. Craig is one of my best buddies, but his idea of a good time doesn't include breaking bones (though it has in the past). Instead of going to the World of Hurt, we went to Telluride.

Despite the fun bouldering to be had, most people are drawn to Telluride by the town and the skiing. Granted, the locals come on friendly, but then again most realtors do. I heard rumor that one in five Telluridians is involved in selling the quaint Victorian houses that make up the town. Mining originally supported the town and the town once supported Butch Cassidy, who withdrew $21,000 from the local bank in June of 1910, his first bank job. Thieving continues to be a Telluride tradition, but now it's the visitors who get robbed—to the tune of six bucks per burger.

Ten years before, we had ventured here on an unforgettable trip. I still cringe at the memory of driving through sleet storms with the windows rolled all the way down. Frostbite seemed a mild price to gain ventilation from Craig's giardic emanations.

On the plus side, I recalled a group of fun boulders at the lower end of the South Fork of the San Miguel River. We drove less than a mile upstream from the noisy gravel-pit operation. The rocks were easy to find again. One boulder on the roadside hinted of the others to be found up the aspen- and fir-covered hillside. The Ilium Boulders are short, moderate, and graced with flat landings. The only blight on the scene is the abundance of fixed carpet patches beneath the boulders: modern tactics, applied with minimal forethought. Most of the carpets were left out beneath low angle or vertical faces, fully exposed to the common summer afternoon thundershowers. Paw them before mounting a problem and you might as well be tapdancing in a pile of cat barf.

The rock at Ilium is the coveted Dakota Sandstone—solid and with good friction on holds of all types: square cuts, slopers, pockets, cracks. Only fingertip flakes are scarce at Ilium. Craig said Dekker had recently told him that "bouldering's no fun because you always have to push yourself" (as if The H-Man doesn't enjoy shoving the envelope). The message was lost on Craig. He was having a blast. I tried to prove Dekker right; I groveled in the dirt on the sit-downs, off-routed holds, threw big lunges, skinned my shins, landed on my ass. To no avail. I was having a good time too.

After the session it was just a five-minute hike downhill to the free campground next to the river. This campground is sometimes home to workers who can't afford the rent in Telluride. On popular weekends it can overflow with visitors. The result has been excessive impact on fragile surrounding areas. Usually there's room in the other free campgrounds upstream. Nearby is good fishing, and in short order, Craig pulled in a limit of cutthroat, brown, and rainbow trout.

A few miles east from the Ilium Boulders is a 30-foot-tall Dakota crag at Society Turn, where the road to Ophir tees into the main road to Telluride. Anyone who doubts that a bat can eat 3,000 insects in one night hasn't seen the glistening pile of black shit beneath the crag's main roof. Fortunately the view up the steep-walled, U-shaped valley toward town is terrific. So is the ceiling problem coming out a bizarre 10-foot diameter cave right of the main roof. The holds are a mix of funky underclings and juggy blocks, many of which rattle when you pull on them. It gets my pick as the most enjoyable roof in Colorado.

Minutes east of town, just past the big mine at the head of the valley, are some popular conglomerate boulders that have been subject to access problems over the years. Dark purple and peppered with knobs and pockets, the boulders lie in a jungle of aspens, ferns, wildflowers, and stinging nettles. There's hope amongst locals that current negotiations might grant legal access sometime this year. Additional cobble pulling can be found on a 30-foot-tall conglomerate cube just beneath Bear Creek Falls.

Another mining community turned ski town is Frisco, Colorado, home of *Frisco Buttress* and *Via the Hot One*. Both of these tough problems are perched on a Lilliputian crag overlooking the westbound on-ramp where Frisco's Main Street traffic turns onto I-70.

I was there one Labor Day weekend, trying *Via the Hot One,* when who should show up but Bob Williams, a high-security-clearance missile mathematician and long-time boulderer. He was there just to look, but found *Frisco Buttress* so appealing that he borrowed a pair of my boots.

At first, he couldn't do the problem, so he resorted to drastic measures to reduce his weight. Now Williams is a cultured and well-mannered individual—the kind of guy who says "Darn it, I fell off," instead of "Festering boils of venereal origin, that hold's slicker than a Firestoned possum head"—hence I was shocked to see him disrobe in view of the crowded holiday traffic just 50 feet away. In nothing but Fire Ballets and a pair of flesh-toned BVDs he attacked the blunt arête. What can I say? It worked.

It takes more than sticky rubber and beige grots to make it up *Via the Hot One*. The wall immediately right of the buttress (the buttress is on-route only for the feet) took Steve Mammen, one of Colorado's most respected boulderers, two years of attempts before success. "The Hot One" refers to Mammen's weed burner, which he used to dry out the weeping seam and warm the holds prior to his late-fall ascent. At 9,000 feet elevation, *Via the Hot One* would seem an ideal summer project. Not so. It faces east, allowing the early morning sun to warm the black rock, including a critical sloper finger edge on which you want as much grip as possible (unless you can do a one arm pull-up on two tips stacked in an inch-deep V-slot). More important than good conditions on the second ascent was The Scottrope, who gave me the confidence to invert in extremis and chuck a foot over my head, an option the spotless Mammen didn't have.

For the beginning to intermediate climber looking to break up the drive along I-70, I recommend the Wolcott Boulders, a pair of firm Dakota Sandstone cubes, one big, one small, situated a mile west of Wolcott (20 miles west of Vail), on the south bank of the Eagle River. On both my visits to these rocks, the fisherman's camp that surrounds them has been filled with noisy chowderheads. If any of the local fish were being caught, it was certainly not from being outsmarted.

The 20-foot boulder is ideally suited for taking big whippers off. Botch a foot smear on a steep bump, or rip out of an opposition move, and at least you can count on a flat landing: either on dirt, in the mud, or atop an RV. The 12-foot-tall boulder is short enough to push yourself on (once you learn the descent route). The left side of its south face is a challenge if you shun the good holds on the left edge.

If you're looking for quality climbing on a big Dakota boulder, head for the northern outskirts of Durango. Known for good mountain biking and a narrow-gauge railroad, Durango is home to The Boxcar, perhaps the best single chunk of Dakota in the state. Length and height are similar to a boxcar, but it's twice as wide and the expansive east face tilts over like the sucker's derailing on top of you.

My first visit taught me that The Boxcar is a poor choice for summer bouldering; after twelve hours of solid driving from L.A., I tried to hop the freight car and was railroaded by all but the most incut of problems. I spent most of my time at the base. Rubber-armed and goggle-eyed, I stared at the lineup of easy-looking problems that were thwarting me. The trees surrounding the boulder weren't tall enough to shade the problems, but they did provide a humid microclimate perfect for buttering up the big sloping square cuts and turning the summit mantels into Mazola nightmares. At least I had the comfort of knowing the medical center was located just five minutes south down the trail.

I returned in mid-September to make amends for my poor performance a month earlier. The Scottrope couldn't make it due to a stomach flu and when I saw The Boxcar I too felt like hurling. It had been defiled. There were paintings of symbols and serpents all over the south-facing warm-up wall and some on the classic east face. I asked the other climbers I met that day and even inquired at the local climbing shop as to their origin, but nobody I asked knew who did these phony aboriginal "artworks." That morning, the sun turned the east face into a giant hibachi. I had a great session despite the heat, tearing up the problems that had spanked me before. Even so, I left feeling bitter, pissed off at how this great boulder had been urbanized.

Fortunately, that afternoon I got my first chance to climb at Durango's other developed area, the Turtle Lake Boulders. Five yards from the road a short boulder with a stepped, Gunksish overhang beckons you into the oak forest beyond, where half-a-dozen sandstone boulders from 10 to 25 feet tall await. I had a great time in this cozy boulder garden, which is packed with amusing problems catering mostly to beginner and intermediate climbers. The rock is soft and the holds rounded and sometimes sandy. Hard problems can and have been done, but beware small holds: they have the life expectancy of Salman Rushdie at a Tehran book signing. If there were as many rock bands at Woodstock as at Durango, the concert would still be going. I left wondering how many more Boxcars are out there waiting to be discovered.

Colorado Rockies bouldering is filled with variety. Fed by the slopes of a host of fourteeners, the Arkansas River flows through the heart of the Rockies and past some bitchin' boulders. Three miles downstream from the town of Granite and on the east side of the river lies a boulder field. Dozens of granite blocks nestled amongst pine trees tempt one to cross the river, but on second thought the water looks awfully fast and the boulders may be too small to climb on.

As it turns out, a handful are big enough; in the 12- to 15-foot range. The rocks are on Forest Service land, but the road to them crosses private land. After driving through three "No Trespassing" signs, Chris Jones, Roland Foster, and I reached a ranch house, which I approached to ask permission. Ordinarily, I'd have begged the "My long hair might freak them out" excuse, but the absentminded Jones would probably forget what to ask, and Foster's breath could've knocked out Evander Holyfield. Miraculously, I made a good impression, and the owners graciously gave us permission to cross their land.

The granite is sound and not too rough on the skin. Some of the landings are great (jagged blocks, loose round cobbles, tree roots), some are smooth and boring. My favorite problem is *The Floater*: technical footwork, dynos to fingertip edges, continuous difficulty, and a "great" landing all combine for a complete make-or-break bouldering experience.

On the same day trip, we climbed 20 miles downstream from the granite rocks, at a group of rhyolite boulders on the east side of the river 5 miles south of Buena Vista. Only one, the Buena Vista Boulder, is big enough to be of interest. Some 20 feet tall, the tilted block is laced with pockets on its overhanging side.

The nearby prison lent inspiration. *Chained Heat* is the obvious challenge, involving quick pocket-poking topped off with a meaty jug slap. Just 6 feet left, a problem starts off the right side of the 7-foot block that props the overhang. Not much to look at, but a falling climber would get clipped and flipped by the boulder beneath, therefore the name: *Life Sentence*. *Light Sentence* should be the name of the tame jug haul a step to the left.

Speaking of light, that's just what I expected from the Redstone boulders 19 miles up the scenic Crystal River from *Climbing* magazine's headquarters. Given the amount of time the magazine staff has to spend whipping my writing into shape, there's surely no time left to exercise. Therefore I didn't expect much in the way of high-powered cranking at the local boulders. That's before I heard Jeff Achey lived in town and had been working them.

The glasses don't fool me. I know Achey is the spawn of some master-race experiment. The Aryan features, the log-like arms, the door-width shoulders: Achey looks like He-Man with a haircut. He's milked the four Redstone boulders, two no bigger than a bathroom, for an amazing 100 problems. Most are absurd contrivances, but Achey, a local teacher, has the right attitude. He says, "This place has an incredible number of classic problems for climbers with nowhere else to go."

Achey met me at Redstone's maroon conglomerate boulders and showed me his favorite problems. Flawlessly he cruised through problem after ruthlessly dialed problem. It reminded me of films I'd seen of the Euro-stars climbing, where any trace of struggling or hesitation is snipped. Two of Achey's best Redstone creations are *The Corkscrew* and *Guns and Roses*.

The Corkscrew has the most bizarre sequence I've ever seen performed on rock. Achey spun out the roof with a series of palm moves, shoulder contortions, and crotch-rending leg splits, on the way completing a 360. Next it was my turn. Achey, a boulderer's boulderer, completely enjoyed his sandbag. I faced outward, arms spread, leg twitching in a fruitless attempt to plaster a foot under the roof. I must have looked like Samson, palming mightily against the pillars to topple the roof of the Philistine temple, yet my strength proved less than heroic, and it was I, not the roof, who fell.

Guns and Roses was more my style, a brutish low traverse with lots of span moves that show off the biceps at their best angle. The kind of problem you like to do in front of an appreciative audience of the opposite sex. A problem worthy of the moniker The Ripper of Redstone. Achey drifted across it, then in a few tries I thugged it.

After a session that was much too short, we headed back to Carbondale. I'd have to rest up for another session with the Hellcat Bitch Editor the next day.

Sure enough, The Hellcat didn't like the way I'd identified one of America's premiere alpine climbers simply as "the bankrupt sport-climbing promoter Jeff Lowe."

"I've got a problem with this," said Hellcat.

"Yeah, problems," I thought and my mind drifted to places I'd never climbed. I'd heard of boulders at Crested Butte and some near Redcliff. Then there was The Cannonball, a 50-foot-diameter globe of virgin granite hidden in the woods near Leadville. I realized the world was full of problems, and I couldn't wait to get on them.

Climbing, June 1992

Pumping Sandstone: The Sequel

What isn't new in Front Range bouldering

Every now and then, a climber comes by whose accomplishments are so ahead of his time that his own generation doesn't know what to make of them. Jim Holloway was such a climber. At the time this was written his accomplishments had the rare distinction of remaining unrepeated nearly two decades later. No other climber could claim that. Nevertheless Jim Holloway was virtually unknown, his name having somehow fallen through the cracks of history. I still don't think most people realize how far ahead of his time Holloway was. I hope this article brought him some of the recognition he deserves.

THE GAP BETWEEN HOLDS WAS HUGE, but so were John Long's lats. Grasping a doorjamb finger edge with his right hand, he levered off that arm, forearm braided, triceps knotted, and strained left to a first digit slot. In an instant the scene was immortalized, the photo of the resultant iron cross gracing the cover of *Climbing* #46. This was the famous *Ripper Traverse*, 20 feet of smooth, hard sandstone, and one of the problems Long had ventured to Colorado to test himself on.

In 1977, Long, aka Largo, ventured to the famed bouldering gardens of Colorado. He documented his Front Range pilgrimage, from Pueblo to Fort Collins, in a treatise entitled "Pumping Sandstone" (*Climbing* #46). No modest shrimp, the perennially shirtless Largo filled the glossy pages with photos of his corn-fed physique and praise for the bouldering accomplishments of John Gill. Both were impressive.

Largo has a habit of stretching the truth, however he did not exaggerate when he wrote that "Gill had indeed mastered the intricacies of dynamic movement." John Gill's reputation as the forefather of modern gymnastic bouldering is well deserved. His testpieces throughout the Front Range (though some argue his hardest problems lie outside Colorado) are still the standard by which one's bouldering is measured. The Eliminators, the Mental Block problems, the *Ripper Traverse*—all are mandatory ticks for any lifer. Though punched out by some of Gill's stiffer problems, Largo handily scaled the standard classics, listing them for the benefit of *Climbing*'s readership. Yet, presumably unbeknownst to Largo, his article on state-of-the-art bouldering was sorely out of date.

Jim Holloway. Very few climbers recognize the name. Nevertheless, in the four years prior to Long's pilgrimage, Holloway did moves on the boulders of Colorado so extreme that even in these days of sticky rubber, steroids, and sponsorships, nobody has come close to repeating them.

In photos from the mid-1970s, Holloway sports long hair, muttonchops, and a lanky physique. He appears an unlikely candidate as a superclimber. Contemporaries, however, remember smoothness and determination, in addition to gymnastic power thought to be achievable only by short men. Holloway remembers "drinking beer, eating junk food, and smoking dope."

The 1970s were a golden era for Colorado bouldering. The activity had finally been recognized as a worthy end in itself, due in part to Gill's standard-setting accomplishments in the 1960s. Despite Gill's fecundity, there were still lots of plums left, and plenty of boulderers to pick them. Holloway, Jim Michael, Sandy Stewart, Scott Blunk, Dan Oliver, and Dave Rice, to name a few. Although their primary objective was to have fun, they bouldered exceedingly hard. Holloway, for one, admits, "I wanted to put up problems nobody would ever repeat."

Before we try to catch up with Holloway, let's return to the original "Pumping Sandstone." As the article ended, Largo was east of Pueblo, in a desolate canyon filled with cholla, quicksand, and Dakota sandstone, a rock type easy on the skin, but hard on the muscles. Bulging, straining, and rippling, the Big Man finger-traversed along the lip of the *Juggernaut* roof, a Gill classic. There was nothing but air for his feet and a long way to go for the trailer-hitch horn above. After failing him on a previous attempt, his arms, so immense they could only be called Largonian, heaved on the fingerslots, launching Long through space. He nailed the horn then triumphantly continued to the summit. On top he got a yearning to write his parents. Alas, he had nowhere to send the letter. "My folks left no forwarding address after moving," wrote Long.

When today's climber tops the *Juggernaut*, his mind is also filled with worry, though of a more urgent, less depressing nature. The question on his mind all day, forgotten only briefly while hucking the monstrous crux dyno, is this: would the rancher who owned this desolate canyon catch him trespassing, and if so, what gauge shotgun barrel would the hapless rock poacher be staring down?

Humor aside, trespassing is a serious offense, not to mention a violation of landowners' privacy. Regrettably, all of the classic Pueblo boulders mentioned in "Pumping Sandstone" (the *Ripper Traverse*, The Penny Ante Boulder, The Fatted Calf) are privately owned. For the dedicated boulderer, missing out on such historic masterpieces is a tragedy, but unless you can secure permission from the landowners, one that must be endured. Of course, clandestine sorties to these boulders are not uncommon.

Despite the quality of the problems around Pueblo, Boulder, the capital of Colorado climbing, gets the most bouldering traffic. Thick with yuppies, Dreaded Trustifarians, ultra athletes, and greedy landlords, Boulder is the most trendy, politically correct city along the Front Range. If you dare visit this buzzing burg, be prepared to feel old and fat.

Most Boulder bouldering occurs in two locations: Eldorado Canyon and Flagstaff Mountain, though the 8-mile stretch between these is also rife with boulders. Eldorado Canyon is most famous for its splendid leads on smooth, hard, red Fountain Sandstone. Nevertheless, some folks, like Steve "5.15" Mammen, go there for the bouldering. Author of many of Horsetooth's hardest problems, Mammen was one of the few serious boulderers active during Colorado's otherwise slow mid-1980s scene. One late spring evening, after an unremarkable afternoon of climbing, Mammen exited the steep-walled gorge at dusk on his sleek, new Japanese motorcycle. Reaching the paved road at the edge of the dilapidated resort town, he opened the throttle on the 750 cc crotch rocket. Tucked over the gas tank, feet back on the pegs, Mammen was in a hurry, passing a Saab Turbo like it was VW Bug.

Suddenly, a six-point buck leapt out from the bushes beside the road and froze in the bike's headlight. With only 10 feet to brake, the Honda Sabre soon lived up to its name. The halves of the deer went flying, as did Mammen, at 70 miles per hour.

"I remember the most horrific thud when I hit the deer, then nothing but silence," says Mammen. "I thought I was dead for sure."

The driver of the Saab watched Mammen flip three times head over heels before hitting the road. After what seemed to be an endless slide, Mammen stopped 100 yards from the impact zone. His sweats and rugby shirt were shredded, several square feet of skin had grated off, his sneakers had blown off, and his ankles were ground down to the bone. If there was any thing to laugh about it was that his socks were still on but stretched out 3 feet long. Mammen hobbled back to the bug-covered carcass and pulled the halves, found 50 feet apart, off the road. Then, covered in blood, entrails, fleas, and ticks, he staggered over to the Saab, reached over the shocked and shaking driver, grabbed the car phone, and dialed 911.

While Mammen was recovering from his monumental road rash (miraculously, he broke no bones) he read an article in *Outside* magazine that listed the "impossible" feats in outdoor sports. For rock climbing it mentioned a 15-foot face on the Milton Boulder in Eldorado Canyon. The holds were there, prompting many attempts, yet were so small, and the sequence so devious, that nobody would ever scale it, said the article. Mammen had seen the problem before. Not a man to suffer fools, he called bullshit on *Outside*. After six weeks of intense effort, he finally managed an absurd, half-blind double dyno off the ground (one hand lunges for an inverted layaway, while the opposite foot kicks for a nickel edge), and linked it with the tenuous twin sloper thumb underclings above. It was a classic example of Mammen's famed perseverance and outstanding footwork. He dubbed the problem *Never Say Never.*

Across the river from *Never Say Never* lies West World, a group of five king-sized boulders hidden in the trees beside the West Ridge. Those who have seen the Yul Brynner trash-action movie the area is named after won't be surprised that West World is full of hazardous amusement. With few exceptions, the problems are tall, the landings rocky, sloped, or both, and the cruxes high.

West World's big draw is *Germ Free Adolescence*—seldom attempted, less seldom topped. *Germ Free* is a sweeping 16-foot, 60-degree overhang, featuring a landing which slopes away dramatically toward the creek a hundred yards below. In the middle is a suitcase-sized flake, followed by a series of evenly spaced, but decreasingly smaller holds leading to a four-finger wide, doorjamb-width edge perfectly situated at the lip. Above that the holds continue to shrink. Topping out is the crux—basically, a nightmare for both climber and spotter. A favorite ploy to rattle would-be ascensionists is to wait until they've grasped the initial jug, then tell them the tale of Rufus Miller.

"You heard about Rufus Miller on this one?"

"Who?"

"Big Roof. Former gymnast. Built like The Hulk. Clamped the lip, cut his feet loose, then pulled half a one-arm giant before dismounting. Sheez, he looked like Superman flying in reverse. I thought he was gonna clear the river for sure."

Sometimes this ploy works. The climber gazes down the steep hillside, glances up at the lip, then lies to his partner. "You know, this doesn't really look like the best line in the Front Range. Let's check out the Whale's Tail." Both then hurriedly vacate West World and head downstream.

The Whale's Tail is a 200-foot-tall pyramid of rock located across the creek from The Bastille. No doubt its popularity as a bouldering site stems from its proximity to the Pumphouse (a much-frequented socializing spot), not the pleasantness of its problems. Long before the first climber set foot in Eldorado Canyon, these problems were submerged in Eldorado Creek, which did a thorough job of buffing the holds. Even today after hundreds of years of exposure, the holds still have a like-new polish worthy of a Turtle Wax commercial.

Two problems on the left side of the Whale's Tail's base stand out as modern testpieces. First is a route I like to call the *B-K Double*—a problem every bit as greasy as its fast food namesake. *B-K*, however, stands for Bachar-Kaptain, not Burger King. The famed Californian John Bachar was the first to master this double lunge. More-fortunate climbers ticked it when it could still be done in sneakers if you had the timing dialed. Then the huge foothold disappeared. The first person to subsequently repeat it was Neal Kaptain. Known for sandbagging at Flagstaff (his incredible crimp strength allowed him to smooth most of the desperates in double boots), he also proved himself a guru of the double lunge.

Five feet left of the *B-K Double* is a twisted creation from the mind of Darius Azin. Known simply as *Darius's Route,* it has the most sloping hold ever pulled on in the history of Front Range bouldering. Apt punishment for thinking up such a monstrosity, Azin spent months on it before succeeding. Imagine climbing out the wheel well of a car, trying to match hands on the outside of the fender then dynoing for the hood when your feet cut loose from the suspension.

For Boulderites who don't like polished holds, there's always Flagstaff Mountain. Flagstaff looms over Boulder, sprinkled with boulders and bristling with pines. It's one of Boulder's most heavily used recreation sites. By day, runners pant up the well-worn trail while cyclists challenge the 3½-mile leg-pumping climb up the 1,000-foot grade. At night the panting and leg-pumping continues, as Flagstaff is the town's favorite make-out site.

Flagstaff is Mother Nature's practical joke on Boulder climbers.

While smooth, firm, stout Dakota Sandstone hogbacks run for over a hundred miles up and down the Front Range, in Boulder the Dakota is faulted out. That leaves Fountain Sandstone to boulder on, which would be fine if it were of the quality found in Eldorado. Alas, at Flagstaff, the Fountain is sharp, pebbly, and frequently loose. Sharktooth flake cranks, knuckle-busting pebble squeezes, finger-creeping pocket pulls—all define the Flagstaff experience. Should one suffer their way to the top of a Flagstaff boulder, he will often be faced with a slap for a rounded summit. Improperly executed, it's a slide down the barnacle-encrusted piling of life.

Forget looking for tricks to get up the rock: success on most Flagstaff problems depends on raw finger strength, not technique. One boulder that epitomizes the Flagstaff style is the Red Wall. Short, sharp, and slick, all the problems require a stern effort to succeed. When that isn't enough, some climbers cheat, or try to.

Bob Williams considers himself to have been the most successful (not necessarily the best) boulderer in Colorado from 1969 to 1973. A University of Colorado grad student at the time, he amassed an impressive record of repeats, including second ascents of many Gill routes, as well as adding some harsh problems of his own. On Flagstaff he left the *William's Mantel,* the *William's Pull,* and most impressive, the *William's Bulge* (aka *Bob's Bulge*—none of these are names he bestowed). There was only one major line on Flagstaff he hadn't mastered—*The Right Side of the Red Wall,* at the time considered Flagstaff's hardest. A single move problem, it forces the climber to lock off on a scoop the size, shallowness, and slipperiness of a soap dish. Williams is an exceedingly competitive fellow, and this problem bugged him more than a burr in the briefs. One day he came up with a scheme to conquer it.

All he needed was a little glue. Not to add a hold—climbers were above such tactics in those days—but to adhere his fingers to the scoop. Unfortunately for Bob, glue technology was not as good as it is today. During a long wait for the adhesive to set, who should wander by but one of the era's top climbers, Steve Wunsch. Getting caught with sticky fingers was degrading enough, but being caught by a reigning hardman doubled the humiliation. Two decades later, Wunsch barely remembers the incident. Williams, however, let the story leak and is haunted by it to this day.

For most climbers, this embarrassment would be enough to make them quit the sport. Not so Williams. For him it took a force beyond anyone's imagination at the time. It took Jim Holloway.

It's ironic that Holloway credits Williams for much of his inspiration.

It was Williams who showed Holloway what serious bouldering was all about. It was also Williams who invited Holloway to go bouldering in Pueblo with the Big Boys, most notably John Gill, who would become Holloway's greatest inspiration. Soon after this induction, Holloway would eat, drink, and sleep bouldering. In a few years he was climbing as well as anyone and was obviously only going to get better. For the competitive Williams, the joy of bouldering diminished. "Jim was just too good," he said. It would be over a decade before Williams would touch rock again.

In the meantime, Holloway flourished, obliterating the standards at Flagstaff and throughout the Front Range. Flagstaff's hardest problem is *A.H.R.* (Another Holloway Route), climbed in 1975. Located on Cloudshadow Rock near its east end, it follows a very specific line of on- and off-route holds. All those attempting repeats have failed. Recently, top British climber Ben Moon was purported to have repeated it, but according to accounts strayed right onto off-route holds, avoiding the hard climbing on *A.H.R.* In Moon's defense, it seems likely he was misguided as to where the real problem climbs.

Amongst one group of hardcore boulderers, *A.H.R.* is known as one of the Big Three, a trio of problems of such difficulty that in a decade-and-a-half nobody has come close to repeating any of them. The holds on all three are in virtually original condition and, with one exception, all within reach of an average built climber (at 6'4", Holloway's height has been used as a common excuse for other's shortcomings). What makes these Front Range testpieces more remarkable is that Holloway established all three in EBs, a boot which, if we were all forced to trade in our modern sticky shoes, would trim three or four letter grades off our ability.

At first glance, *A.H.R.* looks doable—just undercling up to the three-finger pocket with your right hand, crank on it to gain a fingertip edge with the left, then shoot twice for the top. Looks easy till you get on it and realize why Holloway could have done it in EBs: there are no footholds anyway. Like many Flagstaff problems it's heinously contrived. Even Holloway calls it "gross." Nevertheless, it attracts climbers with the lure of undistilled difficulty.

Another potent shot of Flagstaff heinousness is Skip Guerin's low traverse on Pebble Wall, a pebble-milking test requiring great endurance and technical ability. *Over Yourself* is easily the hardest traverse on the mountain. Guerin named it such so he could ask people, "Have you gotten *Over Yourself* yet?" Guerin's accomplishments are doubly impressive in that he frequently disappears from the climbing scene for months at a time. The rumors have him partying at levels that would shame most sailors on shore leave.

Flagstaff does offer problems for the less masochistic, but they make for boring reading and besides, the smart climbers in Boulder (or at least the ones with cars) head south to Morrison to do their bouldering.

Morrison is a quaint town in the foothills west of Denver that banks on antique stores and dinosaurs. Though some climbers flock there for the Morrison Inn's killer margaritas, most go there for the overhangs. No other bouldering area in the Front Range presents the concentration of overhanging Dakota Sandstone as does Morrison. Enormous west-facing overhangs line the hogback above town, shielding the problems from precipitation, shading them on hot summer mornings, and acting as a giant tanning bed on cold winter afternoons.

The Black Hole is currently the fashionable hang at Morrison. It's a 10-foot-tall by 30-foot-wide overhang lousy with sizeable holds, all of which seem to slope the wrong way. Like most walls at Morrison, strong individual lines are scarce. Instead, dozens of fascinating variants crisscross the wall. Only one easy way exists out this roof, the *Breashear's Route*. Left of this is the 5-foot-wide *Cytogrinder* face. Finding any way up *Cytogrinder* is a chore, so much so that a young wannabe named A.J. recently chipped out a crux undercling so he could climb it, in the process turning the hardest *Cytogrinder* variant into the easiest.

Speaking of variants, rocket scientist Bob Williams has found twenty-two ways out to the lip of *Cytogrinder*. Yep, the same Bob Williams, now forty-five, who gave up climbing in 1973, has made a stunning comeback in the last four years. Silver bearded, he's invariably clad in white corduroy shorts and a blue T-shirt which says "Age and treachery will always overcome youth and skill." William's ability to keep up with climbers half his age has gained him a reputation as the "Nolan Ryan of Front Range bouldering." Unlike Nolan, however, Williams has trouble concealing his joy when he fans some skinny twenty-year-old.

Joining Williams in the Black Hole is absentminded physicist Chris Jones. Put Ray Charles in roller skates and he'd have better footwork than Jones, but nobody has better power. Jones is noted for doing terrifically hard move sequences, then stopping short of topping a problem and being perfectly satisfied with his achievement. Recently he's taken on the project of sorting out the history of Front Range

Bouldering, a task Sisyphus wouldn't trade for. At present, his nearly completed guide to Front Range desperates is an underground publication. Much of the misinformation in this article doubtless came from him.

Of the many climbing clans which currently call Morrison home, the most conspicuous is Boulder's Hate Group. Lest readers take the name seriously, let it be known the Hate Group, a gang of Jim Karn's buddies, jokingly fed the name to a reporter profiling Karn, hoping to bolster the sport-climbing ace's bad-boy image. United by their poor haircuts (everything from purple dreadlocks to a Zippy the Pinhead bow-tied volcano plume), *Thrasher*-approved musical taste, and ability to pull down the rads, the Hate Group is stuck with a heavily worked crag. Despite their talent, their most impressive accomplishments at Morrison are in the line of variations and link-ups doomed to obscurity. By no means is this their fault; nearly all the distinct lines were done when they were still watching *Sesame Street.*

The king of Dakota Sandstone areas is Horsetooth Reservoir, one of Gill's favorite haunts in the 1960s. Horsetooth is located just west of Fort Collins, a college town less pretentious than Boulder, but catching up. The reservoir stretches 7 miles north to south behind a series of Dakota hogbacks, the gaps between which have been dammed. At the south end of the reservoir lies the Horsetooth Inn with its cold suds, but more importantly, up the hillside east of the Inn is the Flute Boulder.

The center route on the Flute's east face might be Horsetooth's best. The face is corrugated like a steel shed, forcing the boulderer to bear hug and Gaston up the blunt narrow ribs. Falls are unavoidable. Without a quick shove from the spotter to alter one's trajectory, one's heels will surely clip the big block at the base. It's a long crawl through the snake-infested brush back down to the road. Maybe this is why the final dyno has been done unroped just three times, once from the left (Holloway), then nearly two decades later from easier set-ups straight up and to the right (some poltroon).

Competing for title as the best problem at Horsetooth would have to be the classic lines on the Mental Block and Eliminator boulders at Rotary Park. Most of these lines were pioneered by John Gill in the 1960s.

The Mental Block is one of America's finest boulders. A six-pack of standard classics, plus numerous variants attack the overhanging face, most topping out with sloping mantels. In his article, Long mentioned four of the Mental Block classics as requiring "considerable gunnery to succeed," adding that at Fort Collins in general "static efforts will insure certain failure regardless of strength." Eat your Wheaties, Largo. All six have been done static, but only by Holloway. Especially impressive is the *Pinch Overhang* static—imagine pinching a brick plastered to a 30-degree overhang, then locking it off with one arm below one's solar plexus. The other hand is powerless in its efforts to help with the pull. Once you give up on trying it static, try the committing lunge, followed by the more committing mantel. On the driest days the mantel is a terror; on a humid summer day be prepared for an instant jaw reconstruction. If you survive that, try the unrepeated *Winch and Pinch,* a left to right traverse of the entire overhanging face finished up with the *Pinch Overhang.* It was considered a Last Great Problem since the seventies. Interest in it then was so keen that one local, Jerry Wedekind, would string lanterns across it to practice the moves after work on dark winter evenings. Not only did the lanterns illuminate the holds, they warmed them as well. Despite many strong efforts, it wasn't climbed until the summer of 1990.

The Eliminator is the size of two semitrailer-trucks parked side by side. Unlike the Mental Block, it doesn't have a route ascending it every 4 feet across. Nevertheless, it has a nice flat summit, which upon topping out provides a striking view, particularly when one pulls their head over the lip to see a coconut-oiled coed soaking up rays.

Naturally, Gill left his mark on the Eliminator. The *Right* and *Left Eliminators,* at opposite ends of the west face, are two of his most famous testpieces. The *Left Eliminator* is particularly stout, rewarding half-assed lunges with tail-busting plunges.

The most difficult problem on the Eliminator (and at all of Horsetooth) is the *Meathook,* one of the Big Three. This problem lies left of the *Left Eliminator,* and follows a line straight up from the ground to the dogleg crack above, the same crack which the *Left Eliminator* lunges to. Unless told otherwise, climbers seriously eyeing the problem assume it to start off the dishwasher-size block that gives *Left Eliminator* its hazardous landing. Standing atop this rock and digging your tips into the face-level underclings, it feels reasonable— until you try putting both feet on the rock. The first foot toes under the overhang with ease. The other foot feels like it's bolted to the starter block. The thought of climbing up to the underclings from the ground, as Holloway did, blows the mind.

In the summer of 1991, Scott Blunk repeated the upper part of the *Meathook,* after many efforts starting from the 3-foot-tall block;

the closest anyone had come to repeating one of the Big Three. As usual, many folks pooh-poohed Blunk's ascent, signing it off to the 6'7" climber's enormous reach. What really got Scott up it was his enormous talent. To grab the underclings on the *Meathook* is to wish one's fingers were thinner—Blunk's are the size of frankfurters. Next take into consideration his weight—215 pounds. If that's not enough to keep him grounded, he works in Wyoming forty to fifty hours a week as an honest-to-goodness cowboy, throwing hay bales, tossing steers, branding calves, and cutting the nuts off bulls—pretty physical stuff. Then there's two nights a week teaching martial arts, plus a third training. His size and lightning reflexes have earned him a reputation as the world's best spotter. His climbing deserves equal recognition, but Blunk merely shrugs at his lack of celebrity. As he puts it, "I guess I just grew too tall to be famous."

Scott Blunk proved the top half of the *Meathook* could be repeated. Steve Mammen followed suit, proving a mere 6-footer could do it. Then, in less than 250 tries, this author made it up, proving a mortal could do it. What none of the Club Meathook '91 members could do is come close to scaling it from the ground.

Also infrequently scaled are the score of problems in the Vast Wastelands, the miles upon miles of Dakota hogbacks north of Fort Collins. The routes tend to be tall, committing, and just loose and lichenous enough to make the bowels feel like a wet sack full of canned goods. In other words, typical Mark Wilford and Steve Mammen problems. The nature of Vast Wastelands climbing drives most climbers away. The landowners drive away the rest. When asked by a rancher what was he doing on his property, Wilford said "just bouldering." The rancher snapped back, "Well you just boulder your ass on out of here."

For those willing to explore, the Front Range is full of potential. Boulder Canyon and Button Reservoir have granite problems, while more sandstone can be found at Carter Lake, the Lyons quarries, Mount Sanitas, the Flatirons, and even Garden of the Gods. Holloway tapped into this potential in 1977, when he would run up to a little-known boulder 200 yards uphill from the Cube in Boulder's Flatirons. He was working on what would become the last of the Big Three, a route he would name *Slapshot*.

To look at it now is a lesson in humility. Only 12 feet high, it's an undercut bulge with but two features: a ¼-inch layaway flake (better now after breaking off and being reattached) and a thin horizontal crack just shy of the top. A search for footholds comes up with nothing more than a knuckle-sized blunt projection beneath the bulge. The ground has eroded, making the first reach impossible for sub-6-footers, yet to build it back up or use a cheater stone would seem an act of hubris; the move is that astounding.

At the time he was working on it, Holloway would run a mile uphill to the boulder, hoping to sweat off weight and thus tilt the scales in his favor. This would be the last of his difficult Front Range boulder problems, as his interest turned from bouldering and smoking pot to running and eating health food. After more trips up than he cares to recall, he finally bagged it. He pulled off his EBs, laced on his running shoes, then sprinted down the hill. Behind he left the hardest move ever done on American rock.

(To my knowledge, Slapshot, A.H.R., *and Holloway's ground-up sequence on* Meathook *are still unrepeated as of 1998. Holloway's name for A.H.R. is* Trice.

This piece was unusual in that I remember winning several of the fights with my editors. At the time I was very incensed at the state of American climbing. All sense of fair play and rising to a challenge had seemingly been flushed in the rush to bag bigger numbers. Before this reached print, Climbing *never allowed me to mention chiselers by name or the fact that some climbers were using steroids. The sport was experiencing big time growing pains, and I felt the media worked too hard painting an unrealistically rosy picture of what was going on. I'm glad they let me name the dweeb who chiseled* Cytogrinder. *This bit of peer group pressure seemed to work.* Climbing, *however, never let me take the big name chiselers to task.*

On a lighter note, after much squabbling, Hellcat allowed me to retain the Nolan Ryan reference. It surprises me how mainstream sports illiterate my editors are. Hellcat actually hadn't heard of Nolan Ryan. You didn't have to be a sports fan to figure this one out—at the time Ryan was spraying about Advil every few minutes on primetime TV. As America's poster child for aging athletes, he needed no introduction, nevertheless Hellcat wanted me to write "Nolan Ryan, the durable aging baseball hero" or some such muck. One day I figure I'll submit a piece in which I say, "his long hair and beard made him look like Jesus, the famous son of God.")

Climbing, *February 1992*

The Biggest Boulder
in the World

A little history never hurt anyone

*Style-wise I went out on a limb with this one, but I wanted
to catch that "this is your brain on desert bouldering" feel.
Several readers have told me this was one of their favorites;
others asked me what I'd been smoking.*

IF ONLY VAN TASSEL HAD BEEN elected president, the Integratron would
have been completed and my fingers would be feeling mint right now.
It had been fifty-three years since the last well-publicized death at
Giant Rock, and I didn't want to be the one to break the streak. My
strength was ebbing, however, and it looked like I'd peel off this gargantuan boulder and join Critzer, if not in as many bits. Solgonda,
where are you when I need you? Damn, this desert sun is hot.

I didn't even come to climb this rock; it was the boulders down
the road I was hot for. But there I climbed like a mummy just stirred
from a 5,000-year nap, so I called it a day and moseyed down to
Giant Rock.

This was it, just an hour drive out of Joshua Tree—the biggest
boulder in the world. At least the five articles paving my desk make
that claim; everything from a Yucca Valley history text to the 1953
souvenir program from the Eighth Annual National Turtle Races. They
estimate it to be anywhere from 25,000 to 100,000 tons. Assuming a
2.65g/cc density, my back-of-the-envelope calculations have it weigh-
ing in at a little less, something like 300,000 kegs of beer.

Seven stories high it is, but Frank Critzer chose to live in the basement. The World War I U-boat mess boy had emigrated to the United
States, and sometime between 1927 to 1930 went out into the desert

with his grubstake and started digging. When done, he had a three-room, 400-square-foot domicile entrenched beneath the north face of Giant Rock. It would range from 25 to 115 degrees Fahrenheit outside, but inside Critzer lived with a tenth ton of dynamite in a comfortable 55 to 80 degrees.

One of Critzer's concrete runoff collection gutters was staring me in the face at the lip 20 feet up. For some reason I had to climb this boulder, even though I knew it really wasn't the world's largest. One move to pull the lip. Grabbing the gutter would be bad style. So would falling on my head. I'd already thrown a couple of Parkinson's dynos, weak, twitchy tosses to holds I should have been able to reach statically. This was crazy.

Giant Rock does that to people. Folks thought Critzer was a couple of draws short of a sport climber. There he was, living in the middle of nowhere, days from the nearest town, no valuable minerals, hardly any water, and he was single-handedly scraping a 120-foot-wide, mile-long runway out of the desert. And the planes came. Local flying clubs, Amos and Andy of radio fame, and maybe some night flights from Mexico.

Dope. Illegal aliens. Critzer's a smuggler. The rumors swirled. No, not a smuggler. He's a damn Kraut. Look at that radio he's got. He's a Nazi spy. He's running saboteurs into America.

An iron pipe jutted out from the lip a few feet to my right. A pull-up bar. Swing over, grab it, and mantel up. Like a needle and spoon it beckoned, promising salvation, promising peace. A sucker move if I ever saw one, but I was too whipped to do a muscle up even on that.

"I swore when I came here, I would never go out alive," Critzer told Sheriff McCracken and his deputies. It was July, 1942, and gasoline and dynamite were missing from construction sites in the next county over. Even though he had no jurisdiction in San Bernardino county, Riverside county's McCracken was bringing Critzer in for questioning.

"This wire is attached to 200 pounds of dynamite. It is enough to take us all."

The rock is dark brown, and the fingertip holds beyond the lip were roasting. Each edge, each dent, was cradling a thin deposit of sand—tiny tan ball bearings urging my fingers to roll off. Over and over I reached up, then scurried back down to the lip.

Wire touched terminal, electrons raced to the blasting cap, and the laws of chemistry reduced Critzer to 140 pounds of scorched spaetzle plastered underneath Giant Rock. McCracken was blown out the doorway, his uniform replaced by 100 lacerations and contusions. The deputies' eardrums burst. Fire raged under the monolith, setting off gunshells like Jiffy Pop.

No going back. Critzer had known it. Now I did. I had my chance to back off and didn't. Foolishly I pushed upwards. A nine mil strapped to my back would get me down from the summit, if gravity didn't first.

George Van Tassel, the next resident of the cave under Giant Rock, says it didn't happen that way. Critzer was clean, and a genius to boot. Critzer's manuscript, *The Glass Age,* containing formulas for plastics not yet invented, was, like Critzer, a pile of ashes. Critzer, after arguing with the lawmen, conceded to go with them. He went into his hovel to get his coat and closed the door behind himself, blocking it with a two-by-four. Sensing resistance, the deputies lobbed a tear-gas grenade through the window. The grenade came to a halt under the kitchen table, right next to Frank's case-o'-dynamite footrest.

In addition to explaining Critzer's demise, Van Tassel reconciled science and religion. A former test pilot for Douglas Aircraft and Howard Hughes, Van Tassel obviously had a scientific mind, but he had help as well.

No help up here, but that hungry-looking, stringy-haired scarecrow of a desert rat I saw earlier might drag me to a hospital. Then again, he might not . . . Lose that thought, focus on the move, not the fear. Not the fear, I said.

August 24th, 1953. Van Tassel and wife were sleeping outside in the warm desert night. Up came a man to the foot of his bed. Strangely the dogs didn't bark.

"I asked the man what he wanted," recalled Van Tassel in his book *The Council of Seven Lights,* "thinking his car might have given him trouble and he had walked into our remote airfield as many others had done before. At the same time I sat up in bed. Beyond the man, about a hundred yards away, hovered a glittering, glowing spaceship.

"I knew then that he was not having car trouble . . . "

Van Tassel then toured the spacecraft with his new friend Solgonda.

The sketchpad shrunk to a napkin, as did my confidence. What I would have given for a "perfect-defense, piezo-electric crystal battery" like Van Tassel said Solgonda had to protect him from danger.

Grab the tinies, roll over that arête, weight that foot, and the shaking will stop. On three. Slabsville, baby. One, two . . .

Meetings with the aliens continued. Van Tassel held annual Spacecraft Conventions at Giant Rock. Eleven thousand people showed up for the 1959 gathering. By this time the space people had trained George for a higher calling than running an airstrip 15 miles north of Yucca Valley.

Van Tassel for president in 1960!

... three. I was onto the slab and could rest my arms as long as my legs didn't jackhammer me off. If it were at ground level, it would be a mick. This is easy, just walk up the ripples I told myself, but my legs were fevered pistons and my mind had thrown a rod.

The saucer dudes were feeding him the secrets of rejuvenation. Three miles from Giant Rock, Van Tassel started building a 40-foot-high, 50-foot-wide white dome. This was no ordinary dome. This was a machine, a high-voltage electrostatic generator that would supply a broad range of frequencies to recharge cell structure. We're talking the Big One. Longer life! Youthful energy! The Integratron!

At last it eased to a trot. The top was uneventful. A foot of 1-inch steel stock protruding from the summit and a few old names etched in the varnish. A breeze came from the north, where artillery reports had come from all morning. I looked out at Critzer's runway, a crazy, yet broad straight swath hewn through the creosote and stretching away across the dry lake bed to the south. I felt like I should hang out on top of "the world's largest boulder," but what for? To look at all the penises spray-painted on the rocks below? To work on a melanoma? To mull on what a stupid stunt I'd just pulled? Better to get it over with. I cleaned up some old rope left on top, then started rapping through the sea of epoxy smears left over from Giant Rock's brief bout with glue-up mania. In the late 1970s, the BLM plowed in Critzer's cave, tore down the airport buildings, then turned the area over to the vandals. Must have been the sun.

I coiled my rope then twisted a baseball cap onto my head. Probably over a few more gray hairs. Nothing the Integratron couldn't fix, but the puzzle's final piece is still missing. Van Tassel died in 1978, before the extraterrestrials gave him the final instructions. Some say it was a heart attack. Some say mysterious causes. Some charge murder.

Climbing, September 1995

A Tale of Two Thimbles

Of the hundreds of thousands of climbs in America, few ever reach legendary status. The Thimble is such a climb. In much of my writing I strive to promote history and keep legends alive. That retelling of legends is important was driven home the other day when I bouldered with two teen phenoms who knew who I was, but had no clue what the Eiger was. I was flattered and scared at the same time.

TO THE LAYPERSON, THE THIMBLE is an unprepossessing nub of knobby granite dwarfed by hundreds of towering spires in the Needles of South Dakota. A mere 30 feet tall, its northeast face resembles a kitchen mitt, gently leaning over the parking lot at the Needle's Eye turnout. To the boulderer it towers above everything around. This is where John Gill, the father of modern bouldering, proved to the climbing world that he was a boulderer by choice, not because he lacked the right stuff for the longer routes. By climbing the Thimble in 1961 he validated bouldering as a legitimate subsport of climbing, and one to be reckoned with.

Pat Ament, writing about the Thimble in *Master of Rock*, said this: "Gill had transmuted into art a demon of desire, some kind of turning of the soul. Through the efforts of his imagination, Gill had found a line where one might never have otherwise existed . . . Gill had left in the Needles a tradition of excellence, and the Thimble seemed to represent the degree to which he was able to surrender his inner self to climbing."

Master of Rock, the biography of John Gill, was our bible, though I was too cheap to ever buy the first edition. When I grew up at Indian

Rock in Berkeley, the older, wiser boulderers would tell Gill stories. None had met him, and I don't think any had ever seen a Gill route, much less done one, but the stories would go on. The blankest of walls was pointed at, with the declaration that "Gill would climb that."

Gill was mythical, the essence of bouldering wrapped into human form. And not just any form, but a body like Hercules. *Master of Rock* was filled with photos of the mighty Gill in action. Perhaps most famous was one of Gill performing a one-armed front lever, body horizontal to the ground, goateed jaw mildly clenched in determination, eyes cooly checking his feet to be sure his toes were pointed for full credit. My favorite, however was on page 52: Gill at Pennirile Forest, Kentucky, in the mid-1960s. In it, Gill has just stuck a lunge up a slightly overhung wall, capped by a giant black roof. His left arm is outstretched straight to a hold below his waist, his fingertips lightly touching it as if to say "thanks." His right fingers are latched on a similarly small hold, arm cocked and flexed. His shoulder looks like a casaba melon, his biceps only slightly smaller. Despite the power that arm exudes, Gill appears weightless, feet hovering 3 feet from the wall and 4 feet from the ground. So effortless does the move look that one can imagine Gill reading the graffiti on the wall before him. No Michael Jordan tongue wag for the master. No Tiger Woods fist pump. Just pure cool. To me, that photo embodied bouldering; the skill, the power, the grace, the focus; it was all there.

Even though that photo spoke to my soul, it was the Thimble that called me. Royal Robbins, if not the best climber of his day, then certainly the most competitive and driven, felt the calling too. Desirous to prove he could climb anything anyone else could, he traveled to the Needles in 1964 and locked horns with Gill's creation. Over a quarter century after his attempt, I talked to Robbins about it. "I consider my greatest failure to be my effort on the Thimble," Robbins told me. "I could see that even if I worked at it forever, it was very unlikely that I'd ever climb it."

The Thimble had stopped the Great Robbins cold. This shut up everybody who, until then, had labeled Gill a "mere boulderer." Not only did it shut Robbins down, it shut everyone down for decades. Eventually the guardrail was moved away from the base, lessening the risk. Still the overpowering reputation the Thimble had built was enough to scare off most suitors. A few climbers scratched up it on a toprope, but an unrehearsed, unroped repeat still stood as one of the great prizes of American bouldering. By comparison, *Midnight Lightning* was a trade route. One by one, Gill's other problems saw repeats, but the Thimble stood apart. I don't care if you'd flashed the *Ripper* or soloed the *Juggernaut,* the thought of committing to the upper cruxes on the Thimble was enough to make you wet your pants. Not only would you be taking on a formidable problem, but also you would be tackling an icon of the sport. Repeating the Thimble was tantamount to scoring with the Virgin Mary. In some ways you imagined the joy of standing on top, in other ways a repeat, though inevitable, smacked of heresy.

In 1991, I traveled to South Dakota to try the Thimble. As befits a climb steeped in mystery and legend, there were many rumors surrounding claims of a repeat. Some climbers swore up and down that it had been repeated, others said it stood inviolate. I tried without success to confirm the rumors. Nevertheless, I was convinced it had seen a repeat. Maybe by the Southern boy with the cat on a leash—the one who said "we jump off stuff bigger than this all the time back home." I liked that story. There were many others.

At that point in my life I felt I was American bouldering and American bouldering was me. I had no doubt that I was put on the planet to climb boulders and for no other reason. I was damn good at it and completely devoted. To the sport I sacrificed my body, my relationships, and any chance of gaining social skills. I pissed people off with my rigid ethics—a code so strict that only a fanatic would live up to it, and only I was that fanatical. Every slight to the sport—every cheater stone, every chipped hold, every tick mark—I took as a personal affront. My destiny was in bouldering and I was powerless to change. And I felt it was my destiny that I should climb the Thimble.

My first attempts were cautious, climbing up to a good blocky hold the size of a milk carton. Gill calls this the "Hold of Commitment." I was swapping turns with Mark Wilford, another talented high boulderer. In our respective home areas, Hueco Tanks for me, Horsetooth Reservoir for Mark, we would take turns trying to scare each other off our unrepeated high ball problems. It was bouldering mumblety-peg, with a trip to the ER if you flinched. Mark was first to step up on the Hold of Commitment. From this point it was easier to retreat by traversing left into a groove, than by downclimbing. We both tried to crack the moves above the Hold of Commitment, but both escaped to the groove repeatedly. Mark lost interest, but I continued until my strength was gone. End day one.

The exact chronology is lost to my withering memory cells, but I think it was the next day that we met the Local Expert. Most areas have one. He's the guy who can tell you every move on every climb and every rating, yet never seems to climb himself, lest his omnipotent aura dissipate in the throes of a subpar performance. LE insisted that the escape route left into the groove was indeed the famous Gill route. He was positive. If so, I had already repeated the Thimble six times. I strongly doubted this was the case, so that night I called Gill from the pay phone next to Sylvan Lake. Gill confirmed my suspicions. Though his memory was less than perfect thirty years after the fact, he was positive that the whole idea behind his climb was to stay out of that groove. I was happy to have my opinion confirmed by no less than Gill himself. When the next day I told LE about my conversation, he stated flat out that Gill was wrong.

After a rest day I went back. I pinched the finger holds, toed off the crystals, clutched the Hold of Commitment, slapped for the clamshell bump, hiked my foot high, and again stood up face-to-face with the crux. Off to the right, protruded an enticing knob—the key to further progress. On my left were three feldspar crystals the size of sugar cubes. It was a stretch to get to them, and always my right hand ended up on the cube I wanted my left hand on. If I just cared to dyno for the key knob to the right, it would be no big deal. On a toprope I wouldn't hesitate. But this was broken leg territory, almost the wheelchair zone. Friends had begged me to use a rope. Friends who had toproped it and knew its difficulty. One friend had snapped a key hold off up high and fell onto the rope. I didn't know how fragile the key knob was, or how positive, so I only wanted to grab it statically.

The morning wore on, the heat increased, and still I could not find a static set-up. I bailed left into the groove again and again. Finally I quit. The Thimble was beyond me. Some more guts, maybe a screw loose, and I might have tossed for the knob. It would be an easy toss, but one shot only. The entire idea behind high bouldering is that one takes everything he has learned through the years, and applies it such a way that he never falls. My prowess as a high boulderer would be more in evidence if I backed down, than if I threw a move without 100 percent chance of success.

This was a downer. Destiny unfulfilled. Confidence shaken. Ego emasculated. It was our last day in the Needles. Mark wanted to do *Super Pin,* a scary Pete Cleveland testpiece down the road, so I packed up my gear and we left the Thimble. I followed *Super Pin,* then to reassure myself that I wasn't a complete chickenshit, I led *Hairy Pin,* another runout Cleveland horror show. Feeling a little better about myself, I downed a Foster's oil can as we packed to drive home. We drove up the switchbacks and through the tunnel leading to the

Thimble. The sun was sinking fast and the temperature dropping. Conditions were good for an attempt. I asked Mark to pull over for one last shot.

The Thimble is off limits to climbing during midday, because of the crowds it attracts and the subsequent traffic jams they cause. We were past the witching hour and fortunately no cars were parked under the route. I unfolded my sketchpad, at that time an open cell foam and carpet job, flimsier and smaller than today's store-bought ilk, and positioned it where I thought I might fall. The chance of hitting it was pretty small, but it just might make the difference between a standard fracture and the compound variety. Boots on, hands chalked. A crowd of tourists started coalescing away from the base. "Honey, get the camcorder."

The first half was well wired by now. Soon I was at my sticking point. I fiddled with the sugar cubes then stumbled upon a triple hand switch that positioned my left fingers on the hold my right had stubbornly hogged before. I brought my feet up to the 20-foot level and was poised to statically reach the knob of temptation. This was the sequence, the key twisting in the lock. Click. As I reached toward the knob, the door opened.

What happened next is hard to explain in words. I stepped onto a different plane of consciousness. I was flooded with self-confidence and focus. I was bonded to the rock in a way that went beyond the laws of gravity. There was no tug from below. And though my muscles contracted and my mind charted out each next move, there was no feeling of effort. I was Gill at Pennirile, suspended mysteriously in impossible terrain. The tangible world fell away. I heard voices from the crowd. I remember somebody saying, "Just look at him. He climbs like a monkey." But the voices sounded as if they came from the far reaches of an infinitely long hall, from another world. I could hear what everybody was saying, but it registered no more than a TV in the next room; you knew something was going on, yet it just drifted past.

The feeling lasted the next move. Feet planted just as I'd visualized for the last few days. The balance was exactly as I imagined. My left hand arced slowly to the next knob. My fingers squeezed. The rock was dark, the light fading. Intermittently, bright flashes from the tourists' cameras lit up the face. Like their jabbering, I was perfectly aware of it, but on an immaterial level. The level of the last echo of a voice in a canyon. Everything was crystal clear in my mind— overwhelming clarity. Each move seemed as if I'd rehearsed it for a lifetime. My right hand caught a knob, my feet moved up. My body and my mind seemed separate, like I was watching myself climb from a position hovering behind my shoulders. I eyeballed the big quartz shaft poking out of the summit ridge, then the door slammed shut.

Immediately, the seriousness of the situation struck me. I was back to normal. Mortal. Sketchpad looking like a napkin on the pavement. Fingers tensed, brow furrowed—one move from the hospital, one move from the dream. Gravity back from vacation. I wasted no time and slapped for the cue-ball-sized crystal. Latched on, pulled up, grabbed the ridge with my other hand, tossed my left foot over, and scampered the last move or two to the summit.

I don't remember standing on the summit. I'm sure I did, probably dizzy. I do remember sitting there for a long while, staring vacantly at the granite walls around, trying to make sense of it. Not of the out-of-body stuff, but just out of the climb itself. Did I really climb the Thimble? Is this what it is all about? I felt very strange. Confused, with a light warm emptiness. Heavy with gravity sticking my butt to the summit. I sat there for awhile, thinking I must, if for no other reason than it took sixteen years of bouldering to get there. Sixteen years of pulled tendons, broken bones, scuttled relationships, and fleeting love. Was this the feeling of fulfillment? Was I even smiling? Or was I too shocked? Did I really climb it? It all felt surreal.

Eventually, I scampered down the easy backside before it got too dark. On the ground the smiles came, the sense of relief, the sense of accomplishment, the pride. Sometimes I regret not descending sooner, and catching up with some of the tourists to get the video they shot. At other times I'm glad I didn't. I'm sure watching it on film would look ordinary. I didn't want to break the spell. Nevertheless, it didn't last long.

Shortly thereafter, I was visiting my friends at *Climbing* magazine. Excited by my ascent, my editor grabbed a tape deck and started pumping me for details to print in the news section. Again and again, he tried to get me to say I had bagged the second ascent. I didn't believe this. "Don't make it sound like I'm claiming a second ascent," I told them, "because I'm not." I went to lengths to recount the rumors I'd heard. Nevertheless, the write-up in the news section declared my ascent to be the second. I was fuming and immediately wrote a letter to *Climbing* stating that the claim of a second ascent was theirs, not mine. They chose not to print it, instead printing a number of letters stating that I was full of shit demanding credit where it wasn't due.

To have put so much into a climb. To dream of it for so long. To climb outside of myself to accomplish it. And I was getting trashed. Even five years later somebody asked me if I had climbed the Thimble. I said, "Yes." They replied, "I heard there was something fishy about your ascent." What should have been the crowning achievement of a career became for years a source of bitterness and embarrassment because the media couldn't leave a good story alone, but felt the need to embellish it. Maybe that fueled an even greater desire to prove myself.

Later, when researching my book *Stone Crusade,* I finally tracked down some prior ropeless repeats. Greg Collins from Wyoming had done it in 1981, twenty years after the first ascent, and ten years before mine. He too was inspired by *Master of Rock* and too cheap to buy a copy, having stolen his from the Anchorage library when he was sixteen years old. His was the earliest repeat I unearthed, though there may be earlier. As befits this problem, there will always be some mystery surrounding it.

In time the wounds associated with the reporting of my ascent healed. I'd lie if I said there were no scars, but with each passing year I think more about the climb than the aftermath. The letter Gill wrote me, congratulating me on my ascent, is a cherished possession. There is one other bit of memorabilia I wish I had. Three years ago I adopted a very cute, very loving shepherd/Doberman mix from the Fort Collins pound. I named her Thimble. Small, but tough. She has done more to change my life than that 30-foot mitt of granite ever did. She is my best friend and mood leveler. I carry her photo on dangerous climbs to remind me to come back. When thoughts of hurling my body off Bridalveil Falls inflamed my mind, one glance at her extinguished them. At first, however, I wasn't sure it would work out. I'd had her but a month when I visited Gill and his wife Dorothy at their home west of Pueblo, Colorado. After supper, John and I were sitting at the dining room table talking. I sensed something amiss and peeked under the table. There was Thimble, happily chewing on Dorothy's shoe. At the time I was utterly mortified. Gill was a god, which made Dorothy a goddess, which made Thimble . . .

Anyway, I wish I'd kept that shoe.

previously unpublished

Tales from the Gripped

"THIS IS NOT NEGOTIABLE."

Tom Cosgriff was on the line, feeding me some bull.

"Listen, we had a deal," I said. "Remember? We were going to climb illegal desert spires until we got caught or you had to go back to Norway."

"No. We gotta climb A5 in the Fisher Towers." Cosgriff was adamant.

"Tom, you aren't getting me anywhere near those petrified turds. Besides, they're legal. What fun will that be?"

"This is not negotiable. We're going to the Fishers."

Damn him. How could I say no? He never does. Like the first climb we did together—*Gorilla's Delight,* a classic 5.9 in Boulder Canyon— me with a knee that bent only 60 degrees, Cosgriff with a cast on his wrist. No problem. Now the poor bastard spends most of the year stuck behind a desk in Norway, eyeing some plump blond secretary gobbed in makeup. I relented. Nevertheless, deep down I knew this was his way of getting even for that time I visited him in the Yosemite jail, the time I asked if I could borrow his haulbag, since he wouldn't need it for awhile.

He did bend an iota, though, and I got my sentence reduced. We'd climb the 350-foot Gothic Nightmare, hidden far behind the Titan in the Mystery Towers group of the Fishers. Endwise, it looks like one of the Coneheads wearing a jester's cap, dangly bells sprouting out of the top. From the side it resembles a sailfish fin. The Gothic was still unrepeated after two decades, a fact that appealed to Cosgriff. It was rated only A3, a fact that appealed to me.

There was one hitch: we needed gear, lots of it. Hence my descent into the abode of the Evil Doctor, Tom's pal, *Climbing* magazine's gear editor, Duane Raleigh.

Had I not been with Tom, Raleigh would surely have never let an arch-traditionalist like me in his house. As it was, Duane was nervously trying to keep an eye on me, his gear, and his wife, all at the same time. Back in the spare room I found his chisel collection and actually touched one of the grade reducers. It moved me to eloquence better left unprinted. My comments were not well taken. Duane pulled Tom aside and whispered the doctor's orders: "Make him suffer."

At first, the suffering was limited to humping gear up the long approach, dumping it at the base, and hiking out. Then it intensified when we went for beer and pizza at Moab's famous Poplar Place. The jalapeño, garlic, and green pepper combo was, said Tom, "the most evil pizza I've ever had." Tougher to swallow was the wimpy 3.2 stout. The waitress assured us, "A lot of people are really happy to find beer like this in Utah." Yeah, that's like the happiness one feels when he's in jail, and only gets "befriended" by the little guy.

The next morning we both passed a hibachi's worth of glowing briquettes. We tried a new, uglier approach through several inches of snow. Conditions on the Gothic were wretched. All around, the snow was melting, loosening stones. Those stones hit others, until thunderous rock slides ripped down the walls of the Mystery Towers cirque.

We had reached the base, and were now committed to bucking out double loads in defeat. We hadn't climbed an inch. There was no sense in lugging out the beer, so we sat in the saddle between the Citadel and the Gothic Nightmare and swilled. By the time we had split a six of King Cobra tallboys, tons of debris had worked its way down, and our psyche had worked its way up. Tom started leading.

Only the thought that Tom was suffering more than I was made the shady north-face belay stance bearable. He beat knife blades into millimeter-thick calcite seams. With enough pounding they'd go to the hilt and hold body weight. Stepping on a drilled pin, he blew the hole apart. This was Tom's idea of a great vacation.

A few hours later he was at the belay, and I was following. I could've cleaned the pitch with a Fisher-Price hammer. Now it was my lead.

"Dammit. This isn't funny." My yelps only made Cosgriff laugh harder. "Shit shit shit shit shit." My voice was getting higher. "Watch me." It was 20 degrees Fahrenheit, I was in tennis shoes and thin wool gloves, and I was free-climbing vertical mud. Not out of my own free will. The perfect #3 Friend placement I had excavated from the mud, jump-tested, and moved up on had just exploded, leaving a depression the size and shape of a chili bowl. The only reason I hadn't fallen was that one foot was stemmed onto a knob. Now I was stuck: one foot on the knob and my shoulder pressed against the opposite wall of the dihedral. All the nearby holds were covered in dirt from my attempts to excavate the next placement. The pump flooded in.

Every piece was a time bomb, and if I fell, it would be onto the anchor. Earlier, Tom had stopped me climbing so he could tie off the belay line. He hastily punched another bolt in the anchor because the old ones were oozing out under his weight.

"If I get down to that last piece, I will lower off, let Tom finish this, and retire from aid climbing forever." Such were my thoughts, and "What if I don't?"

I reached down below my feet to the last piece, my balance bigrack, clothes-bundled, tilt-out awkward. My hands and feet were slipping on the dirt. I could grab the stem of the Friend, but knew that it would rotate out if I tried to lower onto it. My only hope was to clip on some aiders and step in.

I clipped aiders to the placement, but couldn't reach down far enough to guide one over my foot. I had one lousy inch of nylon to step through but it was lying flat against the wall like it was glued there. I tried to flick the aider away from the wall and kick my foot through, usually an easy trick, but not with the top step. The curses spilled out of my mouth in angry tones, plaintive tones, and tearful pleas.

One lousy inch of nylon.

The pump clock was ticking down. Then, like in some MacGyver script, when he defuses a nuclear device with a pocket knife as the timer reads one second left, my foot slid through. I eased my way down, clipped into the piece, and rested my helmet against the wall.

The panic vanished, replaced by a nervousness about the piece I was resting on. Then came a bigger fear. Not the threat of imminent injury, but the fear that if I didn't go back up, I would be a chickenshit forever.

I can't remember how long I hung there, regrouping mentally, forcing the decision, willing courage. Finally, I stood up, grabbed my hammer, and started gouging at the crack through the mud, waiting to hear that scraping sound when I reached real rock, my mind focused on one thing: making that next piece stick.

The summit ridge offered sunshine and snow and no evidence of how Bill Forrest and Don Briggs traversed it to its faraway highpoint.

All we found was a hawser-laid rap sling encircling a pile of rubble; twenty years ago it was a sturdy pinnacle. We sat on the ridge, with nothing to do but listen to the intermittent rumble of the towers and walls eroding around us. Four trips in and out, a 200-mile beer run to Grand Junction, and two short, frigid pitches on the north face were all for naught—we bailed.

What possessed me to go back? Or should I say, who? Not Cosgriff. He was pecking his keyboard, sneaking peeks at chunky hips and painted lips, and suffering through economically induced sobriety (seven bucks a beer) in Norway. No, only one other person could drag me back to the fudge-brownie and stale-bread summits of the Mystery Towers. My partner of countless Eldo epics; the man who sent me on my first heading and hooking lead on El Cap (without telling me the first ascensionist decked on the same pitch); The Provider who lent me a faulty portaledge that sent me on a headfirst, 4 A.M. wake-up call a third of the way up El Cap; Mr. Confidence, Mr. Cockiness, and lover of all that is ovine—Robbie Slater. The Team was back together.

This time it was June. The beauty of the maroon-walled, Roadrunner-Coyote approach canyon was lost in the heat, loose sand, and shoe-sucking quicksand.

Our objective was all three Mystery Towers: the Doric Column, the Citadel, and the Gothic Nightmare.

First was the Doric. Say it fast and it sounds like Dork, which is just what it looks like.

Kor was first to try it, but backed off when he saw how much drilling would be required. Forrest and George Hurley then bagged the first ascent in 1969, sneaking onto the summit while their British partner Rod Chuck, tired of being bombarded at the belays, rested on the ground. The Yanks pulled their ropes on the way down. Chuck was not amused. Twenty-three years later, a fellow Brit, Steve "Crusher" Bartlett, avenged the injustice, making the second ascent with George "Chip" Wilson.

The first pitch was mostly free climbing. A 5.7 dirt mantel gave me brief pause, half an hour or so, for reflection. It wouldn't have taken so long if I didn't keep glancing down to see our half-naked companion sunbathing at the base. Knowing Rob's penchant for flat-chested blonds, I had no worries about him being distracted from his belay duties.

Soon, the anchor was cause for thought. Crusher's bolts, now two months old, were already coming loose in the soft rock. I drilled another, feeling the vibrations through my feet. Later, I could feel Rob clean pins 40 feet below.

The next three pitches climbed a mud-encrusted chimney/groove that resembled the inside of a giant gutted fish. Here, the second-ascent crew had freshly riveted Forrest's bolt and bathook ladder for us, so progress was quick and easy for the leader. For the belayer, it could never be quick enough. Mud clods bombarded the belayer's helmet every few minutes, and goggles, bandannas, and long-sleeved shirts couldn't keep the dirt from grinding against the teeth, plugging the ears, and invading every pore. Days after the ascent my nose continued to produce twin strands of red-brown mucus.

On top we basked in the late-afternoon sun, strolling about the spacious summit, clambering up the boulder marking the high point. Forrest and Hurley, not having known they'd bag it the day they did, had not left a register. Crusher had, however, with a note that said, "The Citadel is next."

The Citadel and the Gothic—both unrepeated, both prizes, both tottering piles of choss you could piss a bolt hole into. Crusher might come back any day, so the Citadel was next.

The Citadel looks like an Olympic medals stand viewed in a fun-house mirror, the kind that would make Danny DeVito look like Manute Bol. The first pitch appeared to be a casual dirt scramble, so I volunteered for the lead.

Off-route from the start, I had soon paddled across a dirt slab I dared not reverse. I had no gear in, and below was a series of 35-degree dirt shelves with 6-foot drops between them. It would be an ugly fall, like rolling a 165-pound baseball down ten flights of stairs.

As the dirt under my feet continuously gave way, I slowly walked in place. I desperately needed pro, but the only weakness in the rock slab at my chest was a seam thinner than a pencil line. I had no RURPs, so I pounded two knife blades in. One actually went in half an inch, before it busted off the side of the seam. I tied off and equalized the pins, then agonized over the flexing mantel shelf in front of me for another fifteen minutes.

I figured I'd rather fall going up than going down, and figured I had little choice. What I didn't figure was that the dirt above was dark brown, facing south, and now heated to over 100 degrees. When I got there it was too hot to hang onto. Fortunately, the angle was low enough that I could chop steps with my hammer, like ice climbing in the Sahara.

A hundred feet of zigzag climbing had netted me only 40 feet in elevation. The next anchor was half a rope away so it was decided—I don't remember by whom—that I should lead up to it and get us a full rope off the ground. Had I read Hurley's 1970 article on the Mystery Towers in *Climbing* prior to our ascent, this would surely have been Rob's lead. In it, Forrest recounts the fall he took on this pitch when a quarter-inch bolt broke under his weight. He had removed the bathooks below, and the only pro left between him and a lengthy fall was a fold he tied off in the mud curtain. Miraculously, the thread held.

I had read about the Mystery Towers in the guidebook, however, and was aware of certain tricks used to ascend them: the curtain tie-offs for one, pins forced in calcite veins for another, and angles driven into the mud tent-stake style. Within 30 feet I had employed techniques two and three, as well as some steps gouged in the mud. I reached a bolt and promptly backed it up with the worst bolt I ever placed.

Next came a blank section. The only hint of passage was a couple of millimeter-deep dimples, the remnants of bathook holes. Given that most of the old bolts were now hanging about an inch out from the rock due to erosion, I figured that Forrest drilled bathook holes roughly an inch deep. At first I tried to preserve Forrest's pattern: two to three holes, then a bolt. In the last two decades, however, not only had the rock changed, but so had the technology. Bathooks were no longer in vogue, so as Crusher had done on the Doric, I put rivets in my freshly drilled inch-deep holes. An ethical quandary ensued. Forrest had taken more risk—his hook holes were empty after he passed them. He had nothing to stop a fall except a bolt every 15 feet or so—small consolation in this rock. At least I had eight cents worth of soft steel carriage bolt plugging every hole, plus thicker bolts backing up his quarter-inch coffin nails. It didn't seem sporting, even if my rivets were the weakest money could buy.

I stopped backing up Forrest's bolts, and began tying off their exposed shanks and using them as rivets—the ones that didn't pull out in my fingers, that is. I nailed whenever possible. Fifty feet above my last bolt, I shuddered, looking down at the string of bent rivets and shaky pins beneath me. A long stretch and I hooked the pick end of my hammer through the rotting belay slings and gingerly pulled up on the anchor.

Slater chuckled up the next pitch, in the process performing the impossible—he fixed a pin in the Fisher Towers. Half an hour of pounding wouldn't get it out. Half a year of erosion probably will.

We were keeping the same pace as the first ascent—100 feet per day. In the guidebook, the Citadel is listed as Grade V, even though it is only 400 feet tall. At the rate we were going, it would be a Grade VI. Every bit of work done by the first-ascent party had to be redone. The old pin scars and bathook holes had long since eroded away, and only a handful of original bolts still supported body weight.

Day three on the Citadel. We started up the fixed lines early—the thermometer read a mere 95 degrees. The long summit pitch was mine, the endless belay session Rob's. The first 80 feet was mostly putting in rivets, the only fun coming when I plucked out the old bolts—some in only a quarter-inch—with my fingers.

I reached a shoulder on the arête and balanced across a door-mat-width mud gangplank to the final headwall. Sheer walls dropped away on either side. If the ridge should crumble, I thought, I have to fling myself over the opposite side, so the rope would catch me. At the base of the headwall, I clipped the old bolt anchor, gratefully. I had plenty of rope left so, after hauling up some water, I kept going.

Above, the rock was so decomposed that it was turning into mud in situ. I went to work on a ¾-inch crack. A few taps sent in a 1-inch angle. Fingers pulled it out. Ditto for the 1½. Ditto for the 2-inch. Ditto for the 3-inch bong. Now I had a fist-sized hole in the crack pouring sand. I might as well have been nailing a giant sugar cube.

Twenty-five feet up was a three-bolt ladder to the solid capstone summit crack. The only way up would be to nail the mud curtain. I grabbed the 3-inch Longware bong, a historic borrowed piece of iron, angled it down slightly, and pounded it in until only the sling on the eye poked out through the mud. It went in like a dull knife punched into a jack-o'-lantern.

Pounding in the next bong, I could feel the whole curtain shake. I returned to the ridge to test it, a pattern I would keep up as long as my chain of aiders would reach.

The line went straight up, and a fall would certainly intercept the ridge; I would end up draped and broken over it. Either that or I'd pound onto it then fly down the exposed face on the right or ricochet down the steep flute on the left.

The last 12 feet had taken four hours. I had drained the water bottle at the ridge. We had enough light to make the summit, but I didn't have enough nerves left. In my exhausted and dehydrated state, it would be easy to blow it. Day three ended 20 feet shy of the top.

The next day I went back up, shoving a few of the placements back in with my hands. Soon I was grabbing the rappel slings snaking through the crack at the summit. They came free in my hands, rotted through by twenty-three years of sunshine and wind.

As Rob pulled over the lip, he declared it the coolest summit in the desert. Just like he had with the Doric Column. Just like he had on every spire he'd climbed. We sent the temptingest trundle in celebration.

We had run out of time. The Gothic Nightmare would have to wait for another trip.

Eleven months later it was a race. With the exception of the Titan, the Fisher Towers had been virtually ignored for two decades. Now they had become trendy among some of the Boulder crowd. Rob had ticked nearly every Fisher Tower in the guide, and in his outspoken way, had declared his intention to be first to top them all. Others soon declared their intention to beat Rob, then begged him for beta and pin lists. "The race will be over when I finish," was all Rob would tell them, "no sooner."

I just wanted to do the three Mystery Towers and in the process settle my score with the Gothic, preferably with the second ascent.

Rob had been in the Fishers every weekend for four months. Loyal to The Team, he had been saving the Gothic to do with me. Our experience on the Citadel convinced us this would be more than a weekend project, and Rob had a Monday-through-Friday job. Hence we extended honorary Team membership to Mike O'Donnell, Rob's *Sea of Dreams* partner. A soft-spoken, red-haired brute from Boulder, Mike had a list of wild escapades rivaled by few, including a failed attempt at the Gothic in which an expanding flake both he and I had previously nailed came loose on its own, fell 25 feet, clocked the retreating Mike in the head, and split his helmet from one end to the other. Mike and I would fix up to the summit ridge, then Rob would meet us and triumphantly lead to the top.

The changes a year makes. The popularity of the Moab area had spread like a cancer, and Onion Creek had been "discovered" by the hoi polloi. Tents and campers filled every turnout. Mountain bikes jammed the road. Little TP prayer flags fluttered in the bushes—signs of the reverence Joe Six-pack pays the wilderness.

When Cosgriff and I had approached the Mystery Towers two years before, we saw not a single footprint. The canyon was wild, the approach inobvious, the directions in the guidebook poor, the towers hidden from sight until halfway in. It felt as if nobody had walked this wash since Forrest and crew had rolled in the wheelbarrows supporting their ballsacks.

Now Mike and I followed numerous foot and pawprints up the approach. Mike explained that this had become a popular day hike for the "Kumbaya-ers," the crowd of hippie mountain bikers who now call Moab their own. He started mimicking their behavior, whistling as if calling a dog, and saying, "Dark Star, come here, boy."

We turned the corner where you get the first view of the Doric, and saw a party rapping down—the fifth ascent in less than a year. The Mystery Towers were a mystery no more.

The rock on the Gothic makes the Titan look like granite. Once again I drew the first pitch, which entailed tied-off knife blades, expanding blocks, and dirt-dagger free climbing. I hadn't nailed for a year and was pretty spooked. In the South, they'd say I was shaking like a dog shitting peach pits, but this was more like a dog passing sea urchins. Fortunately, it was a short pitch.

Mike methodically worked out the next pitch, knocking off loads of mud and rotten rock. Most fell to the side of me, but one chunk exploded on my belay plate, making me happy I hadn't opted for a hip belay.

After nailing the expanding mud-block traverse the first-ascent party had bathooked, Mike started chain-smoking. Belaying me on the next lead didn't help matters, though I did my best to help him quit; from 20 feet up I dislodged a chunk of rock that whistled down to knock Mike's "twitch stick" from his lips.

I wriggled into a short chimney between two narrow ridges. It was like chimneying between slightly open scissor blades, and I could easily peer down both the north and south faces. O'Donnell was belaying on the north side. The chimney expanded on the south side. I said, "Listen to this," planted my left foot on the north face, then shoved lightly with my right. A portion of wall the size of my body slowly tipped off like a tree being felled, then traveled 300 feet before creating a thunder that echoed through the valley for minute after satisfying minute. A fine trundle is a rare and beautiful thing. I was reminded of Kor's words when asked why he climbed the desert towers: "Not so much because they're there, but rather because they may not be there much longer."

Even more of the Gothic disappeared when I groveled on top of the knife-edge ridge the next day. I punched and shoved until the ridge was a foot lower, and the medium I would mantel onto resembled rock. A short stroll along the dirt ridge, similar, but wider than the Citadel's gangplank, got me to the anchor and the end of my leading commitment.

Now Rob had joined us, and went to work. After 60 feet, he stopped at a saddle between two gargoyles, midway along what the first ascent dubbed "The Traverse of the Goblins." The saddle was composed entirely of cobbles, a 3-foot-thick layer, every one of which you could pull out with your fingers. No way to nail it or drill it, and free climbing would be nuts. Luckily for Rob, a storm was moving in, and his partners called for a retreat.

The weekend was over. We sat in a Mexican restaurant discussing our plight. I wasn't about to leave. O'Donnell felt likewise. Outside, the streets of Moab were flooding. This, and a job commitment, convinced Rob to flee. He drove us out to the Onion Creek road, where my van was parked. It was a moonless night and still raining. He dropped us at the first stream crossing, then left us to die.

The first crossing turned out to be an insignificant tributary we had never seen water in. We didn't know this until we reached the real Onion Creek. We stood on the bank—what was left of the road—and listened to boulders rolling down the torrent. It was so dark I wondered if we were listening to my van floating by. We stood in T-shirts, shorts, and flip-flops, me with a bag of provisions, Mike with a borrowed tent, and Rob long gone with the tent poles.

I wrapped myself in the tent, Mike wrapped himself in the fly, and we hiked back to the highway. No cars. Was it flooded now, too? Closed for the night? The Rob-left-us-to-die jokes turned into serious talk about what to do next.

I'm not one to throw away beers, even if they are Utah 3.2 road-pops, but I ditched the sixer, something I would do only in the most dire circumstances. The nearest ranch house was 7 miles distant. We started hiking.

Finally, a caravan of rafters drove by and took pity on us, two drowned rats wrapped up like nuns with tents over our heads.

"What are you doing out here?" they asked.

"Rock climbing," we replied.

"Climbers? That explains it."

They dropped us off in Moab, where, once again, we knocked on the door of the patron saint of Moab mud-nailers, Kyle Copeland. If it weren't for his hospitality and gear, we would have never gotten into this mess.

Betrayal. The Team ripped asunder by filthy lucre. Rob knew that next Friday was the only day I could go back. O'Donnell was going to be there. I told Rob he must call in sick, especially since he'd already told his competitors that the second ascent was a done deal.

"You've got to wait until Saturday," Rob pleaded. "I'll lose 6,000 dollars if I don't go to work on Friday."

"Don't give me this bullshit about chicken feed. This is the second ascent of the Gothic we're talking about."

O'Donnell and I went back alone. Forrest had told Slater that from the summit ridge up it was all drilling. Indeed, the only pins he placed were lost arrows pounded into bolt holes; the rock was so bad in places that inch-and-a-half long bolts wouldn't cut it. I finished Slater's lead. Mike led to the glorious summit.

The very top is the size of a park bench, and perfect to sit on. It was time to lift a Mount Everest malt liquor, toast the first ascensionists Forrest and Briggs, toast ourselves, toast Rob who would jug up the next day, and toast all those who have sought adventure in these most stupendous of choss heaps.

"Here's mud in your eye."

(Robbie showed up later with Pancho Torrisi to bag the third ascent of the Gothic.)

Climbing, October 1993

Ice Capades

The innocent, easily excited phase of a climbing career is too short, but by dabbling in several disciplines one can experience it several times. I wasn't writing at the time of my first hard boulder problems, first long free climbs, or first big walls, so this is the only piece I've written that explores the awe and innocence of a rookie pushing his limits. Should I be daft enough to attempt an 8000-meter peak, then I might write another. As for ice climbing, the innocence is gone, but the awe remains.

I WAS DAMN NEAR CHOKING to keep the vomit down. Sheets of rain washed across the black ice in front of me and it was dark. My hands clenched into a death grip as my neck slowly lithified. Marginally attached to this world, I waited for the accident, reaching a state of fear and angst Marc Twight would be proud of. Problem is, I had yet to step out of the car.

One's first drive into Keystone Canyon is supposed to be memorable. More than once, the reaction of an ice climber glorying in the splendor of Keystone's frozen waterfalls has been likened to a rock climber first beholding the walls of Yosemite Valley. My thoughts, however, lay not with the crystalline promises flashing us from the shadows beside the road, but with the slips and drifts of the Aerostar and dark red dreams of the Jaws of Life. Fifty-mile-per-hour flashbacks of four-lane near-death donuts fueled my mental meltdown, drawn out to agonizing lengths by our 15-mile-per-hour descent down Thomson Pass. I couldn't handle the adrenaline jolts each parting with the pavement produced, so I disengaged the wheel from my grip and let Rob Raker drive. Huge mistake. Ignoring the abominable road conditions he doubled my speed. Not that he would know, because half the time he was turned around looking for us in the dark of the back seat to make a point, both hands off the wheel gesturing like Dick Vitale. My pleas that he grip the wheel and decelerate were for naught; the only thing that could slow him down was when he thought he glimpsed big ice next to the road.

My mind a mass of sledgehammered Gummi worms, we reached Valdez around 11 P.M. and descended on Andy Embick's house. Andy, one of Valdez's ice pioneers, greeted us at the door, a glass of Macallans scooped in his left hand and a thin smile breaking a half-inch above his Abe Lincoln/C. Everett Koop beard. A bearskin hung on the wall to his right and the semblance was not lost. Embick is stocky, thick-limbed, and powerful-looking. Perhaps his ursine physique has helped him sneak up on the bruins he has shot. He quickly made us at home, showing off the guest quarters and sauna in the basement, the drying room upstairs, and running through a few quick house rules.

The next day dawned in the upper-30s, but at least it had stopped raining. We headed up to Keystone Canyon, the center of Valdez ice climbing. Size-wise, Keystone Canyon more closely mimics Eldorado Canyon than Yosemite Valley. The guidebook lists over five dozen ice formations in the canyon, from 50-foot low-angle smears to thick, fat, 650-foot monster lines. Contrary to most ice climbing areas, Keystone's approaches are measured in yards, not miles. It almost seems unsportsmanlike to walk a hundred yards, mostly downhill, to get to some of America's best ice climbs. Die-hard ice jocks will want to visit when the Lowe River is breached, and one must wade its icy currents to reach the climbs on the east side of the canyon.

Horsetail Falls is the most climbed route in Valdez so we felt obliged to hop on it. It is 260 feet long, if you don't count the hundred feet of horizontal snow leading from the parking lot to the base. From a narrow cleft at the top, it spreads out in a wide, low-angle apron of ice forming a shell over a plentiful flow beneath. Rob and Annette Bunge cruised up the steeper ground on the left side, while Bruce Hunter, tired of waiting for me to emerge from behind my camera, soloed the right side in about fifteen minutes, or roughly double the seven-minute record time.

Horsetail Falls behind us, we set our sights on *Hung Jury*, a ten-minute stroll down the road and across the river. We took advantage of the still day to hop on this notoriously windy climb. On most days, the wind at *Hung Jury* blows so hard it carries ice chunks *up* the wall.

It also causes the ice to form arches up to 30 feet wide that resemble multiple band shells hanging from the flow. These arches, called "bells," "parachutes," or "umbrellas" by the locals, lend a beautifully spooky architecture to the climb. Usually one can weave their way through the bells, staying on solid ice, but not always. Two years ago, local heavies John Weiland and Brian Teale were on *Hung Jury*, positioned inside one of the bells near the base to escape the wind. Warm conditions followed by a flash freeze had made the ice brittle, so when Weiland placed a tool in an icicle, the vibrations caused a different icicle 20 feet away to collapse. All hell broke loose, raucous and white, as huge blocks of ice fell out of the ceiling and walls of the bell. They exploded against each other and rained on Weiland and Teale. One chunk smashed into Weiland's foot, crushing bones and ripping the heel off his boot. Meanwhile, another block hammered Teale, smashing his scapula before tossing him off his feet and pasting him into a wall. He could feel the quick snapping of his ribs as they caved in, puncturing his lung. Pinned under the block, Teale shoved it off immediately, stood up then collapsed, realizing he couldn't make it down the short hill to the river and road. Weiland had to crawl down to get help.

The previous night's rain left a 2- to 4-inch stream flowing over the ice encasing the Lowe. Donning crampons gave just enough clearance to keep our boots from leaking. Having heard the story of the falling bell, and wary of above-freezing conditions, Bruce, Annette, and I postholed up the snow well right of the fall line. In a hurry to wait for us, Rob trusted his luck and blasted straight up through the line of fire. The climb was wet, but more fun than a barrel of monkeys on acid.

That night and the nights to come we got a chance to know Andy Embick better. Embick, through his scores of first ascents, his authorship of the *Blue Ice and Black Gold* guide to Valdez ice, and his spawning of the annual Valdez Ice Festival, has done more to popularize ice climbing in the Valdez area than anyone else. A doctor, Embick moved to Valdez in 1979. The Alaska pipeline, which terminates in Valdez, was completed the year before and the oil boom fostered a Wild West atmosphere. At the time there were only two other ice climbers in Valdez, John Weiland and Bob Pudwill, and Weiland was in temporary retirement from the sport. Hence, Embick took to introducing non-climbers to the sport. He offered ice climbing and other outdoor activities as a healthy alternative to the other winter recreation to be found in Valdez, such as marathon swilling sessions at the Pipeline Club or the Acres. And even if it wasn't really that safe, Andy was there to stitch them up. Of the dozen or two tyros he took out, half a dozen stuck with the sport, some climbing up to grade V ice before they ever touched a rock climb. Eventually, the ice climbers who stayed in Valdez after the pipeline construction days found themselves getting older, getting married, and repopulating. Embick blames "kids and other near-death experiences" for the current decline of the local climbing scene. Nevertheless, it may be the kids he delivered who will be the future of Valdez ice. Embick himself rarely ice climbs these days concentrating more on kayaking, hunting, and biathlons.

I had heard wild stories about Embick, the most outrageous being when, while lecturing at a black tie American Alpine Club affair, he started disrobing to point out his muscles to the aghast audience. I'd also read his *Blue Ice and Black Gold*, in which the about-the-author blurb runs two full pages. I was expecting a raving egomaniac, but the Andy Embick I met did not live up to this reputation. I'm not saying he was humble, but he told just as many stories about others as about himself and his personal stories are sprinkled with self-deprecating humor that may escape some of his detractors. Besides being an accomplished storyteller, he is full of good advice; for example, rubbing purple ski wax on ax handles for better grip with neoprene gloves. And one thing even his detractors grant him is that he is generous to a fault. He has had up to forty ice climbers crashing in his house at one time. He gives them free use of the sauna, access to the kitchen, use of tools and a workbench, and so on. All he asks in return is that they obey the posted house rules and help shovel snow off the driveway and roof. All winter strangers wander in and out of his house. When his wife Kathy asks her daughters, "Who's that downstairs?" they say, "It's just ice climbers." I couldn't help suspecting that if Andy is as smart as his fellow Rhodes Scholars, his generosity toward climbing bums will be tempered in about ten years . . . when his daughters reach their teens.

The Big Two had to come next: *Bridalveil Falls* and *Keystone Greensteps*. These 650-foot twins dominate Keystone Canyon. One hundred yard downhill approaches, pitch after pitch of aquamarine ice, minimal avalanche danger—the thought of my editors OD'ing on Ex-Lax couldn't have cheered me more.

I'd dreamed of *Greensteps* since I'd started swinging tools a few winters ago. I was antsy, so I grabbed the first lead. Warm temperatures had softened the ice so one swing would sink a pick two inches; the only limit to your speed was how fast you could clean your tools and how often you wanted to hang out and screw in pro. Having led only a dozen pitches of ice before, I was intent on each move and anxiously drove the picks in deeper than necessary. My world was a 10-foot diameter patch of ice in front of me. The steep walls beside me, the exposure below me, the majesty of the rent in the earth I was climbing out of—I was oblivious to it all. Swing swing, kick kick, my focus and rhythm produced a strange monotony. Had I been more relaxed, I could have reveled in the surroundings. Had I been more gripped, I could have basked in my fear. As it was, the one thing that separated human from automaton was the cool macerating squish of leather gloves on skin. I had a spare pair for the next pitch, but I knew Embick was right again—neoprene gloves were the way to go at these warm temps.

The first ascent of *Greensteps* (Jeff Lowe, John Weiland, 1976) was a three-day affair, complete with a brandy-warmed bivy in an ice cave. Today, even ice rookies such as myself can manage the route in a day, especially with 100-meter ropes. The four steps of ice break up as to allow the route to be done in two 100-meter pitches. This melts down the psychological barrier to a puddle you can hop over. Nevertheless, 100-meter ropes have their disadvantages. First, even with a dozen screws, you have to run it out over 30 feet between placements if you want to have any left for the belay. After twisting in the anchors at the first belay, I hadn't so much as a snowflake left on my gear sling. Secondly, despite the one-swing hero ice, it seemed like I could have shaved twice before Bruce arrived at the belay. He was motoring; it just takes awhile to climb that far. He then led the next 300 feet so I had a few more hours to hop and stamp on my belay pad in the snow. Lastly, the degree a rope tangles does not rise linearly with rope length; it increases exponentially. Coiling them is wasted effort, it's best to just stuff them in a pack (leaving the ends out), let the leader take the end on top, and feed the rope out of the pack as he or she goes. When the pack's empty, the second tosses the camera, thermos, etc., in and follows. Stuff the rope back in the pack at the end of the climb.

Bruce stopped at a fat fir tree 30 feet shy of the lip. Many parties rap from this tree, but we felt compelled to pull over the top. Between us and the top, however, was 20 feet of decreasingly coherent ice, then the alder zone.

To withstand avalanches that pluck out more rigid trees, alders have evolved with thin, whippy trunks and branches rarely more than a few inches in diameter. The branches point downhill, so to tie them off it's best to lash prussiks around them. By avoiding a nasty bushwhack traverse over to Bruce's belay, I had saved time, but hadn't collected the cordage from him. When I reached a bunch of alder branches poking out through a 10-foot snow bank atop the climb, I had no way to sling them. Virgin alder climber that I was, I figured I'd just reef up on the branches and be on top in no time. When I pulled on the branches, however, I wouldn't move up, they'd move down. It was like working out on a lat pull machine instead of a pull-up bar. I felt none too secure bouncing around on the limbs with no pro. I dug back to get to the branches where they thickened. Here they were less flimsy, but I was creating an overhang of snow above me. The snow wouldn't support my weight and it looked like it might take hours to dig my way through to the summit. Finally I clued in that if I didn't sweep the snow away, but punched it into the cliff face, that I could create platforms that, if I mashed my shins against them, would just support my weight. Ordinarily, I enjoy being on the steep part of the learning curve, getting better each time out on the ice. This time was scary. It's best to learn such techniques on the dull end. Notwithstanding, it was a necessary lesson used many times in the next two weeks.

The next day *Bridalveil* beckoned. Like *Greensteps*, it is tiered, and like *Greensteps,* the first ascent (Carl Tobin, Clif Moore, and Jim Jennings, 1977) was a multi-day affair. Carl Tobin described it thusly in *Climbing* (Nov–Dec 1980): "Having never seen the falls, and not possessing any knowledge of the climbing history of the area, the three of us set off from Fairbanks in mid-December, determined to "fast lane" our way up *Bridalveil*. However, it took three days of hungover, drugged climbing to grope our way up the route. The long vertical section of the fourth pitch weighed constantly on our thoughts."

"None of us quite understood the intricacies of protecting a long vertical section. Extreme winds slowed us down (100 km/hr is not unusual in Valdez). We started at noon on the first two days (we experienced trouble controlling our drinking). And it was necessary to rap down in the dark each day at 4 P.M. (Happy Hour began at 5)."

"None of us had seen ice like *Bridalveil*'s. My Banff experiences had not taught me how to protect long vertical sections. We could not figure out a method Chouinard would approve of, and so, on the final day, starting at the predawn time of 8 A.M., we decided to do it our way, unprotected. At our experience level, there was a good freakin' to be had by all."

I hadn't seen ice like *Bridalveil*'s either. Following Bruce's lead, I reached the second tier. It was the smoothest sheet of ice that size I'd seen, like a vertical hockey rink freshly Zambonied. The warm, wet ice had already healed from Rob and Annette's ascent the day before. Bruce's efforts had strafed the wall with tiny star cracks rising to the left. The other flaws were no bigger than door dings, the former pickholes, mere navels in the ice. It was glorious to be on such a splendid wall, such a world-class climb, and not have it all pigeonholed like the classics in Colorado.

While *Keystone Greensteps* had been of consistent difficulty for its entire length, *Bridalveil* was more varied, the harder sections being harder than on *Greensteps,* and the easy sections being easier. Slabby romps bridged the gaps between pillars and afforded me the opportunity to look around and trip on what a tremendous position I was in. A good freakin' was had when I reached the top of the *Killer Pillar* pitch. I'd followed weaknesses from right to left, tracing a steep half spiral up the ice. When the angle relented, a hole in the ice greeted me that a sports car could drop through. From powder blue to aqua to navy and indigo then black, the gullet descended. A Jonahesque bait fish view if there ever was one. The shell of ice was glowing and Bridalveil Falls poured down the gap between the gently ribbed ice and the chunky black rock. The thought of busting through was inescapable. Could a person climb back out against the deluge, or would the climber drown or freeze to death first?

Many parties rap from above *Killer Pillar,* as the route eases considerably at that point, but again we felt obliged to top out. This meant another posthole session to get to the descent gully, but at least we knew not to try the "direct line" we had the day before. Instead we hiked straight uphill to the road beneath which the Alaska Pipeline is buried, then traversed this west to the avalanche chute descent. One doesn't get near-virgin ice for free.

Modern gear and 100-meter ropes have brought *Bridalveil* and *Greensteps* down to a level doable by a fairly fit and moderately experienced ice climber such as myself. Not so the Keystone Wall. Just left of the big two, this 80-degree diamond-shaped face lies less than a shortstop's throw to first from the highway. The foreshortening caused by viewing it from the base of the narrow canyon causes it to look small, but it is nearly as tall as Longs Peak's Diamond. Flat laid slabs of stone form a face broken by thin dihedrals, ledges, and roofs. A paisley motif of moss blebs and verglas stains decorate the slabs.

Up to the mid-1980s, Valdez ice climbing was focused on the prominent flows and pillars. Then in 1987 Steve Garvey broke new ground with his ascent of *Sans Amis* on the Keystone Wall. Everyone we talked to agreed that Garvey is currently the hard ice guru of the area. On *Sans Amis*, he climbed long sections of ice no more than an inch thick. His best protection consisted of snargs pounded in the bigger "moss clouds." On the upper pitch, he surmounted multiple roofs involving leaning off tools levered in beneath the overhangs, then scratching up the thin smears above the lips until he could get his feet back on the wall. Thus started the assault on the not-so-prominent lines: the ephemeral drips, the thin pro-less smears, the mixed nightmares, the strings of frozen moss clods. Despite assurances that frozen moss, being a fibrous composite material, was bomber compared to a similar-sized chunk of frozen water, I had no intention of dulling my tools and/or punching into the snow at the base of Keystone Wall. When we were there, however, several Alaskans were vying for new lines on the Keystone Wall, including Teale, Paul Turecki, and Chuck Comstock.

It seems every Alaskan ice climber has a Chuck Comstock story to tell. I first met Chuck in the Bridalveil parking lot with Brian Teale. Teale knew I was there on *Climbing*'s behest, and I assumed Chuck knew it too. Comstock came trudging up the embankment to the parking lot, shoulder-length dreadlocks dripping from a ratty old wool cap and framing a long, thick bushel of red beard. He was attired à la army surplus and his skin looked bleached. I wasn't climbing that day and dressed in forest green canvas pants and an orange jacket. He gave me the once-over then asked, "Are them those fancy fashion pants?"

I was taken aback. Here I was, torso a $400 glowing Gore-Tex ember, and he's flipping me shit about my pants.

"Them's cotton?"

Comstock seemed leery of people, or was it just reporters? Either way, the ploy worked. I was so uncomfortable I wasn't about to ask him for stories. Besides, I had plenty fed to me by others already.

Comstock, an Iowa farm boy, arrived in Valdez as a Coast Guardsman and never left. Prior to his arrival he had no climbing experience but soon became, to use Embick's words, a "neophyte member of a loosely bound group of bored, eager, and ignorant Valdez ice climbers." Comstock's propensity to get into dangerous predicaments was the stuff of legends. I'd seen a hairball series of photos of him escaping off a multiton fractured ice pillar just in time to watch it collapse and burst on the ground. When I asked Brian Teale if Comstock liked taking unnecessary risks, he said, "I don't know about that. He just doesn't like to go do stuff and have an ordinary time. Chuck likes to have epics." Embick and others had recounted many of these epics, both on the ice and off. Every time, Comstock gets in deep shit then pulls through. Paul Turecki claims Comstock "has some kind of guardian angel looking out for him." Brian Teale provided the proof.

One night, Comstock was soloing *Bridalveil Falls.* "Chuck takes pride in having shit for gear," Teale told us. As usual, Comstock was climbing without a third tool. Part way up he broke a tool. For most climbers this would mean curtains, but Comstock kept going with a single ax. Sure enough, salvation arrived 25 feet later when Comstock found a tool left by a Navy SEAL who backed off the route earlier that day.

While we were in Valdez, Embick never missed a chance to tell us how fat *Wowie Zowie* was this winter. One only has to take his spotting scope, one of his many toys, a few yards from his front door to confirm this. First done by Tobin and Embick, *Wowie Zowie* was the big name climb of the early 1980s with a reputation for steepness, unprotectability, and poor consolidation. On the first ascent, Tobin climbed around the backside of the pillar, hacked a window through thin ice to the front, then crawled through the window and onto the overhanging pillar above. The pro was miserable in bubbly Swiss cheese ice, and twice Tobin slipped, catching himself on just a single tool.

Wowie Zowie is still taken seriously. When Boulder big names Kevin Cooney and Michael Gilbert visited Valdez in '93 they churned up the standard classics in short order. Throughout, they allegedly refused to swill any booze until *Wowie Zowie* was in their coup bag. And indeed they came back singing of its praises and its horrors, though one wonders if an ascent done after a week of sobriety can be considered to be in good style.

A rest day was due, so we slapped boards on and headed up Mineral Creek to view *Wowie Zowie* up close. We skied up the deep and broad V-shaped canyon. Crack, rumble—avalanches serenaded us in stereo from both sides. We could smell the snapped alder branches on the close ones. In the course of a few hours we witnessed thirty to forty slides including one right over *Wowie Zowie,* and two barreling down the gully a hundred feet left of it. We also slapped a few mosquitoes.

Certain climbs are so visually striking that one redefines their level of acceptable risk. Standing beneath *Wowie Zowie* brought that scary feeling of excitement. Huge fangs of ice coalesce to form the most striking pillar of ice I have seen. On the dark overhanging walls on either side hang dozens of white bayonets, casting an evil, gothic look about the climb.

I wanted *Wowie Zowie*. I psyched myself up, telling myself I was good enough to lead it, and if not, at worst I would leave a tool to back off. Every now and then the thought would seep in, "What if the ice is too shitty to get back off gear in?" I didn't have an answer for that other than downclimb and pray. It was in rare shape, thick and plump, and I spied a groove creasing the notorious final pillar. All this fueled delusions of grandeur. If only I could talk my partners out of it, I could lead this thing. Work up the weakness, stay cool, find the rests. Crack. Another avalanche cascaded down the gully 100 feet left of it. Okay. Find a good warm-up pillar to test yourself on, then come back when the avalanche danger has settled and the temp drops below freezing.

Had the stock market dropped as fast as the temperature in Valdez, they would be calling for a wet cleanup on Wall Street. One day it was all soft and drippy and Horsetail Falls looked like Madonna's jeans (1986). Two days later it was fully frozen. We had ducked the avalanche danger by climbing in Bear Canyon and Hole in the Wall Canyon. More great ice, but without the sporadic traffic noises of Keystone Canyon. Hole in the Wall is particularly pretty, a deep, winding gash in the bedrock, with a small stream bubbling through it. At places the canyon walls are but 30 feet apart, and rise over 200 feet.

By the time avalanche danger had subsided, conditions were so frigid that huge pillars had sprouted vertical fracture lines and otherwise easy climbs shed placements on large-pizza-sized dinner plates. We were spared our appointment with *Wowie Zowie,* at least for this year. We also missed out on avalanche-prone Sheep Creek, where some of the really long climbs lurked. The canyons around Valdez are well developed, but the potential for new routes elsewhere in southeast Alaska boggles the mind. In most cases, long ski-ins or snowmachine approaches will be required. Steve Davis tried to combine the two, having one person drive the snowmachine (called snowmobiles in the lower 48) while the other person is towed along on skis behind the vehicle. As it would be ridiculously pumping to hang onto the tow rope for the 9-mile approach, Davis attached himself to the rope with a fifi hook. The skidoo took off and Davis's heel popped out of one of his Ramer bindings. The roar of the engine drowned out his cries, so he was flying along behind the snowmachine on one ski. Finally he crashed, and still bound to the rope, got towed behind the rig. The cowboy-behind-the-horse stunt went on until the driver thought his engine was starting to run rough. He stopped, only to look back and see the human sea anchor behind.

To cap off our trip, we decided to hit the beaches near Homer. Jim Sweeney, a garrulous and lively character from Anchorage, had given us the hard sell on this area he did much to develop. He jokingly put down the big ice in Valdez to pump up the Homer climbs. Furthermore, he billed the town of Homer as "Berkeley of Alaska," and coaxed us with tales of the wild nightlife there. His cheap tactics worked. We drove back to Anchorage, then headed south down the Seward Highway. Ordinarily, dozens of roadside ice climbs would have presented themselves to us along the Seward, but scant groundwater flow and high temperatures conspired against us. There wasn't even enough ice to do the stand-atop-the-car-to reach-the-bottom-of-the-flow trick to get started.

Homer was pretty sedate when we visited. No tear gas, nobody offering us acid, none of that stuff I grew up with in Berkeley. In fact it pretty much lived up to its self-proclaimed moniker "The Halibut Capital of Alaska." There were no nose rings (we only saw one in our two-week stay in Alaska) and the militant feminazis must have flown south for the winter. The only hint of Berkeley we saw was the blatant lesbian couple at Neon Coyote restaurant. At least Sweeney was right about the ice climbing. Though no taller than 120 feet, the routes at Ninilchik (one of several seaside areas near Homer) were wild.

Approaching the routes involved a mile-long stroll along the beach south of a small fishing hamlet. Depending on when waves last washed over the sand, it ranged from frozen hard as concrete to a crusty slush prone to foot-deep postholing. Under the former conditions I found donning the spikes to be a favorable alternative to cratering on one's ass. The end of the beach gave way to near-vertical cliffs dropping into the tidal flats. Every 30 yards or so, a flow of ice would adorn the wall. The ice was impregnated with sediment from the soft mudstone. One drip would be gray, the next one brown, the one next to it snot yellow. At high tide waves would lick away at the base of the routes, so several were devoid of ice for the first 4 or 5 feet. The fatter flows looked simple, but the subzero cold made them exciting. Repeatedly, I'd get gripped as a dinner plate flashed within inches of a neighboring tool placement. The wind was so stiff it gave me instant ice cream headaches and blew my tools off trajectory in mid-swing. I had to stem out with my right foot to keep the gale from barn-dooring me off. Unless I kept them constantly twisting, screws would freeze tight in mid-placement. Add frequent stops to warm numb hands and the going was slow. Eventually I got in my token Ninilchik lead, set it up as a toprope, and lowered back down.

Slow going is no big deal on most one-pitch climbs, but not so when the tide is coming in. Rob went up to clean the pitch. Between my extended sojourn on the sharp end, and his difficulty getting out the screws, we had chewed up a fair bit of clock. Waves of Slurpee consistency were marching up the beach. One or two of these splashing into you could cost you some appendages. Bruce and I moved the packs away, hanging them on tools sunk into the soft, icy stone. The waves were 30 feet away, then 20, then 10 when Rob stepped over the lip and I gratefully abandoned the belay and immediate vicinity. Rob got himself down and somehow deftly managed to retrieve the rope without it blowing into the soup.

The actual climbs at Ninilchik were not as impressive as the surroundings. Large driftwood snags draped in icicles adorned the beach as did hundreds of icebergs from twelve-pack to jukebox size. In the water a school of seals played king of the ice floe while the sun set over the snow-clad volcanoes across Cook Inlet. It was hard to leave, so we trucked over to an attractive little smear above the high tide line. Bruce was bouldering around on the 30-foot vertical formation when brittle ice and bottoming crampon placements convinced him to climb down. Midway up was a basketball-sized rest knob that snapped when Bruce stuck it with his ax. Bruce hung on but the knob didn't. It hit the snow slope at the base, and instead of tumbling straight down, it followed the path of our footprints and plowed right into my pack, breaking my sunglasses and powdering the filter on my camera lens. I was choked. Rob stepped up and gave the block a righteous kick that didn't faze the block, but broke his crampon. Bad juju was in the air. It was time to go home.

Climbing, November 1995

The Fab 50

Verm faces objective dangers, '90s style

IT USED TO BE ALL YOU HAD TO DO to make a name for yourself in climbing was to bag the first ascent of an 8000-meter peak. Now it's not so easy. You name it, it's been done—climb the highest peak on each continent, send *The Nose* free in a day, ski the Black Ice Couloir, parapente off Everest, tack a sit-down start onto the *Zodiac* . . . These feats were cutting into my own plans to be gloriously famous, universally envied, and high on America's most-eligible-bachelors list.

Lack of funds deflated my scheme to inner-tube down Nanga Parbat's Rupal Face. Hence, I started looking for some less expensive mission: one within range of my prematurely aging van. There didn't seem to be many left. This led me to the '90s definition of "objective danger": I was in danger of having had all my objectives ticked by someone else.

Then it hit me. Ten years ago, I couldn't get anyone to go to Hueco Tanks because it was "a well-known fact" that Texas had no climbing. Even today, several states are rumored to be climbing-free. Tim Toula's *Rock 'n' Road* lists no developed climbing in Delaware, Louisiana, North Dakota, or Nebraska. For the past decade, I lived out of a van touring America in search of the next bouldering fix. Although I wasn't thinking much about it at the time, this fixation, I realized, has put me in an excellent position to be first to do a technical rock climb or boulder problem in every state.

On the surface, this appears a reasonable, fun goal. In reality, it is a way to visit some of the worst climbing areas on the planet. Take, for instance, Florida Caverns State Park, a spot once listed in *Rock & Ice* as having the potential to be a "legitimate bouldering area." Florida Caverns has a few cliff bands up to 15 feet tall. Swamps caress the base of the rocks and poison ivy thickets crown the topouts. Mosquitoes encourage the visitor to keep moving. Nonetheless, I knew I'd have to stop long enough to bag one problem and tick Florida.

I chose a squat but overhanging limestone lump next to the road. This 10-foot-tall boulder was chosen not for its aesthetics or challenge, but for its relatively lofty position above the water table. I set up my tripod and camera, then quickly tiptoed through the poison ivy, racing the self-timer to the base. The holds resembled third-world "barbed wire"—the broken-glass-and-cement icing atop courtyard walls in less affluent countries. I pulled on the dirtiest holds, counting on the cushioning moss to prevent lacerations. Had it been an inch over the state line into Alabama, I would have never touched the thing.

This detour from sane and worthy climbing could be justified in only one way—by continuing my quest for the Fabulous 50. Be forewarned: if you want to prove you're as moronic as moi, you're in for some bad climbing. But think of the glory of being "first." Nowadays you're lucky to be the second person in your office to do the Seven Summits.

By now you're probably thinking of quitting your job and joining the race. As with any race, there must be rules. As the founder of the Fab 50, I will do my duty and set them out right now. (The best way to win any contest is to make the rules yourself.)

To qualify a climb must be on natural rock and natural holds (no buildings or home gyms allowed).

It must contain fifth-class moves. (No biggy—my moss-covered jug haul in Florida probably tipped the scales at 5.6. It counts.)

It need not be a roped climb.

You must not tick all fifty states before I do.

Sounds simple, right? Wrong-o. This challenge contains three more rules than the Seven Summits. As well, it could and should take more time than ticking the Seven Summits.

As Larry Bird once declared in the locker room before a three-point shooting contest—you are all just fighting for second. Larry won that day, and I virtually have this title wrapped up. There's just one hitch: Louisiana.

Louisiana is a great state and a credit to the nation: home to Tabasco sauce, Zapps potato chips, Mardi Gras, and LSU baseball (we'll be big and forgive them Albert Belle). At this point, I've been on three recon trips to the Bayou State. The first time I had a line on some rocks big enough to create waterfalls. They had to be big enough to count. The rock turned out to be a 3-foot-thick sandstone band with 15 feet of clay packed beneath it. Still, if I could make it up the slimy packed clay and mantel the rocky shelf above, it would count. The ascent looked tricky and dangerous. Before lacing up, a quick perusal of the map told me what the road signs failed to mention: these "crags" were actually ten minutes across the border into Mississippi. I was safe, temporarily.

I figured I could trace the same rock formation into Louisiana. Back West, this exercise would take a few hours. But these were the Deep South woods, full of vines, poison ivy, old tires, and spooky bogs. I could hike to K2 quicker. I drove back into Louisiana and found a streambed. Imagining I saw vertical terrain around a bend in the creek, I parked the car, and thrashed down through the underbrush, making a line for a sandbar that promised an easy path toward my niche in history.

Every year climbers perish in avalanches, fall into crevasses, or get clobbered by rocks. Being first and foremost a climber, I always thought that dying for the sport seemed noble. But as the sandbar liquefied beneath me, I could see the headlines: Man Swallowed by Quicksand on Approach to America's Worst Climb. I struggled out, barely retaining my shoes. This wasn't worth it. I'd find rock elsewhere in Louisiana.

I now got scientific and procured a geologic map to the state. One look at the map drove me to drink. (OK, that's not that hard, but you get the point.) The entire state was covered in floodplain sediments from the mighty Mississippi. Nothing but silt and clay. But wait. Just as I was about to give up I noticed a squiggle on the map, marked sandstone. The words "Rock Quarry" were on the map inside the sandstone-bearing formation.

An exiled climbing buddy and I drove north for several hours. From the highway there was no hint of rock. I asked at a gas station. "Rocks?" They looked at me like I was a haulbag short of a wall climber.

We cruised back and forth along the back roads near the gas station, straining for a glimpse of rock. It was beginning to look hopeless when by chance we spied a sign for Rock Quarry Road. I felt the sweat break on my palms. We would just pull up at the first house and ask where the rocks were.

The first house was a ramshackle affair sporting a number of abandoned cars as lawn ornaments. Three men were out front. Brothers, fathers, maybe both. The eldest was seated next to a pickup, fondling a large chainsaw. He had the sort of physique that only overalls can cover. The younger ones hadn't yet crested the 300-pound mark, but were due any day. One of them hefted a large wood-splitting ax.

Doubtless, we looked just as strange to them. Furthermore, I asked strange questions about rocks. Obviously, I wasn't normal. I hope I didn't scare them too bad. As to where the quarry was, the answer was "long gone." But, they offered, there were some big rocks by the houses down the road.

We drove in the direction indicated and damned if Ol' Haystack wasn't right. These were the biggest rocks I'd seen in the entire state. There were a couple I doubt I could lift, and one I figured I'd need a running start, well maybe a step or two, to jump over. Furthermore, the rock was good solid sandstone, reminiscent of the Dakota Sandstone at Horsetooth Reservoir. I got the sinking feeling that Louisiana may have once had rocks big enough to climb, but they had all been turned into building stone. Recon Two came to naught.

I burned two more tanks of gas following leads on Recon Three. Again I confounded the natives with my questions. Hiding their fear behind awkward smiles, they'd say, "I think there are cliffs at the other end of the lake." There never were.

What if Louisiana had zero climbing? Forty-six states into my quest, I couldn't let this stop me. I asked myself, "What would Dick Bass do?"

Probably buy his way out of it. Bass is the multimillionaire ski-resort owner who was first to claim the Seven Summits. For the cost of those exploits, Bass could easily rent a couple of skycranes and airlift Hueco Tank's famous Mushroom Boulder to Louisiana. Drop it right on the 50-yard line at Death Valley and crank problems off during halftime at a Tigers game. Then he could fly it back to Hueco and thereby foil any competitors. Eventually, guides would form a coalition to truck some pissant boulder from Mississippi to the French Quarter and charge 65,000 bucks a shot to all the doctors and lawyers intent on ticking the Fabulous 50 before their friends.

There was another option. Bass hired a geographer to declare the hill-walk Kosciusko the highest mountain in Australasia. Forget that New Guinea's more difficult Carstensz Pyramid is nearly 9,000 feet taller. I know a couple lawyers not currently engaged in suing other climbers. In exchange for their services in declaring the Louisiana Purchase null and void, I could cut them in on the action with directions to the boulders in Delaware. This plan seemed to have promise, until I realized almost every crux state was part of the Purchase—North Dakota, Nebraska, Iowa, Kansas, Missouri. Not only was the thought of giving this land back to the French distasteful, it exposed another catch: If I wiped out these states, someone else might have unwittingly beat me to the goal.

The Fabulous 50 had rapidly changed from being the "Poor Man's

Seven Summits" to a princely crusade. The days when hard work, determination, and iron will could write you into the record books are gone. For that matter, they may never have existed. Whymper wasn't exactly a pauper, nor was the Duke of Abruzzi. The biggest objective danger in the '90s is lack of funds. Hence, kind reader, I'll have to leave you now while I check last night's lotto numbers.

Aloha.

(As this first went to press, I was visiting Nebraska and North Dakota. The trip was a success—half the footholds didn't break and none of the boulders completely collapsed. Having a degree in geology, I can assure you that what I climbed in those two states was rock, appearances to the contrary. Reaching for the top of a cliff band in North Dakota, I had that same "this could be really stupid" feeling I got while sinking in the Louisiana quicksand.

Later I found a rock to climb in Louisiana that, if you stared at it long enough, bore a strange resemblance to El Capitan, only 3,000 feet shorter. But that's another story.)

Climbing, November 1998

PART IV

CHARACTERS

IF ROCKS AND MOUNTAINS ARE the bread and butter of climbing, then climbers are the spice. Something about hanging off rock faces, spitting in Death's eye, and pretty much doing stuff to prematurely age your parents attracts folks with good stories to tell.

When I pick up a climbing magazine, I want to be inspired to go climbing, not hang out with a media darling. To this end, I'd find a near-death-scrape-on-the-rock tale to be more inspiring than knowing that in Russ Clune's bathroom, the soap matches the towels. Go ahead and laugh, this last fact actually saw print.

The majority of climbers profiled in *Climbing* in the early 1990s were sport climbers. The profiles were all too predictable—each was full of big route names, bigger numbers, diet and training regimens, and some homey facts. Somehow this would take up 2,500 words. I felt I could have done the same job on the back of a baseball card. The sad fact is that while sport climbing may be fun to do, it's terribly boring to read about. None of these guys or girls were crawling down from the Ogre with two broken legs, or watching bus-sized rocks crash down a couloir at them. The profiles lacked action. I wanted to change this, but there was a catch.

I hate writing profiles. For me, they are the hardest and most time-consuming of assignments. It is the writer's responsibility to be sure the subject is portrayed accurately, not just their actions, but their feelings and words as well. The worst fights I've had with my editors came when I felt they were twisting a subject's words to say what the magazine wanted them to say, not what the subject was actually trying to express. Having been misquoted in print numerous times, I'm very touchy about this. Also, I've seen the other side, when I've misunderstood a subject's words, and the resulting article incurred their wrath.

Climbing was hungry for personal-interest stories, and they appealed to me to write some profiles. Temporarily taking leave of my senses, I consented. I agreed to do three feature-length profiles, so long as I could pick the climbers. They said okay. I told them I wanted to profile Mark Wilford, Tom Cosgriff, and Rob Slater. I picked these three because they were from my generation, climbed for similar reasons as myself, and were serious adrenaline junkies. As well, I had climbed with each of them and knew they were the real deal. They had all survived numerous epics, yet kept going back for more.

Later *Climbing* suggested that only the Wilford piece should be feature length, because nobody had heard of Cosgriff or Slater. I went ballistic. The hardest part of any of these profiles would be keeping them down to 3,000 words. Any of these guys could fill an entire book with page-turning anecdotes. I'm sure I said something like, "Just because these guys aren't in any of your frou-frou full-page ads doesn't mean they won't make great reading. Don't weenie out, let's inspire the readers. Give me a chance." Despite my lack of manners, they did.

After the Slater article was printed, a stranger told me they had got that issue and eagerly went to the profile on column-inch-queen Robyn Erbesfeld. He said he couldn't finish it. Discouraged, he flipped to the Slater piece, though he'd never heard of Robbie. "After reading that," he said, "I was so stoked to climb." Compliments like that kept me writing.

After the Adrenaline Junkies profiles, a long time passed before I felt like writing about another climber. By this time, I had my own column and the flexibility to escape the profile format. In the past *Climbing* did not like to print question and answer interviews, preferring profiles instead. But a subject of such huge interest and personal nature thrust forth that I felt it could only be done justice in the subject's own words. Hence, the Bobbi Bensman interview.

Up through 1997, Bobbi Bensman was best known for her sport-climbing achievements and her tremendously ripped body. Great material for a photo shoot or news flash, but not enough for a full, engaging interview. Then, in 1998, she shocked the climbing world by getting her breasts augmented. Despite the fact that Bobbi is a terrifically talented climber and funny individual, it was the new boobs that everyone was talking about. The public was having their say; Bobbi deserved a chance to respond. I felt I was the only the climbing journalist out there man enough to handle the job.

The Wilford Case

*This profile was written during the height of the sport
versus trad years. Wilford was one of the few trads who
stayed pure. I was another. Ironically, back in college days we
couldn't stand each other. Eventually, we discovered we had
more in common with each other than with most other climbers. The petty differences from dorm days disappeared and
we've been good friends since. I wrote this because I felt
Wilford set an example that reflected well on traditional ideals.
I also liked the palm-sweating anecdotes.*

*Some background: the first big international sport-climbing
competition to be held in America occurred at Snowbird in
1988. The final quip about Wilford beating J. B. Tribout was
edited out when this was first published. My editors did not
want me to reveal that Wilford had outclimbed one of the
world's top-ranked sport climbers that day. I felt it was a great
line, showing Wilford's sense of humor. He doesn't spout off
about himself much, but he got a kick out of beating Tribout
at Tribout's own game. Just like he gets a kick out of honking
at cows.*

A FRIEND OF MINE ONCE REMARKED, "If God exists, then He must spend
a disproportionately large amount of time on The Wilford Case." The
speaker had a point. Wilford's climbing career has been liberally punc-
tuated with bold ascents and life-threatening near misses. Ken
Duncan, a hotshot 1970s Colorado climber, calls Wilford "another
Tobin Sorenson, but with better luck so far."

Consider the record. Wilford has survived four automobile

rollovers (the subject is quick to note that he was driving in only three of these). He pulled the car-door-sized flake off the *Salvation Roof* in Eldorado, ripping out all of his gear except for a quarter-inch bolt hanging halfway out of its hole in the roof. Then there's the first time he tried to do a winter solo of the entire East Face of Longs Peak— the time a whiteout moved in and Wilford started down, faster than planned.

Attempting to set an anchor, Wilford let go of his rappel lines. Suddenly he slipped, and pulled backwards by his heavy pack, he blasted headfirst down the face. The ropes raced through his brake system, flipping around so he couldn't grasp them. His only hope was the tiny overhand knots he'd tied in the ends of his 8 and 9 millimeter ropes. Given the force his fall would put on these knots, the small diameter of his ropes, and the large gaps in his carabiner brake system, it seemed a futile safety measure; when he hit the end of his ropes the knots would cinch into knuckle-sized balls and squirt through his brakes. There would be a slight jerk on his harness, then a 200-foot free fall to the deck.

As fate would have it, this wasn't Wilford's day to die. An instant before the knots reached his brake system, a piton dangling from his rack sucked into the space between his brake biners. The pin filled enough of the gap to stop the knots from squeezing through. Wilford rode out the rope stretch and ended suspended in the middle of the blank granite face. Two A3 anchors later, he was on the ground.

In a climbing world increasingly obsessed with big numbers and risk-free ascents, Wilford stands apart as a climber who seeks more, one who is not afraid to climb himself into trouble and force through it, all the while pushing his mental and physical limits.

Wilford is best known for his alpine achievements, in particular the first American solo of the North Face of the Eiger; however, to call Wilford just an alpinist is akin to calling Bo Jackson just a football player. Randy Joseph, a Colorado climbing guide and frequent partner of Wilford's since high school, puts it this way: "It really doesn't matter what Mark's climbing on, boulders, rock, ice, or mixed ground, he's state of the art."

Wilford is modest about his achievements. Talk to his friends and partners and you're sure to hear many Wilford stories he wouldn't have told himself. When pressed for details surrounding these tales, Wilford recounts the facts in a straightforward and simple manner. Annoyed by braggarts, Wilford prefers understatement to exaggeration.

In climbing, Wilford is outspoken about one subject, his traditionalist beliefs. He's determined to protect certain crags for traditional climbing and has backed up his words with a bolt-hungry crowbar. He believes means are just as important as the end; hence, he won't hangdog. "I consider it cheating," he says flatly.

Some people view traditional climbers as "conservative." Nobody who has met Wilford would give him that tag. His wildness, on and off the rock, is legendary.

Wilford grew up in Fort Collins, Colorado. His engineer father located the family at a safe distance from his workplace—the nuclear weapons plant at Rocky Flats. Wilford's first snow climb was at age eleven, his first foray onto rock at thirteen. People who met Wilford later, in his twenties, are astonished to learn that he had been a clean-living kid ("pure as the driven snow," declares one early partner). As a teen, Wilford's penchant for risk earned him the nickname "the Wacko Kid," bestowed by his fellow Horsetooth Hardcores, a group of local boulderers bonded by a ritual January 23 dip through a hole cut in the ice of Horsetooth Reservoir.

During high school, he often bouldered with his mentor and fellow Hardcore Steve Mammen, a Front Range bouldering legend. Not satisfied with Horsetooth's treacherous landings, Wilford and Steve discovered a way to add extra fear to each spring day's session. They called it icewalking. The goal was simple. Walk across the ice to the opposite bank of the reservoir, half a mile away.

At first it was easy. There were few cracks in the ice and the surface felt solid. As spring wore on, the ice thinned. Soon the surface was laced with cracks, the chunks of ice were held together like a jigsaw puzzle. With each step, the surface would flex and creak. Should a section come loose, it would be curtains. When it finally became a matter of leaping from floe to floe, and in heading to solid ice the pair broke through on their first three steps from the shore, they mutually decided to call it quits. In retrospect, Mammen, a frequent risk-taker himself, calls it "the most dangerous thing I've ever done."

In the fall of 1977, Wilford enrolled at the University of Colorado in Boulder. College did nothing to quiet Wilford down. To the contrary, it introduced him to the joys of partying. One night around about 11 P.M., Wilford returned to his dorm room from partying downstairs. He started packing his climbing gear. It was winter (Wilford's week-old beer chunks were still frozen to the windowsill) and Wilford was inspired to climb the First Flatiron—that night.

His aggressive driving having resulted in the suspension of his license, Wilford was forced to hike to "The First" from the dorm. The extended approach warmed Wilford up. At the base he stripped off his warmer layers of clothing and stuffed them in his pack. He tied the pack to one end of a haul line, clipped the other end of the line to his harness, and then started up the snow-plastered slabs. Climbing sans headlamp in the dark, he worked his way up until the haul line came taut. He stopped to haul his pack, which became stuck partway up. Unable to free it, Wilford cast the haul line off and continued up, convinced that the exertion of climbing would make his spare clothes unnecessary.

Things went well for several pitches until Wilford found himself atop a 4-inch wide by 18-inch long flake, unable to crack the moves above, too gripped to reverse the moves below. It was 1 A.M. and the winter sun would be a long time in rising. Unanchored, he stood atop the flake all night long, fighting off sleep and hypothermia.

Morning dawned, but the light gave no clues as to how to free-climb off the flake. In desperation, Wilford cut off the shoulder sling of his alpine hammer by hammering the webbing against the rock. He then removed his belt, made of 1-inch webbing, and tied it to the shoulder sling. Looping these over his bivy flake, he had just enough webbing to tension traverse over to a nearby crack and escape from the face. He was late to class that day.

Engineering studies were eating into Wilford's climbing time. A decision had to be made. Would it be a life of button-down geek shirts, Pencil-Pals, and calculator holsters? No. Wilford opted for a career as a full-time climber. For the next decade he worked as little as possible, and only to support his habit.

For starters, he dropped out halfway through his second semester and went to Yosemite, where he traded Valley honemaster Jim Bridwell "something illicit" for a pair of wall boots. He then started up the *Salathe Wall* with Colorado's Charlie Fowler. Conditions were abominable, but while other parties bailed, Wilford and Charlie persevered. By the time they reached the top, Wilford looked like a tertiary syphilitic—his leg was bruised and swollen from a wrecking ball swing into Hollow Flake; his hands were twice normal size and oozing pus from numerous infections; the constant soakings in frigid meltwater cascades had whitened, wrinkled and softened his skin to a pasty mush reminiscent of cauliflower gone bad; and to top it all off he was enveloped in a rash of itching, weeping blisters courtesy of the poison oak bushes on Mammoth Terraces. Things could have been worse, though; he could have been in midterms.

Wilford seems not to *want* to climb, but to *need* to. He devours rock in huge quantities and is particularly drawn to the extra challenge of first ascents. One project was to free the *Diagonal Direct* on the Lower East Face of Longs Peak, a grade V he had done the first winter ascent of during his high school days. Now out of college, but still in his late teens, Wilford teamed up with Boulder's Pat Adams for the attempt. The crux pitch is a dicey proposition, 5.11 tips jams and thin face moves protected by a nickel-thick stopper with only poor gear below to back it up. Wilford had delicately worked through the crux, the first free ascent apparently in the bag, when a hummock of grass he was grasping tore out of the crack. He went whistling, stripping the puny #2 stopper from the crack. The next nut pulled. At the belay, his partner Pat Adams watched Wilford whip by. After Wilford had fallen over 50 feet, the rope pulled taut around Adam's waist jerking him upward against the anchor nuts. They pulled.

A few seconds later both climbers came to a swinging stop, dangling on opposite ends of the rope, suspended by a single nut thinner than a pack of matches. After reestablishing the anchor, Wilford went up again, passed the crux, but was forced to climb back down when his haul line jammed. At that, the pair retreated.

Experiences such as Wilford had on the *Diagonal Direct* gave him the confidence to push himself further in the realm of high stakes, high difficulty climbing. He would, in fact, attack risky climbs throughout his career, not just for a limited period.

One of Wilford's most fearsome creations is *Spinal Tap*, a first free ascent he bagged in 1986. The route lies alongside the Big Thompson River in Colorado's Front Range, on a granite crag of indistinct character save for one perfectly cleaved face, 80 feet tall and 25 feet wide. From the opposite bank of the river, the face appears as flawless as a sheet of plate glass. Only with binoculars can a hairline seam be seen slicing up the center of the nearly vertical face. Apart from a couple of tiny notches in the seam, there appears to be nothing to hold on to besides a thin coating of lichen. When Wilford first tried leading it free, he found a bolt left from the first aid ascent. The first ascensionists, indignant at Wilford's audacity in trying to free their route, tried to scare him off by chopping their own bolt.

To Wilford, the loss of the only good piece of pro on the pitch only upped the stakes, and therefore the rewards of success. Now Wilford's best piece was a 0.5 Lowe Tricam that he filed down to 0.3 size to fit a horizontal slot 15 feet below the crux. Above the modified Tricam, the protection consisted of exclusively #1 and #2 RPs and Crack-N-Ups, all equipped with Screamer fall arresters.

After dicing past the microscopic B1+ crux edging section, Wilford was without footholds. He tossed one dyno, then a second, his feet paddling against the burnished wall. One more lunge and he'd gain the key horizontal groove marking the end of the crux section. He missed.

All the stitches on the first Screamer burst apart, as did the cable on the RP it was attached to. Then the next piece shot from the crack. When Wilford hit 30 feet, the third Screamer blew apart, stitch by stitch. It slowed him down until, with only a few stitches left, he came to a stop dangling from a Crack-N-Up.

It took Wilford five attempts spread over two years to finally succeed on this testpiece. Graded 5.13- R or X, *Spinal Tap* has yet to see a second lead. Mammen, who seconded the first ascents of both *Spinal Tap* and Colorado's most famous mind control challenge, *Perilous Journey,* says, "If someone pointed a gun at my head and said, 'you have a choice, I'm going to shoot you, you can climb *Spinal Tap,* or you can climb *Perilous Journey.* What's your choice?' I would take *Perilous Journey* by far." And his second choice would be getting shot? "No. I'd take *Spinal Tap.* Who knows, I might luck out."

Wilford has based his 5.13 rating of *Spinal Tap* on the amount of effort it required, both physical and mental, to lead from the ground up. He feels that the Yosemite Decimal System (YDS) "has been bastardized" because "you can't equate traditional climbing and Eurostyle climbing." Wilford has proposed that Eurostyle ascents be given European (French) grades, and traditional ascents be given YDS grades.

Asked why he sticks to traditional climbing even though it lacks the glitter and glory of sport climbing, Wilford says, "I haven't compromised my style to be competitive." Several years ago he was tempted, when it seemed like everyone and his grandmother were out cranking 5.13. Everyone except him. His self-confidence sagged, but returned in greater measure when he realized that it was just numbers increasing, not standards. Sure, people were ticking bigger numbers than he was, but in what style? When it came to an accurate measure of a climber's ability, on-sight ascents, most of the overnight sensations he met had nothing on him.

Wilford believes the dividends gained from traditional ascents are worth every bit of extra effort. He credits traditional climbing with teaching him self-preservation, respect for the rock, and the value of trying hard and not giving up. "Traditional climbing actually makes you a better climber because instead of hanging on bolts you've got to learn how to downclimb to a rest, and how to rest,' he says. "You have to be more of an on-sight climber—you're not going to have so many opportunities at a crux section." The ability to downclimb, a skill Wilford feels is being lost, is essential in high bouldering, mountaineering, soloing, and necky leads. If it weren't for his mastery of this skill, it seems certain Wilford would be maggot food by now.

"Climbing has given me the best times of my life," says Wilford. "I owe the sport something." He intends to repay the debt by preserving certain areas for the evolution of traditional climbing. In the past he has spoken out in anger over the bashing of traditional ethics. One published letter to the editor, prompted by the demise of traditional ethics in Eldorado Canyon, was signed Mark "The Chisel" Wilford. This was back in the days when climbers used chisels to chop bolts, not holds. Penned in haste, his antagonistic words were ill taken by some.

Then came the period when numbers rose and his confidence waned. It was the mid-1980s; hype was king and the trend to be hyped was sport climbing. Wilford remained quiet. At the time, few voices were speaking up for traditionalism. Now he's not afraid to raise his voice, but in a more diplomatic way than before. He tries to relate the positive aspects of traditional-style climbing more than the negative effects of sport climbing, such as overcrowding, closure of areas, and environmental insensitivity. He cites Czechoslovakia as an area that has stuck to traditional ethics since the late 1800s and therefore still has potential for new routes 100 years later. He'd like to see certain areas in the U.S. granted that kind of respect. Yosemite, Joshua Tree, Estes Park, and Rocky Mountain National Park are among those he lists.

"My biggest problem is with bolts next to cracks and rap-bolting in traditional areas," Wilford states. He's removed many bolts he's found offensive, but only after he has led the climb on clean gear. If he hasn't led the route before it was bolted, he has his partner tape off the hangers so he can't chicken out and clip them. "I'd like to see some areas left for traditional climbing," Wilford says, then adds half-jokingly, "otherwise it's going to be a lot of work pulling all those bolts out."

Not all aspects of sport climbing offend Wilford. He has been in several competitions, the on-sight nature of which he appreciates, and he currently makes his living as a climbing gear sales rep, a job that depends on the popularity of climbing. Wilford remarks, however, that "sport climbing doesn't hold the aspect of climbing I enjoy and why I got into climbing, which is adventure, the unknown, and a degree of risk."

Whether Wilford seeks adventure or vice versa is unclear. In 1982, midway through his decade of full-time climbing, he was on the beach at Cabo San Lucas in Baja California when a woman from an Atlanta ad agency chased an errant football into the knee-deep water. Although it was a pleasant sunny day at the beach, an offshore storm was pushing enormous waves up on the shore. She struggled as the first wave pounded her into the sand, then dragged her out to sea. When she came back in on the second wave, her body was limp as a rag doll's. A bevy of onlookers watched in horror as the downshore current swept her toward the rocks bordering the beach.

A rescue attempt appeared suicidal. Randy Joseph, who was with Wilford on the beach, thought about rushing in on the next wave, "but Wilford beat me to it," Joseph recalls. Joining Wilford was a Canadian cyclist. They grabbed the girl, then all three were swept out together. For an instant the trio of bodies was visible inside the translucent wave, being lifted 25 feet up, before slamming into the sand. The force of the impact was enough to rip Wilford's earring out. The girl's jewelry had long since been stripped. A human chain from the beach finally pulled them in, one wave short of being dashed into the rocks.

The woman was in bad shape. She was coughing up sand and seawater. When she came to, the first person she saw was Wilford: the strong chin, the high cheekbones, the dark eyes and hair. "She fell in love with Wilford immediately," says Joseph. When Wilford got back to Fort Collins, a billboard downtown greeted him, proclaiming in 3-foot-tall letters, "Mark Wilford, my lifesaver. I love you. Deb."

Women have always been a welcome distraction for Wilford, especially since high-school days when he lost his virginity in the Fort Collins cemetery (she was alive). "I like girls. I've just had some unfortunate luck with them. They've led me astray," says Wilford, then adds, "I've led some of them astray also." Whether women are attracted to his looks, athleticism, or self-confidence and determination is debatable. One thing is for sure, the constant traveling involved with climbing and repping causes problems with maintaining long-term relationships. Wilford is single at the time of this writing, but expects his heart will be broken several times before this goes to print. "I have an easier time dealing with loose rock," he admits. "It's more predictable."

Wilford, confused about women? Didn't he have it all figured out at age twenty-five when he starred with alpinist Jeff Lowe in the movie *Cloudwalker*? In it Wilford offers this observation: "Climbing gives me something that a female can give me. I feel a great comfort, a completeness there that's almost orgasmic." Says Wilford today, "I was just reading a script. The filmmaker put those words in my mouth."

Many people have wanted to put words in Wilford's mouth or

make him out to be someone he isn't. For instance, they ask him for his ideology on death, believing that someone who regularly solos dangerous alpine routes must constantly brood on the subject. Wilford, however, is a nuts-and-bolts guy, not a philosopher. He presents himself simply, explaining the obvious, remarking on the usual, getting a kick out of honking at cows or, when they don't flinch, facing them down with his car. When it comes to death he just says he hopes to die of old age, though he, not to mention his passengers, suspect his end will come in a car crash.

In 1983 it almost did, on another trip to Baja California, when Wilford was in his mid-twenties and at the height of his wild streak. Mike McCarron, South Side Chicago's best climber, describes the trip as a "three-week binge." Adventure showed up in the form of a black Pontiac Trans Am. Wilford personally prefers compact European sports cars; nevertheless he was awed by the power of the Trans Am's 6.6-liter engine. "I've always liked to drive fast," says Wilford with characteristic understatement. He had already made the speedometer read zero the hard way, but had yet to ease the needle back into double digits when he failed to comprehend a traffic sign. For all he knew, *curva peligrosa* was Spanish for Burma Shave, not dangerous curve ahead. The big black muscle car hurtled off the sharp bend at 80 mph. After one-and-a-half rolls, it came to rest in a dry river bed.

Wilford was knocked out briefly, an acquaintance in the back was unscathed, and Glen, the Southern California kid that "owned" the car wasn't moving. "At that point," Wilford recalls, "I was really bummed because I thought I'd killed Glen." Fortuitously, the next car by contained two paramedics who checked Glen out, then assured Wilford that Glen was only unconscious and would recover. Just as that worry was assuaged, the local police arrived and the real bummer began. (Traffic accidents are felony offenses in Mexico.)

The cops hauled Wilford to a doctor. Despite his patient's multiple lacerations and grotesque hematomas about the skull and elsewhere, the doctor insisted Wilford was faking his injuries. He jabbed him in the butt with a huge syringe anyway. Next, the cops took their prisoner to jail.

The cell was square, 25 by 25 feet. One wall was bars, the others solid, windowless. A hole in the corner and one lightbulb in the ceiling completed the interior decoration. Half a dozen drunks and two blood-caked fighters shared the cell with Wilford. Barely able to move due to his injuries, Wilford desperately hoped that none of his cellmates would mess with him. Only one person got close, a drunk pushed into the cell; for a second he remained upright, spinning like a barely nicked bowling pin, before falling toward the concrete floor. His cranium impacted 10 feet from Wilford, the sharp "crack" heard by all. The cop gave the drunk's head a quick check, then left the cell before blood started trickling out the prisoner's ears.

The next day McCarron showed up to bail Wilford out. "I've smelled better zoos," Mike says, "but Wilford looked right at home in there with his amigos." Indeed, Wilford's clothes were plastered to him with blood, not that changing them was an option. McCarron explains, "He couldn't take his shirt off because his head was so swollen."

The Federales arrived to transport him from the little local jail to the judge in La Paz. It was Wilford's chance to strike a deal. The Federales wanted the Trans Am engine for a patrol car. As it had become obvious that the car really didn't belong to Glen, Wilford and Mike happily turned it over along with, of course, every penny that they had. The Federales then released Wilford.

The climbers spent the next week waiting for escape money to be wired, obtaining all the painkillers that Wilford and his uninjured friends would need, and dodging the local and state police who, jealous that the Feds had received all the bribes, wanted to shake Wilford down for their cut.

As far as Wilford is concerned, money is a necessary evil, whether it's for bribing Federales or funding expeditions to far-flung locales. In the tradition of dedicated climbers, Wilford worked off-season manual labor jobs to support himself—roughnecking in Wyoming, and working high steel in the winter. "High steel work was just like alpine climbing," he says. "I had to wear four layers of pants and seven layers of shirts. My hands were constantly numb. The best part was walking unroped across snow-covered beams 50 feet off the deck. I loved the exposure."

In 1987, Wilford moved back to Fort Collins in an effort to distance himself from the bad influences and wild life of his previous home, Boulder. The move has been effective. What would have formerly been partying time he now spends restoring his Triumph TR3 from the frame up, or collecting rocks, fossils, and old coins. Wilford is calmer now, and shows little emotion other than happy nonchalance or mild exuberance. (The raucous boys in the neighboring frat house might disagree. Shy one window courtesy of Wilford's pitching arm, they could argue that Wilford can still display considerable anger.)

A year after his homecoming, Wilford gave up manual labor in favor of a career as a sales rep in the climbing industry. This job would seem boring compared to his former occupations. Nevertheless, even repping has its risks. On a sales trip last winter in Canada, Wilford managed his fourth vehicle rollover.

Wilford's reputation as one of the world's best all-around climbers helps him in his new job. Clients know Wilford's opinions are based on experience, not press releases. To get this experience means doing a lot of climbing. In Munich, at the 1988 ISPO show, Wilford was given some new ice gear to test. What better testing ground than the North Face of the Eiger?

Wilford's first American solo of the Eiger Nordwand is a well-publicized story. How he got off-route early, then corrected himself and picked up the pace only to run into a group of eight Spaniards, the lowest of whom was dangling from the end of a rope, taking a crap. "That was the first thing they tried to drop on me," recalls Wilford. Fortunately, Wilford dodged the falling debris, caught up with the Spaniards, and managed to climb by some and stem over the rest without losing too much time. Two hundred feet higher, he dislodged a 2-foot thick icicle that crashed amongst the Spaniards, roughing them up a bit and providing good footage for the documentary they were filming.

The tensest moment of the climb was on The Rotten Crack pitch. At this point Wilford almost backed off the wall. The holds were all loose, like a pile of unmortared bricks, and held together only by their own weight and the thin wedges of ice between them. Partway up, a dreadfully exposed bulge confronted him. The only pro was a shaky fixed pin and a sorry-sounding piton Wilford tapped in as a backup. He clipped in to these with a 6-millimeter daisy chain and started bouldering the moves. After trying three different sequences, Wilford reached the lip of the bulge and cleared off a ledge smaller than this magazine.

"I was freaking," says Wilford. As he tried to press out the mantel, his daisy chain had came taut. Wilford uncocked his arms and was left dangling from the lip by numb hands that were pumping out fast. Already he had lost enough strength that he would be unable to reverse the moves. There were only two choices: fall on the suspect pins and likely to his death or cut the daisy chain and free solo the mantel.

What a scene it would have been to watch from above. Two hands visible at the lip, nothing else. Then just one hand at the lip, clamped on for dear life, fingers turning purple. Vital seconds pass and the knuckles bleach white. Just when it appears that that hand will give out and slide off, the other hand slaps the lip. There's a mighty heave and a face appears, eyes ablaze with fear, jaws clenched so tight the teeth threaten to bite through the open pocketknife. Wilford presses the mantel and struggles to lift his foot the extra inch to get the crampons over the lip. He stands up on the ledge, hugging the wall. Backing off is no longer an option.

When the Spanish climbers came across the severed daisy chain, they assumed the worst—that Wilford was halfway down to Grindelwald, or at least parts of him were. As it turned out, the next worst thing happened; Wilford was at the summit quaffing the beer left for them by a thoughtful *compadre*.

While soloing the Eiger Nordwand is a sure way to make the history books, many of Wilford's accomplishments have been lost in obscurity, in particular his bouldering accomplishments. He has been one of the foremost developers of bouldering around Fort Collins where the list of activists include such renowned names as Gill, Mammen, Borgman, and Holloway. Wilford is particularly known for his high bouldering exploits and his willingness to push standards on loose rock. One of his favorite areas is the Vast Wastelands, the miles upon miles of Dakota Sandstone hogbacks north of Fort Collins. The problems are tall, the rock quality variable, the landings bad, and the property owners feisty when they catch you—all factors that appeal to Wilford. To quote Mammen, "You're in for trouble if you try to go up there and follow Mark. You'll probably end up in Poudre Valley Hospital." Wilford's skill at loose rock climbing has kept him alive in the mountains. Nevertheless, he's paid the price to obtain this skill. Numerous dumps into rocky landings have left Wilford's ankles in shambles—the ligaments are so stretched now that instead of his ankles spraining, they simply fold over.

Wilford's latest bouldering accident occurred in Pakistan. He was there to climb Nameless Tower, but was lured by a 20-foot-tall boulder 5,000 feet beneath the summit. Every climber who had reached the final microedging move on this problem had backed off. Wilford was determined to do the move. As it turned out the others had chosen wisely. Wilford slipped, shish-kabobbing his knee on a granite spike at the base.

Wilford was feeling bad. The huge gap beneath his kneecap exposed the bone beneath. Severed nerves let their complaints be known. So did his partner, Aussie alpine ace Greg Child. Child had failed on an earlier attempt on this colossal pinnacle and was in no mood to fail again, especially due to a partner injuring himself jerking around at the base.

As luck would have it, it stormed for the next ten days. Child's anger subsided, and hence Wilford's guilt did the same. Wilford became obsessed with hygiene, douching the wound with hydrogen peroxide and keeping his knee straight for days to promote healing. By the time the weather cleared, Wilford was able to go up on the wall.

Wilford describes the epic he and Child then had as "one of the closest times I've come to buying it." He says this softly, pensively, the memory obviously still fresh and disturbing.

Things went relatively well for nine days. Greg did the brunt of the leading, encountering plenty of hard aid on the way. A thousand feet above them loomed huge icicles that, if they fell, would reduce the climbers to Sloppy Joe filling. The icicles hung in, but the weather didn't. The idea of retreat was discussed, then discarded.

The crack they had been climbing was exquisite, of Butterballs quality for a pitch-and-a-half. Unfortunately, it ended in the middle of a blank face, not the ledge they had hoped for. Wilford pendulumed right to a blunt arête he could hook then nailed up a rising traverse to the right. The light began to wane as sleet lashed the face. It was one of Wilford's hardest aid leads, taking four hours to reach the end. He knocked away a thin sheet of verglas to expose a vertical crack, then hammered in the anchor—five knife blades.

Meanwhile, at the other end of the rope, Child had been stuck at a hanging belay, completely exposed to the storm, unable to move to keep warm. The beautiful crack he was anchored to had turned into a drain spout, drenching him with ice water. The sleet froze on contact with his body, armoring him in ice. By the time Child cut the haulbags loose, he was dangerously hypothermic.

After hurtling around the corner, the haulbags came to rest 80 feet below Wilford. (Due to the zigzag line the pitch took, the haul line traveled a much shorter distance between belays than the lead line.) Wilford leaned back on the hauling system, but the bags wouldn't budge. He jumped. They still wouldn't budge.

Meanwhile, Child tried to follow the pitch. He got nowhere as his jumars refused to grip the rope. It had become, in Child's words, "a wire of ice." He screamed to Wilford to throw him another rope. The only dry rope, however, was in the haulbag.

Wilford redoubled his efforts to pull the bags up. He jumped so hard on the hauling system, he pulled out one of the anchor pins. His only choice was to rap down the free looped end of the haul line to get to the bags. When he reached the bottom of the loop and could descend no further, his feet were just above the bag. Child was scream-ing, "I can't feel my hands. Can't you hurry?"

To reach the bags, Wilford had to flip upside-down. In this posi-tion he could just reach the bags and extract a rope. It was getting darker and colder as Wilford raced up the 8-millimeter haul line. The rope got icier every second. The closer he got to the anchor, the more the jumars would slip. If he didn't reach the anchor soon, he'd freeze to death jugging in place.

Eventually he reached the belay, where he quickly anchored the dry rope then started rappelling sideways across the face, holding on to the lead line to get to the arête.

"From the arête I could see Greg," Wilford recalls, "and he's just fucked—sitting there on his way out."

Wilford tried throwing the rope to Child. It missed. He tried again. Another miss. After many attempts he finally got the cord to Child. Child then had no choice but to cut loose from the anchor and take the terrifying swing across the face, around the arête, and into the unseen beyond. As he put it to Wilford before committing, "If this cold doesn't kill me, the jumar will."

They made it to the anchor, where they managed to get a bolt in and pull up the haulbags. By now it was dark, and their first attempt to erect the portaledge ended when the frame collapsed while they pulled the fly on. Wilford was doing most of the work at the belay because Child was so frozen. To worsen matters, Child had lost a glove. "I was getting panicky," Child admits. Reassembling the ledge became a long ordeal. Child later praised Wilford's handling of the situation. "He was very strong up there. He's very calm. He doesn't get flustered or scared." When they finally got in the assembled portaledge it was after midnight. Child produced some pills that can help prevent frostbite by increasing circulation in the body's extremities. These pills however, move blood away from the body's core and can induce shock if one doesn't get warm right away. They took the pills. Child shoved his hands in Wilford's armpits, while Wilford's feet warmed in Child's crotch.

Meanwhile, back in the sport-climbing world, dozens of would-be champions were ingesting performance enhancing chemicals and stuffing their fingers in training boards, all in the hopes of qualifying at Snowbird. While they had to shun the refrigerator to slim down, Wilford was living in a refrigerator, burning all the fat he could to survive the harrowing retreat off Trango. A month later, he joined the hordes of Saran-wrapped Lycra lads at Snowbird. There he entered the open competition. He had gotten in only a dozen days of rock climbing since returning from Pakistan, and he wasn't given the invitees privilege of resting through the qualifying rounds. Nevertheless, he managed to climb his way into the finals, one of only eight climbers to do so.

"I didn't do too well in the finals," Wilford says. "I placed in the middle." Then the all-arounder laughs at a famous Europup who would gladly swap standings and adds, "but I beat J.B. Tribout."

(Pushing forty has not mellowed Wilford. Since this came out he has returned to climb Nameless Tower and gone on to succeed on Cerro Torre. As well, he has climbed icebergs in Antarctica [for a cigarette commercial] and his rollover count now stands at six [yes, he was only driving in five of those].)

Climbing, October 1991

Riding the Pendulum—
Tom Cosgriff

AT 11 P.M. ON A FRIGID WINTER night in 1972, Tom Cosgriff, the helpful young son, leans over his mother, Kendall, and bandages her eyes. She has just had cataract surgery. An hour later Tom's alarm goes off. He rustles about, making just enough commotion to wake his mom.

"What time is it?" she asks.

"Six o'clock. I'm going to help Gary on his paper route."

As Kendall goes back to sleep, Tom slips out the door and into the Denver night. First he steals a car and drives over to Gary Cupp's. Gary, also in his early teens, sneaks out the window and steals another car. They race out to the whoop-de-doos of County Line Road and play Hogs of the Road at 100 mph. Then they return to their neighborhood, park the cars where they found them, and creep back home.

Inside almost everybody exists a pendulum that, given the opportunity, swings back and forth between the desire for a secure, productive, socially acceptable existence and the lust for freedom, excitement, and no-holds-barred fun. For most folks, the pendulum swings gently, losing momentum with time. By age twenty-one, most Americans have stilled it, and through the bonds of work, debt, and peer pressure, tied it firmly to the side of security. Tom Cosgriff's pendulum still swings wildly and, at thirty-seven, *he* is lashed to *it*.

Cosgriff has had one of the most outrageous careers of any American climber, yet few Americans have ever heard of him. It doesn't help that for the last five years he's lived in Norway, that he is often confused with California's Scott Cosgrove, and that being basically insecure, he is reluctant to beat his own chest.

"I've never considered myself a good climber," Cosgriff says. "I've always been more at the bottom end." Such a viewpoint has prodded him to overachieve. Cosgriff's climbing adventures have spanned the globe from Eldorado Canyon, Canyonlands, and Yosemite to the Alps, the Troll Wall, Jordan, and Antarctica. Unless he's had a few beers, he's more apt to talk about the climbs he wants to do than those he has done—such as the first ascent of *Arctic Sea* on Half Dome, the first solo of the Totem Pole, and the second ascent of the *Arch Wall* on Trollveggen.

The media often portrays accomplished climbers as regular people; as if, were we common folks to try a little harder, or loosen up a bit more, we could be just like them. Few of us could ever be like Cosgriff. He'll prod a partner up that crumbling aid seam, then get him to hop in the cab of a second steam shovel he's hijacked for a game of Clash of the Titans. As the fear of death or incarceration makes his friend queasy, Cosgriff laughs like a maniac, not a hint of worry showing. Ironically, Cosgriff wishes he were more like us—wishes he could steer the pendulum. He's the kind of guy who, after angry Native Americans trundled rocks at him and chased him out of Canyon de Chelly, snuck back in a few days later and bagged the first free ascent of Spider Rock. It's not that Cosgriff has no social conscience. At the office he's a productive member of society, your basic clean-cut, bespectacled workaholic computer nerd. It's that his need for adventure often outweighs his conscience.

Cosgriff started as a young malefactor in Denver. He could easily blame his delinquent tendencies on having grown up without a father figure (his father died of cancer when Tom was a toddler), but he doesn't. He had a very loving family and remains extremely close to his mother and sister. He says his bad acts were simply the result of boredom. The standard sports outlets for youthful energy were ineffective—Cosgriff, skinny and clumsy, was always the last one picked for the team, and only allowed to play in the final seconds of a blowout. Hence Tom and his buddy Gary spent their time stealing cars, constructing homemade bombs, and throwing rock-spiked snowballs at police cruisers.

Tom's mom worked for a doctor named Bill Gerber, who introduced Tom and Gary to climbing when they were twelve years old. At Castle Rock in Boulder Canyon, he handed them a rope and told them to meet him on top. After the boys spent a few hours in unsuccessful attempts to lasso horns and trees and Batman their way up, Dr. Gerber showed them how it was done. That was enough to get them hooked. Rappelling thrilled the boys, and they managed to acquire some biners and 1-inch webbing harnesses, but no rope.

On the way home from junior high, Gary stopped in the local drugstore and spied some nylon clothesline in the bargain bin. Ninety-nine cents a bundle seemed exorbitant, so he grabbed a hank to sneak inside his jacket. The bundles, however, were connected together like sausage links, so he just kept stuffing them all in until he had ten bulging beneath his coat. He bolted out the door, ran home, and called Tom.

The clothesline rated as 100-pound test. Since neither he nor Tom weighed that much, Gary felt it would be adequate for rappelling. A quick test in a tree proved him wrong, so the two ended up braiding three strands together. They then tied off a pipe atop the local elementary school and tossed the rope off the roof. Gary stepped over the side. The instant the rope weighted the edge, it snapped, sending Gary two stories into the bushes. At that, Tom got a Goldline and Gary got a kernmantle. "Now we were dangerous," says Gary. Soon they were rappelling off buildings and Tyrolean-traversing between trees all over the neighborhood.

As a youth, Cosgriff attended a Denver private school that had a climbing club. The school made you wear sport coats and ties, and was filled with Harvard-bound types who had nothing better to do with their money than spend it on drugs. Cosgriff remembers the sounds of the library: the flipping of pages, the squeak of the chairs, the tapping of razor blades. Though he didn't have the money the other kids had, Cosgriff showed a knack for creative financing and soon became fond of getting high. He particularly enjoyed hallucinogens, but any substance was fair game.

"I thought, as all mothers do, that their sons are wonderful and mine could never do anything wrong," recalls Kendall. "Then I found out all these terrible things he had been doing when he was in school." She laughs and refuses to give details, but whatever it was, was enough to get Tom, a bad student anyway, threatened with expulsion.

"Then I got interested in school and started studying," says Cosgriff. "A couple of the teachers were really out for me and all of a sudden I started getting A's and that really drove them crazy. They couldn't figure out how the hell I was cheating." Tom stopped taunting cops as well. Maybe the drugs mellowed him, maybe it was fear of prosecution upon attaining legal age, or maybe it was climbing. Whatever the reason, if he wasn't studying, he was out in Eldorado Canyon climbing. Soon his wimpy frame gave way to broad shoulders and shredded abs.

Cosgriff briefly went to college in Santa Clara, California, then transferred to the University of Colorado in Boulder. At times, it seemed he might be heading toward normalcy—he majored in math and fantasized about getting his credentials and teaching at Fairview High School in Boulder. "Just kicking back," he says. "I wanted to climb and just have a nice quiet life." But the pendulum kept swinging. He started climbing with the likes of Rob Slater, Neal Beidleman, Jerry Greenleaf, Bruce Bailey, Rufus Miller, Skip Guerin, "The Great Matt," and some partners who prefer to remain anonymous. He and one partner would head out on full-moon winter nights to Eldorado, drop acid to keep their fingers warm and enhance the graphics, then climb a 200-foot, mostly vertical 5.9+ route on Wind Tower called *Metamorphosis.* They had no rope for protection, only T-shirts that read "Blotter Is My Spotter."

When it came to substance abuse, another Cosgriff partner, his fraternity little brother Rob Slater, was the antithesis of Cosgriff, never once trying booze or drugs, but both shared a bawdy sense of humor and both were game for scary routes. After teaming up frequently in Eldorado, Cosgriff planted the big-wall bug in Slater. Out in Yosemite they tackled the steep side of El Cap, doing the classic aid walls *Zodiac* and *Tangerine Trip.*

Late in college, Cosgriff fell in love with a smart, comely student, Robin Mainwaring. Her determination to become a doctor inspired Cosgriff to shoot for something higher himself, and electrical engineering classes filled his senior year. He had been roughnecking in the oil patches of Wyoming and Colorado for the previous few summers, and now aimed to get a high-paying engineer's job with one of the wireline companies. He graduated in 1981 and took a job in the oil business, donning the orange coveralls of a Dresser-Atlas wireline engineer. Based out of Houston, he worked offshore in the Gulf of Mexico.

Houston being bereft of climbing, Cosgriff spent his onshore time with Robin or taking climbing trips.

On one of these trips he teamed up with Duane Raleigh for an ascent of El Cap's *Pacific Ocean Wall,* at that time one of El Cap's most feared routes. Out of provisions, the famished duo pulled over the top after five days. They spied a campfire and trudged up to it to beg food. There they met two guys from Houston named Phil Smith and Phil Mayfield. The Phils shared their hot dogs and Budweiser, then around midnight looked at each other and announced, "Well, we've got to be going."

"You can't go now," Cosgriff said. "It's too dark to see the trail."

"We're not walking."

Cosgriff and Raleigh watched the ensuing spectacle from the park-bench-wide ledge just beneath the visor topping the Dawn Wall. As the climbers dangled their feet over 3,000 feet of air, the Phils ran off the summit hand in hand, flew over the pair, and hurtled down the face. Ten seconds later their parachutes opened and they glided into El Cap Meadow. Cosgriff liked what he saw.

Back in Houston, Cosgriff looked up Phil Smith, who invited him to jump off a bridge spanning a ship channel. It would be a relatively safe introduction—a "sack-of-potatoes" jump into the water with a getaway boat and a camera crew from a local TV station lined up. The bridge was closed so they drove through the roadblock. Cosgriff and three others were prepared to jump when the law accosted them.

"You're all under arrest," the trooper yelled.

The first guy leapt off, then the second, then Cosgriff. But Cosgriff didn't drop. The trooper had him by a leg loop and was trying to drag him back over the railing.

"I'd let go if I were you," said Cosgriff as he leaned further out.

Finally, the trooper lost his grip and Cosgriff fell freely, closely followed by the fourth jumper.

On the way to the police station, the trooper told the TV crew that he and Cosgriff were both lucky to be alive, because if Tom had yanked him off, "I would have pulled my gun and shot him before we hit the water."

Ample photographic evidence led to a summons for the jumpers, who eventually plea-bargained their way out of it for 500 clams apiece. Mishaps such as these don't deter Cosgriff. After some plane jumps (gained through forged log books), and jumps off antennas, Cosgriff was ready for his first building jump. His partners and he chose the Allied Bank in Houston. From the air the skyscraper looks like a giant dollar sign. Seventy-two stories high, it was still under construction when Cosgriff and crew sneaked past the security guards at midnight.

Cosgriff opted to dive first. He knew that a rock dropped from the top of the Allied building takes nine seconds to hit the ground. To execute the jump safely, after four seconds he would throw out his pilot chute, which would then pull out his main chute.

Standing on the corner of the skyscraper, Cosgriff bunny-hopped off the cash monument in a head-high position.

"I was having a really good time at this point," says Cosgriff, "because as soon as you jump off, everything's out of your hands—you're not scared anymore." In a second or two he had tilted into a relaxed spread-eagle posture with his head a foot or two lower than his feet; this position helped him soar away from the building. He was in perfect body position, and on four, he tossed out his pilot chute. He was enjoying the thrill of seeing the individual stories race by when he realized he had counted to seven and his main chute had not deployed.

Cosgriff pulled his reserve ripcord, then spread his arms and legs and even splayed his fingers to slow himself as much as possible. He was still trucking at 95 mph when he plunged beneath the top of the tree in the library courtyard across the boulevard from the bank.

A few blocks away, Robin watched from the getaway car. She saw her boyfriend, with no chute open, plummet out of sight behind the two-story library.

Cosgriff missed clipping the library roof by 5 feet, and similarly avoided a 30-foot sculpture and the big tree. Just as he'd written himself off, he felt the tug of the reserve opening. His body jerked upright and swung forward.

"One second I thought I was going to die," he recalls, "then the next second it's like 'Yes, I'm going to live.' Then I saw the arch windows coming up and it's like, 'Arrr, I'm going to die after all.'"

Indeed, Cosgriff had amassed a lot of forward momentum and was now looking at a full-speed Carl Lewis dash through the library's big plate-glass windows.

"Luckily I hit this foot-and-a-half wide concrete arch between the windows."

That was the last Cosgriff remembered. He was knocked out. His feet hit the ground so hard that his sneakers blew into shreds. Deep gashes circled the soles of his feet where the shock wave had burst through the skin.

Cosgriff woke to Robin's hysterical screams. She thought he was dead. Tom thought he was busted. He was looking at a pair of polished boots leading up to a uniformed man. Realizing it was just a rent-a-cop guard, he started crawling toward the street. He emerged from between two parked cars and the getaway car nearly ran him over. He elevated his legs on the way to the hospital; nevertheless, the gashes in his feet bled profusely, and the blood pouring down his legs pooled in the seat of his pants. For insurance reasons, he told the doctors he fell out of a tree while trimming branches at midnight. It was an obvious fib, and the mutterings Cosgriff overheard implied that at first glance the ER personnel assumed he'd had a kinky-sex accident.

Cosgriff spent the next several weeks crawling around the hardwood floors of his apartment in kneepads. He swore he'd never

BASE jump again. When he finally recovered enough to crutch into Dresser-Atlas, his boss told him the good news first.

"You've got an extra two weeks pay, Tom."

A local outdoor store took pity on Cosgriff and gave him a job selling top-of-the-line Marmot sleeping bags and Gore-Tex suits to Texans going out to Big Bend for the weekend. This gave him time to heal, though his feet were never the same again. As soon as he was able, he took six months off to go climbing, ending up in Yosemite where he became the first person to solo *Tribal Rite* (5.9 A4) on El Cap. (It had only had four or five previous ascents.) After he got down he gave Robin a call.

"I did the climb and now I'm in orange coveralls," he told her.

"Oh, you got your job back at Dresser-Atlas," exclaimed Robin.

Then Cosgriff explained that these coveralls did not say Dresser-Atlas, but rather Yosemite Jail.

"You bastard! You jumped!"

There was a resounding click as Robin hung up, terminating Cosgriff's one allotted phone call as well as his link to bail money. Cosgriff had a few weeks to ponder how the authorities had finally caught him.

"That was such an ego crusher," Tom says, "because I downright deserved it. I spent years and years honing my skills at getting away from cops, then I completely broke all the rules that I knew."

It had all started with a few beers on top of the Big Stone. Then he tipsily tripped into a big log poised next to the visor and sent it over the edge. Worried that the log might have wiped the party on Mescalito off the face, he quickly donned his rig and jumped before dark. As he whizzed past, he saw the party safe and sound in a portaledge under an overhang. Shortly thereafter, he flew right over the rangers sitting on the hood of their cruiser parked next to El Cap Meadow. The chase began. He ditched the rangers, no thanks to the tourists who locked their doors when he tried to hop in their cars. The pursuit led into the woods beneath El Cap. This is where he feels he blew it, by not stripping off his suit and running straight back past the rangers in his jogging shorts. After dark, aided by night-vision goggles, the rangers spotted him heading along the base of El Cap in the direction of the bar. Spent from the wall and the chase, Cosgriff got in only a few licks before being subdued.

The two weeks at the John Muir Inn went by quickly. At night Cosgriff ate TV dinners with his cellmates, whom he describes as "really nice guys." He felt a "near-religious experience of closeness" with a speed dealer out of Los Angeles. Days were spent washing and waxing fire engines as his friend Mike O'Donnell sped by, waving from Tom's Turbo Saab.

Though Cosgriff is fond of telling wild stories about illegal activities or drugs, he can just as easily rave about petroleum engineering (he was a 4.0 student, first in his master's degree class). On their third bivy during the third ascent of *Zenith* on Half Dome, O'Donnell looked down at Cosgriff lying back on a portaledge in the setting sun. Cosgriff was buck naked, save for an HP pocket computer and a book of algorithms between his legs. Adjusting his glasses with one hand, madly punching keys with the other, Cosgriff only looked up long enough to exclaim, "This is such interesting stuff."

O'Donnell worked with Cosgriff on the wireline boats. He's seen Cosgriff pull a Clark Kent-ish transformation from boring, hardworking team player to hero. It was Christmas morning far out in the Gulf of Mexico. Cosgriff and some crew members from India had taken a small man-overboard boat out to fix a foul-up in the gear being towed 1,000 feet behind the mother ship. Once they hooked into the gear, the boat capsized, sending them all into the water. Thinking quickly, Cosgriff cut the boat away from the cable, so that it drifted with the men as a huge crosscurrent swept them away from the mother ship. Most of the freshly dunked crew scrambled onto the overturned flat-bottomed boat, but one man, a pudgy non-swimmer, floated away.

"Heeelp me, heeelp me," the man cried in a high-pitched voice. Cosgriff took off swimming and grabbed the guy by the neck. After fifteen minutes, he'd dragged him back. Exhausted, he'd just gotten the victim on top of the overturned boat when an obstinate anticapsizing device suddenly triggered. Instantly, airbags inflated and righted the boat, sending everyone flying again. Cosgriff repeated the ordeal.

It was soon after that things seemed to be settling down. After dating for nine years, Tom and Robin made plans to tie the knot. They had weathered many trials together: Cosgriff's serious immersion in grad school, the stress of Robin's medical studies, and the constant moving about to accommodate her residencies. Cosgriff felt that he finally was in control of the pendulum and headed for a safe and secure life. Even his attitudes toward climbing had changed: he no longer climbed out of control, spurred on by the excitement of the danger; instead he climbed conservatively, placing lots of gear and thriving on being in control in hazardous situations. Because his idea of "conservative" climbing still included healthy runouts and A5 pitches, his friends didn't see much change from the Cosgriff of old.

Perhaps neither did Robin. Two weeks before the wedding, she told him, "I never want to see you again."

"When did you decide this?"

"It came to me this weekend."

Tom never got any further explanation. His friends got terse notes in the mail stating, "The wedding of Robin Mainwaring and Tom Cosgriff will not take place."

Cosgriff was devastated—utterly crushed, stripped-naked-raw-to-the-bone, acid-in-the-eyes, chainsaw-to-the-heart devastated. Cosgriff generally keeps his personal life to himself, instead of unloading on his friends. Accordingly, he packed his worries and his bags, ditched his Ph.D. program, and fled the country. Even seeing mutual friends of his and Robin's, or even places they had been together, was too hard. He settled in Norway where he took a programming job in Geco's Oslo offices.

Cosgriff caved in to his depression and his first year in Norway was hell, black and fetid. Even the climbs he did fit that mold. He went up to the *Arch Wall* route on Trollveggen (Troll Wall), a giant north-facing amphitheater of rock bigger, taller, darker, wetter, and just plain nastier than El Cap. *Arch Wall* (A5) was the toughest route on the wall, and unrepeated since the futuristic first ascent by Ed and Hugh Drummond in twenty-two days in 1972. Cosgriff remembers approaching up snow slopes in sneakers and without an ice ax. The fog was thick. The air repeatedly vibrated and buffeted the eardrums when huge rocks, some as big as washing machines, ripped through the mist and crashed into the snowy scree just feet away. The wall itself is steep enough that rockfall is not a hazard, but waterfalls are. On the first A5 pitch, Cosgriff climbed for five hours through a torrent. The water pounded loudly on his helmet and he had to look down to breathe. Snow swirled about. He and Aslak Aastorp persevered, and after ten days had bagged the second ascent.

Norway has been a huge change from the United States. Cosgriff finds Norwegians to be very conservative. Most vices, other than sexual, are too expensive to partake in—a single beer at a bar will set you back seven bucks.

"I lead a bloody conservative life in front of my terminal in Oslo," Cosgriff says. He takes every chance he gets to ditch the office and go on extended vacations. In the last few years, trips have taken him crack climbing up the 1,000-foot sandstone buttes of Wadi Rum in Jordan, sport climbing on the beaches of Sardinia, and alpine climbing in the Canadian Rockies. Though he dabbles in most forms of the sport, he's driven more by big walls, whether they be long nail-ups or giant mixed alpine routes, than by free climbs that would take a day or less. When on vacation, he views rest days as an anathema. He has an infectious enthusiasm, which gets his partners to push themselves as well. Sometimes, though, his desire to always climb as hard as he can drives less-motivated partners nuts. Cosgriff doesn't worry about this. After one partner got spooked by the soft sandstone of Wadi Rum and refused to climb anymore, Cosgriff recruited an Arab teenager, taught him to belay, and hauled him up route after route. That kid was "the fastest partner I ever had," claims Cosgriff.

Cosgriff is better recognized in Norwegian climbing circles than in America. Because he was the best wall climber in Norway, in 1993 he was invited to go on an expedition to Queen Maud Land, the Norwegian territory in Antarctica. However, there were grumblings that Cosgriff, a non-Norwegian, was on the team. Cosgriff felt he had to butter up the expedition's leader, Ivar Erik Tollefsen, if he wanted to ensure a shot at the 3,000-foot spires jutting up from the Antarctic ice cap. This meant guiding Tollefsen up the Troll Wall.

Tollefsen is a smart, driven man: a self-made millionaire by the age of twenty-five, an expert skier who held the record for the fastest crossing of Greenland, and in his own words "the world's worst professional climber." At that time, his professional status was due not to his climbing ability, but to his genius at rounding up sponsorship. Cosgriff picked the *Rimmen Route*, a 5.10 free route. The two made it through the hard, steep climbing, Cosgriff leading the way, to where they had eight pitches of supposedly easy gully climbing to go. The gully was verglassed, though, so Cosgriff pushed the line up the neighboring wet, mossy faces. The 80-foot runouts were hair-raising, especially after twenty hours of climbing in the perpetual daylight. Then Cosgriff realized he wasn't even on belay. Hearing strange noises, he looked down to see Tollefsen yakking into a portable phone, telling his yuppie friends in Oslo how it was going up on the Troll Wall at three in the morning. Tollefsen then packed the phone, dogged up the rope, and declared, "That wasn't very hard. Hurry up and do another."

"I wanted to throw him off right there," says Cosgriff. He didn't, and two days later was officially invited on the trip.

Photos of Queen Maud Land are enough to make a wall climber forget his worries, his sweetheart, even his dog. The ice cap stretches horizontally to the horizon, white and infinite. Dozens of enormous rock spires punch through the ice like shark fins slicing the ocean surface. Tollefsen, through a year of full-time patron stroking, had put together the ultimate package tour. He'd lined up sponsors for everything from satellite navigation systems to boxer shorts. All the team members had to do was show up a few days early to make sure their new clothes fit.

They flew to Capetown, then boarded a Russian icebreaker. A maker of Aquavit, a potent Norwegian spirit, was helping sponsor the expedition, so it wasn't long before the drinking and arm-wrestling parties began on the back deck.

Everyone was eager to be on the first helicopter to leave ship for the ice cap—until they saw the aging whirlybird. In between trips inside the fuselage to pull on the vodka bottle, its mechanics beat pieces of the chopper together with hammers. Nonetheless, all expedition members survived the shuttle to basecamp.

Antarctica was another world and the surroundings delighted Cosgriff. It was also his first experience with a big expedition and the egos and politics surrounding such an endeavor. The members split up into three teams: a ski team, an alpine-climbing team, and a wall-climbing team. Tollefsen was most qualified to be on the ski team, but felt that the greatest glory was to be found on the North Face of Ulvetanna, the most impressive spire in the region. Being trip leader, he put himself on the wall team. Cosgriff argued back, pointing out that Tollefson's inexperience could be a liability. In the book that chronicled the expedition Tollefsen wrote, "Thomas's objection was possibly justified, but he had evidently forgotten that it was he who was with me and not the other way about. My lack of big wall experience was common knowledge from the outset, but I still had to suppress an urge to heave Thomas overboard."

Tollefsen overruled Cosgriff, then tossed him this bone: "Think of this—if I'm on the wall team, you'll get at least thirty pages written about you in the book."

This was the wrong tack to take. Cosgriff has strong beliefs about how and why climbing should be approached. It should be done for pure motives, he feels, not glory or profit, and anything short of Messnerian achievement doesn't merit ink. He tolerates his cohorts' attempts to glorify him, but wonders why they would want to, because, he says, "I'm not rad. I've never done any hard routes. I haven't done any 13s."

The North Face of Ulvetanna turned out to be nearly featureless. The rock, which looked like Yosemite granite from a distance, turned out to be as crumbly as Fisher Towers rock, yet tough as quartzite on drill bits. In places the rock was too decomposing to aid, so free climbing was mandatory. When the wall came into shadow, the temperature would drop to minus 22 degrees F, so, even though the sun never set, the climbers only had seven to eight hours to climb each day. Pitch by pitch, the wall team disintegrated. It was down to two members when Cosgriff's partner got sick, and he ended up soloing.

Seven hundred feet up the 2,700-foot wall, he concocted a traverse to avoid a monstrous death flake. He got strung out on some of the hardest nailing of his career, then stepped from his aiders and balanced right across a narrow 35-foot ledge that sloped outward. About a body length past the end of the ledge and level with his feet was a flake. It was too far away for him to aid over to it. Moreover, if he lunged for it, it was too rounded to hope to hang onto. Reversing the traverse looked doubtful, and he was determined to see what lay around the corner. Chest plastered to the wall, Cosgriff stood psyching up for an hour and a half. In his hands were two ice Spectres. He looked back to his last pro, a pair of knife blades 50 feet away. Finally he leaned to the right, starting a slow cartwheel off the ledge. It was like that first step off the skyscraper in Houston. Everything was beyond his control. The coarse brown grains of the rock swept by his face as the target approached. He stretched out his arms and stabbed the Spectres at the flake as he fell past.

They caught.

A few moves later, Cosgriff reached a dead end. Hanging from the flake he placed a rivet, lowered down, then hauled himself back to the belay. The North Face remained unclimbed. Later Cosgriff would write, "We came down from Ulvetanna thoroughly disappointed and demoralized. The whole reason I had come to Dronning Maud Land was to climb a big wall, and now that we had failed, I felt that I had no reason for being here and that the whole trip was a waste. I had quickly forgotten how much fun I'd had on the boat with the Russians, skiing around on the shelf ice with hundreds of penguins chasing after us, the fantastic views from the top of Jøkulkyrkja (the "highest peak in Norway"), and the fine ski trip back to basecamp." Before the end of the trip, he, Janåge Gundersen, and Trond Hilde managed to climb the previously unscaled 1,800-foot tooth of Kinntanna. In retrospect he calls this trip the best of his life. He had forgotten how much hard wall climbing meant to him in the four years since he had climbed the *Arch Wall*. Now he was reenergized.

One aspect of the expedition bothered Cosgriff deeply. He felt some members of the alpine climbing team were making too big a deal of the first ascents they'd made. By modern European standards, they were not that hard. The reason they were bagging these peaks was because nobody else could afford to climb there—not because they were great climbers. Cosgriff found this boasting embarrassing and expressed his feelings. Pricking Tollefsen's party balloon caused anger and confrontations, but later he and Tollefsen put that behind them, and became good friends and training partners. It looks like Cosgriff will be invited back to Antarctica with Tollefsen this year.

Meanwhile, Cosgriff contemplates moving back to America. He searches for some control over his life, but the pendulum still calls the shots. It tells him not to move unless he has a firm job offer in the States. He dreams of a good job, a loving wife, even a few kids. Then the pendulum swings the other way. His eyes open wide and a smile turns his lips as he describes soloing the Totem Pole on New Year's Day a decade ago—the Indians screaming at him and banging their guns; the ropes sticking on the descent; and the final acid-laced celebration in a blizzard that night at the Monticello airport. Atop the airport's light tower he clutched onto the rotating beacon like a gargoyle.

"I was all fried out," he exclaims, "King of the Beam—spinning around *in complete control of the world.*"

Climbing, September 1996

Life Without a Net—
Rob Slater

Both this and the following piece, "The Hard Song," are about Robbie Slater. They are probably best read together.

TEN CONTINUOUS HOURS INTO AN A5 lead, Rob Slater is on suspect hooks that might fail any second. The best pieces on this pitch are some copperheads 40 feet below that couldn't catch a falling interest rate. Below that are a bunch of hand-cleanable pin stacks. And 160 feet down is the only gear that will hold, the belay anchor. Rob Slater has an ulcer.

But don't blame it on climbing.

It's pitch black. Rob leaps from the top of a 750-foot antenna and hurtles toward the ground. Going for the maximum rush, he risks a free fall of such length that if his main chute were to fail there would be no time to release his reserve. Three seconds after jumping he throws out his pilot chute. It gets sucked into the vacuum behind his back, and is powerless to pull out the main chute. Another three seconds pass. Knowing it's too late, knowing he's going to die, Rob reaches for the reserve anyway. The resultant twist in his body knocks the pilot chute out of the vacuum. He is falling 170 feet per second when the main opens, just 200 feet above the ground. Rob Slater has an ulcer.

But don't blame it on BASE jumping.

Rob's in the midst of a frothing, screaming, elbow-to-elbow crowd. Nobody is smiling. They're all after one thing—money. And this, "The Floor" of the Chicago Mercantile Exchange, is the place to get it. Millions of dollars worth of bonds, foreign currencies, and frozen pork-belly futures trade hands here every minute. It's no place for the timid. Rob equates working here to "leading an A5+ pitch during an earthquake, with a hundred other leaders fighting you for the next hook placement." Rob Slater has an ulcer.

Blame it on work.

The Rob Slater one meets in Chicago does not look like the kind of guy who has climbed El Cap fifteen times (twice by standard-pushing new routes) or who skydives off fixed objects for fun. The uniform of a Chicago yuppie looks less awkward on his compact frame than one would suspect. When he returns home from work to his cramped studio apartment (tidy by climber's standards), he collapses into a chair, loosens his tie, and runs his fingers through a tangled, thinning mat of blond hair. The Floor and the quest for financial security has exhausted him. Unless the subjects of adventure and climbing are deliberately raised, the romantic ideals he holds of the Heroic Age of Antarctic Exploration and the hell-bent enthusiasm he possesses on the rock are not apparent. Instead, he groans at the thought that his friends will be scarfing pizza tonight, while his stomach begs for mercy.

If Slater had everything he wanted in life—namely, a Ferrari, a house in Utah's Castle Valley, and an alpine-style shot at Gasherbrum IV's West Face, or at least a Taco John's and a soothing A5 lead nearby—he believes the ulcer would go away. Like many of us, he prefers to escape the grind by spending his vacations climbing. But hanging on some puny skyhook, looking at a 100-footer if it pops—is that relaxing?

"In the whole scheme of things, yes," Slater says. "I want to come back from my vacation so wiped out that I have to go back to work to recover."

It was during his high school days in Cheyenne, Wyoming, when Slater first said yes to stress. Then, as now, he wanted nothing to do with the negative effects of booze and drugs. While his fellow high school juniors were conning beers at the local bowling alley, Slater and Bruce Hunter, who Slater had met on summer NOLS courses, were mainlining adrenaline on the North Face of Temple Peak in the Wind River Range.

"Bruce and I decided to be hard alpine masters," he recalls. "That meant climbing with 300-foot ropes. We didn't own one so we tied two 150s together. Of course we couldn't place any pro because of the knot so we just took 300-foot runouts on each pitch."

Halfway up the face the two climbers paused at a small ledge as huge rocks started crashing down. A car-sized block fell between them, chopping their ropes and forcing a retreat. "We got down to the base," Slater says, "and thought, `Wow, this is mountaineering, we've got to do more of it.'"

His mountaineering career would wait, however. During his senior year in high school, Slater visited the University of Colorado in Boulder upon the urging of his dad, a Mini-Mart checker who wanted his son to get the college education he never had. (Or so Slater jokes; actually his father is a doctor.) The very first day in Boulder, he knew that CU was the only choice; at a street corner near campus he was confronted by the image of the Flatirons on one side, the campus on the other, and crossing the street in front of him, at least ten coeds of such beauty that he says, "I'd have married any one of them on the spot, period." He hadn't even seen Eldorado Canyon yet.

Upon arriving in Boulder for school, he immediately blew off dorm orientation day to go to Eldo. His partner left early so he went in search of another ropemate. At the remains of the canyon's old pumphouse, a barren concrete slab where climbers often congregate, he met Tom Cosgriff, yet to establish his own reputation for hard wall climbs and insane BASE jumps. Cosgriff was alone. Nobody wanted to do the routes he wanted to do; they were too dangerous. Slater was looking for excitement.

Just across the stream lay *Wide Country*, then a serious proposition for climbers in EBs and without modern micronuts. The pair ticked the route, the first of many they would subsequently team up for.

During a rainy spring break during his freshman year, Slater happened upon the newly published book *Yosemite Climber*, by George Meyers. Taken by the big-wall photos, he immediately bought a copy, took it over to Cosgriff's place, and announced, "We gotta do A5."

Slater's enthusiasm generally borders on mania and once set upon a goal he won't be distracted. Fortunately, veteran climbing bum Jimmy Dunn was holding his annual "I'm quitting climbing" gear sale. Slater cleaned him out, buying 250 pins, haulbags, a portaledge, the works. Slater had never led an aid pitch before.

He promptly went up Boulder Canyon to Castle Rock to try out aid climbing, but sheepishly backed off the A1 *Practice Roof*. Nevertheless, the rumor was spread that he and Cosgriff were going to become A5 masters. This new passion seemed a convenient excuse to lay off the 5.12s, until a few weeks later he found himself three pitches up the Titan at the Fisher Towers in Utah.

The Fisher Towers resemble the drip sand castles that children make at the beach. Unless the Titan has crumbled before this goes to print, it measures 900 feet tall. "I'd never even heard of the Titan when (fellow Boulderite) Bill Feiges recruited me for the route," Slater says.

Slater learned to jumar on the first pitch, then later led the crux section. During that lead, he pulled out the pitch's only bolt while performing a body-weight test; it spooked him badly. At the belay, even thought they were above the crux, Slater insisted they bail. Feiges told Slater that if he backed off of the Titan, it was a sure bet that he'd never do any of the walls in Yosemite with their loose, expanding flakes and extended hooking stretches. Nevertheless, Slater was adamant and they came down. Feiges was enraged and wouldn't talk to Slater on the seven-hour drive back to Boulder. Feiges's assertion that Slater would never amount to anything as an aid climber only drove him to push harder.

A month later Slater and Cosgriff climbed their first El Cap route, the *Zodiac*. This was the first of five consecutive summer forays Slater would make to Yosemite. During these trips, he climbed the Captain over a dozen times, gaining a wealth of aid-climbing experience. He returned to Utah on New Year's Eve of 1985 and settled his score with the Titan via a more difficult line, the *Sundevil Chimney*.

It was back in Boulder at the beginning of his junior year that Slater met the man who would become his most trusted partner, Randy Leavitt. Conversing with Leavitt one day, Slater, inspired by seeing a BASE jumper whip past him during his first Yosemite trip, announced matter-of-factly that he was going to buy a parachute and skydive off of El Cap. Leavitt, an experienced wall man and BASE jumper, had heard many climbers make this boast. Few ever went through with it. Something in Slater's manic grin and self-assurance impressed Leavitt.

"I could tell he meant it," Leavitt says. "He had guts." Besides, to get to the top Slater wanted to climb *Sea of Dreams,* which was also a goal of Leavitt's. Nobody knew much about the route (it had had only two ascents), other than it was El Cap's hardest, with potential for fatal falls from four of the pitches. First, however, Slater would have to learn how to skydive.

Slater enrolled in "Leavitt's Accelerated Free Fall School," which involved a quick ground course and forging fifty skydives in a log book. Next they boarded a plane in Loveland, Colorado, and ascended to 11,000 feet. With 80 knots of wind howling by, another skydiver was at the door, psyching to jump. He turned to Slater and Leavitt and in a shaky voice exclaimed, "Boy, sometimes it feels like the first time!"

Slater looked at him sympathetically and said, "I know what you mean."

Slater landed laughing and twenty-five jumps later was standing at the lip of the Black Canyon of the Gunnison River. The jump is a difficult one because the canyon is deeper than it is wide and the landing a mere speck of a sandbar. Add to that the fact that the wall is not quite vertical, requiring the skydiver to "track" away from it, and the fact that its height of 2,000 feet allows little time to correct errors, and it becomes a much more serious jump than El Capitan.

Slater's first two Black Canyon jumps went without a hitch and he began to feel bored. To add spice to his third, he and Leavitt decided to launch together, holding hands for the pics, then climb the Painted Wall back out. To safely complete the jump, Leavitt would open his chute one second before Slater, providing vertical separation so they wouldn't collide in the air. However, an instant after pushing out from the lip they lost the desired foot-first position and tipped dangerously head down. Slater felt Leavitt release his wrist and looked over to see Leavitt windmilling his arms like a stuntman to avoid a fatal flip onto his back. Slater went into a headfirst, no lift dive, trying to gain enough speed to track away from the rapidly approaching wall. He was frantically twisting his head in all directions, but could not spot Leavitt, leaving him with the conclusion that Leavitt must be just above him. He tracked away from the wall. Still he couldn't see Leavitt. The ground was rushing up at him, seconds away, but throwing his pilot chute would be the equivalent of slamming on the brakes with Leavitt tailgating at 120 mph.

In the meantime, Leavitt had maneuvered 100 feet to the right at a level 80 feet above Slater and opened his chute. As Leavitt rode his canopy down he witnessed "the most vivid sight of my life."

Leavitt's eyes fixed on Slater's white jumpsuit. The wall blazed by in the background, the thick white pegmatite bands flashing past like stripes on a freeway. He watched Slater hurtle faster and faster toward a messy destiny in the talus, falling 1,200 feet, 1,500 feet, 1,800 feet. Finally, one second before impact, Slater's chute opened. Backwards.

Slater was 150 feet above the talus, but only 80 feet from the cliff and heading straight for it. He cranked the chute around, narrowly avoiding the wall. Reaching the landing site was by now impossible, leaving only three options: smash into the other wall and die, touch down in the grade six rapids and drown, or try to make it to a gravel bar strewn with football-size rocks. Slater chose option three. Unfortunately, it entailed a downwind landing (a skydiving no-no) at a painful 40 mph into the blocks. He survived the impact of the crash but faced yet another hitch—he was on the wrong side of the river.

Leavitt retrieved one of the ropes they had stashed for the Painted Wall and threw it over the torrent. "The water was fast and rough, but I felt the swim across would be no problem," Slater says. "After all, I was captain of the high school swim team."

One step in and he was swept away until the rope pulled taut and swung him over to the opposite bank. Slater's foot, badly twisted in the landing, had swollen to elephantine proportions, so they scrubbed their plans to do the Painted Wall. Instead they spent the next two days hiking out—a hike that normally took an hour and a half. "I think my foot was broken," Slater says, years later. However, instead of going to the emergency room, he headed for Yosemite, where the *Pacific Ocean Wall* beckoned.

In 1982, the *P.O. Wall* was one of the toughest lines up El Cap. Cosgriff had already done the route and stoked their friendly rivalry by repeatedly telling Slater what a fantastic climb he had missed. For a year Slater had stared at the topo of the route that he had taped to his wall. On the topo he'd added the words "SOLO THIS ROUTE." Never mind that he had never soloed an aid pitch over 50 feet long or for that matter that the *P.O.* had never been soloed before. He spent five days climbing it, then jumped off. Sixty seconds later he and his canopy landed in El Cap Meadow. "Right then I knew I'd keep jumping off until I got caught," he says. The next day he started up *Sea of Dreams* with Leavitt.

This time it was Leavitt's turn to break a foot and the pair was forced to retreat from partway up. Slater recruited Coloradoan Mike O'Donnell, a burly survivor of many epics, to finish the route. The pair encountered ten days of continually desperate aid climbing en route to the summit, the last three days without food. "Throughout," O'Donnell says, "Slater displayed astonishing cockiness in the face of death. He'd be on A5, looking down at a pinnacle 100 feet below that he'd impale himself on, and yell down, 'This is nothing but dogshit here, Mikey.'"

On the last day, they tossed all their extraneous gear, including sleeping bags and jackets, from below the summit to lighten the load. By the last pitch, Slater was so weak he could swing a hammer no more than once at each pin while cleaning the last pitch. Leaving the iron, he jugged to the summit. It was dark and lashed by rain. Slater curled up under a haulbag for a long, grim bivy.

Just before dawn the wind calmed, the rain ceased, and the Valley floor was dark and quiet. Conditions couldn't have been better. Slater jumped. The wall rushed by, a faint tan blur in a world of black. He opened his chute and steered away from the wall knowing El Cap Meadow was out there somewhere. Just then a lone pair of headlights came down the valley lighting the pavement beside the meadow. Slater flew right through the lights, landing 30 feet from the car. He heard doors slam.

"You're under arrest. Stop."

Slater hotfooted it across the meadow in his climbing shoes, his chute wrapped around him and dragging through the tall grass and weeds. Behind him were two rangers, the better fed of whom gave up the chase quickly. The other ranger kept up the pursuit, waving his gun at Slater and yelling, "You're under arrest."

Exhausted from the wall and lack of food, Slater began losing ground to the law officer.

"I've never gotten a parking ticket before," Slater thought, "and now if they catch me I'm resisting arrest." Terrified, he jumped into the Merced River and let the current take him. His pursuer ran along the bank waving his large sidearm and hollering. Slater abandoned his skydiving rig. Deciding that his quarry wasn't worth a frigid soaking, or wasting a bullet, the ranger gave up the chase and Slater escaped.

The incident cost him $3,000 in lost gear, but he insists it was worth every penny. It was his last cliff jump. After that, he jumped off of skyscrapers and an antenna to round out the four fixed object jumps one needs to wear the mantle of BASE jumper. He now relishes his status as a retired BASE jumper. Still, at the foot of his bed lies a packed chute, ready to go. "I just sleep better knowing it's there," he says. "If I feel the urge I can just go out and jump." Given his compulsive nature and the location of his office on the sixtieth floor of the Sears Tower, the urge could come any day.

BASE jumping was over, but the fascination with El Cap remained. A year after graduating with his business degree, Slater returned to the Valley to establish a first ascent of his own. When he and Cosgriff were viewing the North America Wall for their first time, they had picked out a line going right up the middle of the map. Coming from Wyoming, Slater has a special affinity for ovines. Hence, they dubbed the line the *Wyoming Sheep Ranch*. After being the butt of dirty jokes for so long, Slater now had a chance to make up a few sheep jokes of his own.

Fuzzy Pile Substitute, *Ewephoria*, and *High Boots on a Full Moon Night* are some of the pitch names. Enjoyable evenings can be spent at the Sheepalope or Wooly Box bivies, complete with authentic fixed Wyoming curios. Speaking of which, one doesn't want to fall onto Cattleprod Pillar. Inspired by the *Sea of Dreams*'s Peregrine Pillar pitch, on which one risks a fatal fall onto the pillar (Slater—"I thought it added to the pitch"), Slater had hoped such a pillar would grace the

Sheep Ranch. If such a fixture were missing, however, he'd brought his own. Now, should one fall onto this 18-inch strap-on substitute one would suffer terminal internal hemorrhaging. Nevertheless, the probable cause of death would be embarrassment.

These antics are all in keeping with Slater's goal to produce a route that was really hard, well put together, and that people would get a kick out of. Doubtless, some prudes are offended. To them he says, "If you don't like the name, then you should have climbed it first and named it something else. If you're offended by the toys, then I suggest you do a different route."

Of course Slater's idea of fun is a little different than most folks'. Take the *Liz Is Tight* pitch on *Wyoming Sheep Ranch*. Four hours after leaving the belay, Slater had gained a scant 40 feet via dicey aid moves up the shattered diorite. It was obvious he'd never complete this radically overhung pitch before dark so he lowered until he was even with his belayer, John Barbella, who pulled him 20 feet in to the anchor. Barbella asked, "So what did you lower off of—a rivet?"

Slater flashed his crazed grin. "Nah, hooks."

Morning dawned and the ropes still rose above to a pair of lone hooks and a few feet of duct tape. Apparently, the night's winds hadn't dislodged them. What had seemed like a neat idea the day before didn't seem so cool anymore. To start the day's climbing, Slater slowly lowered out from the wall, then with 2,000 feet of air beneath him, jugged to the hooks. Above loomed an S-shaped seam forming a pair of 100-foot long labial features on the edge of an orange arête. Eleven hours passed. First copperheads, then expanding knife blades, then more copperheads. He was living his definition of A5: should a piece fail, he'd go at least 150 feet. Now, having spent ten days on the wall, Slater found it increasingly difficult to concentrate on the task at hand. Each placement got harder. His legs were going numb. Near the end of the pitch he was faced with the most marginal of tied-off blade stacks. Twice he pounded them in. Twice he gave them the jump test. Twice they pulled out.

Jolts of adrenaline seared his chest. Acid bit the lining of his empty stomach. In frustration, he beat the wall with his hammer—THAK THAK THAK—pounding out the stress. His fit over, he tapped the stack back in, clipped, leaned out, jumped in his stirrups, and it held. Three placements later the rope pulled at his harness just as the crack ended. Slater reached as high as he could and drilled the belay anchor. For Slater, aid climbing doesn't get any better.

In 1985, a year after establishing the *Sheep Ranch*, Slater moved to Chicago where the father of one of his former El Cap partners set him up with a job on the Exchange. Would mere lucre lure a hardcore climber like Slater to the windswept rockless wastes of Chicago? "Nah," Slater says, "I needed something to do other than watching *Geraldo*."

Whenever he can escape his job, Slater leaves Chicago, often to climb with Leavitt. One of the things that bonds the Slater/Leavitt partnership is their mutual love of E.T.—extensive trickery. To cope with the vicissitudes of aid climbing, Slater and Randy have designed many tools to surmount otherwise unclimbable sections without damaging the rock, tools you can't buy at REI; however, you can get most of the parts at True Value. Perhaps the pair's favorite device is "Lovetron," a North Face VE-24 tent pole with a skyhook at the end. Cheater sticks have long been found in many aid climbers arsenals, but beyond a certain length they become difficult to direct.

The Lovetron solves this problem with a steering cable. With practice, this device can be deadly accurate. See that light switch 15 feet across the room? Slater could hook it in a matter of seconds. "That would be A1," he says. So a hard Lovetron move would be like hooking the top of the molded switch plate? "Yeah," Slater chuckles and his pupils dilate. "Then getting on it." Other forms of E.T. are a guarded secret. You get the feeling that your gullibility is being tested when Slater hints at driving pins with a golf club or hanging on rubber hooks.

Slater and Leavitt make it clear that their routes involve E.T. "You can't go up on *Scorched Earth* with a rack of pins, some Friends, and some wired Stoppers," Slater warns. "You're not going to be able to do it. You have to be prepared to rake the wall with a hook on the end of a 14-foot Lovetron and do any other trickery required. If you're not willing to do that then you shouldn't be on the climb."

Still, some ambitious climbers refuse to let E.T. stand in their way in their attempts to repeat routes. The fourth ascent party of Leavitt and Greg Child's *Lost in America* bragged in the press that they found a way around the Lovetron move all the previous ascents had done, the move that on the third ascent forced solo wallmaster Xaver Bongard into an extra trip to the ground to procure a longer stick. Instead of bringing a cheater stick, which they deemed unethical, they packed a bag of rivets—not exactly a sporting rack on a fourth ascent. Upset at this defilement of his friend's creation, Slater has since Lovetronned past the retro-rivets and removed them.

"Needless to say," Slater says, "Randy and I are not the most popular guys in the Valley."

Scorched Earth, located between *Iron Hawk* and *Tangerine Trip,* was Slater and Leavitt's last Valley wall and they feel El Cap's hardest. The climbing is continuously hard and involves lots of E.T., including a 30-foot sideways hook-to-hook Lovetron passage. Slater takes the traditional view that "aid climbing should be imaginative, that the leader should make every effort to get through a stretch of rock with the least amount of permanent damage." This view is not commonly held in the Valley these days where trenching heads (chiseling holes for copperhead placements) and adding bolts or rivets to existing climbs are increasingly commonplace practices. Slater feels this serves to take the adventure out of wall climbing by reducing the difficulty to a common level he would call A3.

"Eventually the *Sea of Dreams* will be A3," he predicts. "Someone will get out on the *Hook or Book* pitch, get scared, put a bolt in, and ruin the whole character of the pitch. That's the direction aid climbing is going in Yosemite and why I want no part of it anymore."

Now, he's turned his attention to the mountains and the desert. In the desert, adventure is still easy to find. Especially in Navajolands where towering shafts of blood-red sandstone lure like Sirens and climbing is strictly forbidden.

"I have great respect for the Navajolands," he says. "The worst thing that could happen would be to allow climbing there. Where John Q. climbs, destruction follows. The Navajo should patrol the place with machine guns." Would that stop Slater from climbing there? No way. "Worrying about getting busted by Indians, having your windows smashed, getting your gear stolen—that adds something."

On his Navajoland ascents Slater and his partner try to leave no trace of their passing, but if caught, they each carry a blank check in their pocket, ready to write out the $500 fine.

Slater wishes the old days were back. There would be fewer people, less chalk, no Lycra, and only girls would wear earrings. He sees overcrowding of routes and modern tactics as taking the adventure out of rock climbing. So now his goals have come full circle back to mountaineering. A recent forced bivy in the Sierras—of the minutes creeping by, jumping up and down and hugging your partner to stay warm, not knowing if you'll live to see the sunrise variety—has rekindled his psyche for cold weather climbing. His partner, Bruce Hunter, calls it "one of those nights where you're hating life." Slater rates it as "by far the most miserable experience of my life." Both agree that they'd do it again without hesitation.

Slater longs for Shackletonesque adventures, like skiing across Antarctica, pulling a sled, with no radio, knowing if you get lost, or lose something, or burn your tent down, then you're dead. But

Antarctic forays take lots of money. For a hundred grand Slater could buy equivalent misery on McKinley's *Cassin Ridge* in the dark of winter and still have the funds to find himself flashing past Fisher Towers in a Ferrari, slender blonde wife at his side, drifting through the left turn to Castle Valley, smoking the tires, jamming up through the gears, eons from the stock exchange, but just seconds from home.

Climbing, February 1991

The Hard Song

Travels with Rob Slater

I knew that at some point I would be writing a piece like this. I just didn't know which friend would be the subject. Sometimes I thought I'd be lucky and check out first. Such was not the case.

I WAS AT THE RENO TRADE SHOW when I first heard that Rob Slater died descending from the summit of K2. At that moment my world shrunk into a tight sphere while the bustle of the huge convention hall floated on another plane. I didn't want to believe what I was told, but a stern-faced friend assured me he wasn't joking.

Numb, I hurried out before I learned any more details. Robbie embodied the climbing spirit, combining a oneness with the medium with a soaring, irrepressible urge to climb. Despite all the climbers, the gear, the clothes, the plastic walls, the videos, and the hype, there wasn't the least breath of the climbing spirit in Reno. I walked away from the convention center knowing I would not walk back in.

The next morning I drove to the desert seeking Robbie's spirit. The shock of his death made me question my own compulsion to climb. The first boulder I passed was crumbly and homely. I balanced up the loose, dark flakes, moving up in the hot desert sun. The spirit was on top and I felt the oneness and the urge. The next boulders I hit were white bullet granite. Traversing a finger seam, feet smearing the lip of a roof, jagged blocks below—the spirit was strong. I felt it on the way up Wheeler Peak as the cold wind ripped across the rocky summit ridge stinging my cheeks; then again on the descent as snowballs melted to nothing in my hands.

I felt the spirit and I felt the sadness. I felt the rock and I felt my tears. We were The Team and now one of us was buried by the snows of K2, by the power of ambition, and by the realization of a dream.

I've lost friends to climbing accidents in the past, but none that I had climbed with as much as Robbie. Our partnership started around fifteen years ago in the red recesses of Eldo and on the gray granite of Boulder Canyon. We took turns dragging each other up the RP horror shows of the early 1980s. On top of each we celebrated with a simple bark: "The Team!"

We fed on our triumphs and The Team momentum grew. Our success was based more on the fact that we were a strong partnership than on strong individual performances. We drew on each other's strengths, and by encouraging each other we had few weaknesses. Later, Robbie left for the Chicago Board of Trade, but whenever he'd return West we would pick up right where we left off and take things further. He introduced me to alpine climbing in the Winds and the Tetons, and he handed me that rack of steel and copper for my first heading lead. Never mind that it had groundfall potential (Robbie neglected to tell me that the much more experienced first ascensionist had decked), Robbie just told me I'd have no problem and he was right.

Robbie had more confidence in my abilities than I, and time and again he got me to push myself. This was due in part to the fact that we almost always climbed the routes Robbie wanted to do, which weren't necessarily ones I had the experience to do. Nevertheless, I never failed to have a good time climbing with him so I kept saying yes. Robbie was a master at getting his way. When you went on a road trip, it was to his objective, but in your car.

The only time I can remember riding in his car was when I visited him in Chicago. The sedan was sitting at the curb, an official-looking yellow envelope tucked beneath the wiper. Robbie plucked off the offending ticket, popped the trunk, then tossed it on top of a stack of forty or fifty others. I forget where we drove.

Robbie was raw and vibrant. Tact was a waste of time; sensitivity was for wimps. If you didn't like the way Rob was, he couldn't care less. He would say what he wanted to say, do what he wanted to do, and drive those around him crazy with the way he lived by his own rules. He only obeyed societal mores enough to get by, keep his job, and not be committed. Yet he had a respect for the American Way, the old pull-yourself-up-by-the-bootstraps philosophy. Robbie didn't respect whiners, wimps, or anyone looking for a handout. I remember talking to him about K2 shortly before he left. A young climber over-heard our conversation and butted in.

"You're going to K2?" He pointed at Robbie. "Who's sponsoring you?"

"I am," Robbie snapped back. "I've got a good job. Maybe you should get a job too."

One feeling Robbie and I shared was a distaste for how climbing is sinking toward the lowest common denominator. When told that someone added bolts and a fixed line to the Mystery Towers approach in Utah, Robbie was livid. We had humped full loads over that section more times than we cared to count, and never once did we consider busting out the cord. "I can't believe these people call themselves climbers," Robbie exclaimed. "What a bunch of pussies." He spit the last word out like he'd just bitten into a rotten apple. As a member of the Eldorado bolting committee, Rob steadfastly rejected applications to add bolts to existing routes. Rob felt risk was one of the most important components of climbing. If there was no risk involved there was little reward.

Robbie had a passion for big walls, desert spires, Eldorado free routes, and hard alpine climbs, but he had another passion as well. Being a true son of Wyoming, Robbie loved sheep, or so he joked. The two most prominent decorations in his apartment were posters of K2 and cute little sheep dolls. Who but Rob would take a major accomplishment like the first ascent of one of the hardest wall routes on El Cap, name it *Wyoming Sheep Ranch,* leave sexy sheep toys at select anchors, and dub pitches *Ewephoria, Fuzzy Pile Substitute,* and *High Boots on a Full Moon Night?*

Flocks of admiring ovines will sorely miss Robbie, but if the truth be known, his real romantic passion was for flat-chested, athletic blondes. This made him great to have as a friend, because being drawn toward more top-heavy physiques, I knew we'd never be fighting over the same woman. How he'd grimace when I'd ogle a curvy lass. Rob's determination to achieve goals, whether the courtship of a beloved or the scaling of a mountain, was matched only by his joy in reaching them. When a lengthy courtship came to fruition in his car, Rob expressed his fire for life by reaching forward, tipping the rearview mirror, and flashing himself a smile as he gave the big thumbs up. I can imagine him sporting that same thumbs-up grin on the summit of K2.

Because he lived in Boulder and because he worshiped women, Robbie felt the red-hot iron of the feminist militia brand his hide with the word Sexist. That didn't faze him. Time and again he'd tell me he'd just met "the future Mrs. Rob Slater." Then he would wax on about his new flame and how perfect she was, how she fulfilled his blonde-eyebrow fetish, or how she had left a batch of fresh-baked cookies on his doorstep. Rob rarely restrained his bawdy sense of humor, so before introducing any women to him, I always warned them that they would love him or hate him. Invariably they loved him. It must have been his infectious enthusiasm.

Robbie was a master at inspiring confidence, in himself and his partners. He was cockier than most climbers, and this put some people off. This was just Robbie's way of psyching himself up. But no matter how loosely he shot his mouth off, he ended up backing up his words with his actions. When others vowed to climb all the Fisher Towers first, he simply replied, "The race will be over when I finish. No sooner." And he was right. He became the first, and so far only climber to summit all the Fisher Towers. In the end, the people put off by his bragging were more choked by the fact that he backed up his words, than by the words themselves.

Robbie was Robbie—coarse and funny, hyper and driven. He would say what he thought, which was usually not politically correct. Usually I'd laugh, but sometimes he'd say things that made even me cringe. He'd get you pissed off, then he'd back off, tilt his head to the side, look up at you with a sad, pouty grin, clasp his hands in front of his chest and beg forgiveness. That hurt-puppy look always worked on me.

One reason his friends were so quick to forgive was that Robbie didn't judge his friends. Even if he didn't agree with you, he'd say, "You do whatever you want, Chief. You know I'm behind you 100 per-cent." I never met anybody who had so much trust in his friends. It didn't matter whether you were just asking his permission to print a story about him, or belaying him while blazing on acid, Robbie trusted you not to screw up. When someone puts that much trust in you, you don't let him down.

For most climbers, just to do the climbs that Robbie and I did with each other would constitute a very successful climbing career. It astounds me that Robbie had equally strong partnerships with so many other climbers: Cosgriff, Gilbert, Hunter, Hammer, Leavitt, O'Donnell, Torrisi, and many others. To say Slater climbed enough for ten careers is not a cliché, but a fact. He had no patience and a surfeit of energy. I can count the number of times I beat Robbie to the base of a climb, or back to the car, on one finger.

I still can't figure out how someone who stuck so much to his own agenda could end up as such a loyal friend to so many, but Robbie pulled it off. Maybe it was the way he endeared himself to us by calling us "Great One" or "Chief." Or maybe we all stuck around because it was so fun to watch Robbie be Robbie, outraging people with his outspokenness and seedy sense of humor, or exulting upon reaching the summit of another desert spire and saying for the umpteenth time, "This is the coolest summit in the desert." Maybe it was because you knew you would make it up a climb if you were with Robbie, because he wouldn't leave until he did. Maybe it's because you knew Robbie didn't want any friends he couldn't trust, and he picked you to be his friend. Whatever the reason, it was an honor to be Rob Slater's friend.

I miss climbing with Rob. I miss the chants of "The Team," the bowls of Frosted Flakes for breakfast, the dissing on sport routes. I miss the Danny Thomas and John Wayne Gacy jokes. He promised to drink a beer with me after he triumphed on K2, and partake in all his friends' vices they had been egging him to try. He never wanted to do any of these things, and he never had. He didn't need to—he was crazed on life. But after all the hard work and sacrifices and effort, and all the living life on his own agenda so that he would climb K2, he was ready to give up that agenda to please his friends. I don't need to drink that beer with Robbie, because I know he would have kept his word. In some ways it seems fitting that he didn't have to lower himself to that act, even if it was just one beer. Rob's purity remains intact, and therefore so does his spirit.

More than anything in life, Robbie wanted to stand atop K2. As a mountaineer, you can climb no higher. It's the rare climber who succeeds on his first attempt at an 8000-meter peak. To succeed on the hardest of them all is utterly remarkable, though it came as no surprise to those who knew Robbie. Robbie would have topped out if it took ten trips to the Karakoram. Knowing he reached the summit, and knowing how much this meant to him, I feel that Robbie now rests in peace.

When a climber of Robbie's skill and dedication perishes in the mountains, his spirit joins the greater overall spirit of climbing. If the mountains didn't periodically take our heroes from us, the rewards of climbing would be miniscule. Robbie gloried in challenge and risk, whether he found it inching up an A5 hooking lead or grinding up the summit slopes of K2 without oxygen. He was willing to give his all to the sport.

I wish I had written this next line myself, but I stole it from a more poetic writer: "Death is the hard song. We only sing it once, and none of us gets it exactly right." Robbie sang the hard song. If anybody came close to getting it right, it was he. He was on the right stage. He hit every note perfectly. And sometimes I think he felt the time was right. He just sang it too early for the rest of us.

Climbing, November 1995

Bobbi Busts Out

Ms. Bensman on body image, boob jobs, unrequited lust, and the journey from 13D to 34C

Shortly before I did this interview, Climbing *ran a cover photo of a girl bouldering in an undersized bikini top. That issue became a best-seller, as well as generating much criticism in the letters column. It seemed climbers would rather look at and talk about boobs than read about climbing. Seems normal to me, so I was surprised that I had such a hard time selling this interview. I pitched it several times to my editors before it got accepted. It was a classic case of "We love it, but we don't want to print it." What seemed like easy bucks (just ask the questions and write down the answers) turned into weeks of negotiations, edits, and compromises. Thankfully, Bobbi was fun to work with, because I barely made minimum wage on this one. Feelings ran strong when dealing with my editors, but they compromised as well, and though not as racy as the unedited version, this one still captures the essence of the interview.*

WARNING: THE FOLLOWING INTERVIEW contains adult language (I wasn't using these words until I was five) and mild sexual content. If it were made into a Hollywood flick it would come just a slo-mo decapitation or gory disembowelment shy of rating PG-13. If such material makes your blood boil, your face break out, and your hand write nasty letters to the editor, you can thank me later.

On April 4, 1998, Bobbi Bensman returned to the Phoenix Bouldering Contest, a competition she has won a phenomenal twelve times. This year the thirty-five-year-old, twenty-time national sport-climbing event winner came packing more than ever. The talk was not about her previous wins or perennial favorite status however, but about her newly augmented breasts.

Since her surgery, Bobbi has received rude, unsigned e-mails at her Web site and has been the frequent target of pickup attempts everywhere from the health club to Petsmart. As well, her nicknames had changed from Robert Bensman and Bobbi Benchpress to Boobi and Barbie. All this, I suppose, was to be expected. What wasn't expected was that this would draw more attention from the climbing community than any of her climbing achievements. This seems hugely unfair to me. Aside from Lynn Hill, Bobbi has done more than anyone to open the door for professional women climbers. She has done this not only through her competition victories, but also by her frequent successes on "men's routes" and her persistent photo presence in the outdoor sports magazines. When it comes to selling an image, Bobbi's body is her bread and butter. Her truck grill abs, Gummi worm bicep veins, and acorn squash delts are the envy of climbers both female and male. Now she has changed that body and some of her harshest critics are the very women riding Bobbi's coattails through the door of professional climbing. Furthermore, the bulk of the criticism has been behind Bobbi's back. This interview was not just a cheap ploy for me to grasp what she'd done, but also a chance for Bobbi to respond to her critics.

This interview took place just after Bobbi placed third in the invitational round of the contest. A few hours later she would place second on the real rock. Present were Bobbi, myself, her friend Dan McQuade, and mutual friend Chris Dunn. I felt it would be indelicate to ask her immediately about her breasts, so I eased into the subject.

V In an interview a few years back, you said your two goals before you died were to climb Astroman and to find your G-spot. Given your new dimensions, I take it you've already made it through the Harding Slot.

B I definitely made it through the Harding Slot.

V How's the other goal going?

B Well, one out of two is not bad.

V I've seen a lot of women look at photos of you in the past and say, "Wow, I wish I looked like that." When I hear that I cringe and think, "No, I wish I looked like that." Now you don't look like that anymore. Do you think you've let down some of your fans?

B Oh, totally. Totally. A lot of people were really disappointed. I heard that in the women's ice climbing isolation zone at the X-games, I got the shit slammed out of me. Women were saying, "I've lost all respect for Bobbi Bensman, I can't believe she did this." (Bobbi leans forward, her voice gets louder, hurried and more intense as she lets it out.) For all my life, I have been flat as a board, and I didn't want to be that way anymore. I'm into personal freedom and if a person wants to improve upon oneself, then by all means go for it—it's a free world. I've always wanted to do this. I've always been into wearing clothing and hated how I've looked with a flat chest. Now I've got a thousand-dollar new wardrobe. I walked into Victoria's Secret three years ago and they took one look at me and they're like "Honey, there's not a bra in the store that will fit you." I walk into Victoria's Secret now and *I RULE*.

V There's younger climbers coming up that are going to be climbing circles around you any day.

B Yeah, it's awesome.

V But you've got something they don't have now—bigger boobs. Was that part of the decision?

B No. I should have done this ten years ago. But you can't really finance them, you have to pay cash. I had to save up money. I was going to go around the climbing community and ask if everyone would pitch in a little bit. Somebody buy the left one and I'll buy the right one.

V How much did your new breasts cost?

B $4,100.

V They look like a million.

B Oh, thank you.

V What about the change in dimensions? Have they affected your climbing?

B I went from a double-A to a C, and a *nice* C-cup. It hasn't gotten in the way of climbing too much. I still don't feel like I'm 100 percent recovered. I had the surgery December 13 and six weeks after I still couldn't lift my arms. When I did start climbing again in February it was really easy . . . and now I'm feeling pretty damn good. I've already done seven 5.13 FAAs, First Augmented Ascents. On crossover underclings they get in the way just a tad, but otherwise I think I'll be able to climb just as hard as I want.

V How many pounds did they add?

B Probably five.

V Do you have trouble with footwork? Can you see your feet?

B No problem.

V How big are your feet?

B Ooh, they're big.

V Do you think you would have been first today if . . .

B No way. You know getting third today—I'm psyched. I'm in the money and I climbed well. That's all that counts.

V How much money's out there now?

B Not that good. (Sighs.) Sponsorship money is not that good. Definitely worse than substitute teaching. Also the competition money sucks; if you win a national you only win 600 bucks.

V But your sole source of income is related to climbing, correct?

B I have a lot of little streams that run together to form a river. Besides sponsorship money, I do a lot of instructional seminars and then there's my slide shows. That's how I bought my house, by doing slide shows.

V What about modeling?

B I'm doing that as well.

V Are you getting more modeling offers since the boob job?

B No. I haven't tried to pursue that.

V Was any of your decision based on "I could market myself better now"?

B No, that wasn't even a consideration, because now that I'm thirty-five I feel like I need to move on with my life. This was totally a personal thing for me, not to get in *Playboy,* or not to get more pictures taken, or get more modeling jobs or anything. 1998 is my last year of being a "professional climber." Now I'm kind of looking for a job in marketing and sales in the outdoor industry. I'd like to be a sales rep for La Sportiva. Some sort of job that has nothing to do with tits.

V You could rep for Boreal—show up at a store and say "Get a load of these Bambas . . . "

A couple of issues back you wrote an angry letter to the editor, because *Climbing* mentioned Beth Rodden's weight. It said there was too much emphasis placed on body image and that can cause eating disorders.

B Beth mentioned that she looked up to women climbers such as Robyn because they are petite and they're at the top. I was worried that a woman who was a big-boned girl would have to starve themselves to get down to that weight. Today a sixteen-year-old girl won, Shena Sturman. That girl is burly and *it's awesome.* That's the kind of role models we need—people that are not so eating-disordered out.

V People look at photos of you and say, "Wow, she's so ripped, she's so skinny." I think a lot people think you're eating-disordered out.

B I weigh between 115 and 120. That's not eating-disordered out. That's not skinny.

V I don't know. You look like you're wrapped in Saran Wrap.

B Really?

V You'd send the statue of *David* running to get liposuctioned.

B I don't know. I mean, I munch out.

V C'mon, years ago you told me your goal was to get so skinny, your period would disappear.

B It never happened. I've always been 10 percent body fat or higher.

V You got a boob job, but will it stop there? Will you wake up one morning, decide your nose is too big, and go get it fixed?

B No, the boob job thing has just been on my mind for twenty years.

V How would you have felt five years ago if Lynn Hill had gotten a boob job?

B I would have high-fived her. I never had a problem with that.

V What would you say if Katie Brown showed up at the next competition sporting C-cups and told you that you gave her the courage to get them?

B Oh, shit. That's a good question. I think I would feel bad because she's only seventeen. I don't want her to do that. I think you need more time to decide that.

V My sources at the mag tell me you were critical of the *Climbing* magazine "bikini cover."

B No way. I thought it was a nice shot, but I didn't think it was good enough to be on the cover. And there wasn't even an article about her. [Rikki Ishoy] is a really good Swiss climber. She climbs hard 5.13. You don't get to know anything about her except here she is on the cover.

V I thought it was a hideous tease because they didn't show the rest of the boulder.

Having been an outspoken feminist at times, does breast augmentation contradict your feminist ideals?

B I don't think it does. I could see if you did something like this for your husband or to try to get guys that it would. In this situation it didn't have to do with any guys, it had to do with me. I was completely solo on this. Even back when I was a women's studies major I wanted this. It's your own personal choice. That's empowering. That's a feminist issue right there. I can see how (feminists) think I sold out and that I sold out for men. But if you do this operation for men you're a fool.

V If you lived on the Isle of Lesbos . . .

B I'd still do it. You are definitely the Howard Stern of climbing. Has anyone told you that?

V I'd rather be compared to Frank Zappa than Howard Stern.

B (Lifts Verm's shirt, prods beer gut.) I still like to check your belly out every time I see you, every couple years. You should have seen John Sherman when I first met him fifteen years ago. Do you remember him? Fox. *Fox.*

CD It was the 1980s haircut.

B I remember seeing him on a route and thinking, "Who is that guy?" I just fell in love. He was skinny and tan and lean with long hair. You're one of the only guys I never could get. Isn't that funny? (Addressing others.) He's a total tit guy. You couldn't get him if you were flat-chested.

V But I talked to you anyway and I'm still talking to you now.

B Oh yeah, you were always a good friend. You liked me, but didn't do anything about it. What was your problem?

At this, Bobbi left to watch the young men compete. Boob job or no boob job, Bobbi was still the Bobbi I'd met fifteen years before: goal-oriented, hard-working, fun-loving, and a wee bit saucy. I came away convinced that her boob job wasn't a marketing ploy hatched by a climber no longer assured of cashing first-place checks. I believe she truly did this just for herself. I thought, "How lucky to be so happy with your body that you would only change one thing." I contemplated my own physique. Alas, I was no longer the boy of Bobbi's dreams. That's okay; I still have my dog Thimble. "What do you think, Chief?" I addressed her. "Would you get a boob job for me?" She folded her ears back and gave me a worried look. "Naah, you're right. I love you just the way you are. Besides, to get all your tits augmented would cost, let's see . . . $18,450. Heck, for that price I could get lipo-sucked, dewrinkled, hair-weaved, and artificially tanned. Bobbi couldn't take her hands off me. I wonder what the boys in 'iso' will say?"

Climbing, September 1998

Afterword

"JOHN SHERMAN ROSE OUT of the ranks of the lumpenproletariat (I had to look it up too. —V) in a fiery maelstrom of vulgarity and dynamic witticisms. He's since made a living at it." —*The Mountain Yodel*

In the winter of 1995–96, I was honored to be the poster child for the United Dirtbag Climbers' Fund. This nonprofit organization is the brainchild of the minds behind the less-than-non-profit Mountain Yodel—*the one climbing journal that has the wisdom, integrity, and class to have never published my articles. The UDCF's plea seems an apt way to wrap this book up. It was accompanied by a beer-foaming-from-the-mouth picture of me on a K-Mart chaise lounge/portaledge taken during an aborted attempt at wall climbing in Australia. The plea reads thusly:*

Do you know me?

Sure you do. But you probably don't recognize the man in the picture. That's because it was taken back in the glory days.

Well, there haven't been many glory days in the past few years because now I have a job. I'm a climbing journalist. Of course that's not what I tell my parents—they think I coordinate shuttle landings for NASA. I had to spare them the shame. I can't tell you how demeaning it is writing for the glossy climbing rags, but they're the only ones who will pay for my "meaningless, rude, obnoxious, immature diatribes" and then only after they've censored them. I tried contributing to The Yodel, but they're too smart to run my drivel and too cheap to pay anyone.

That's where you come in. Your magnanimous contribution to the United Dirtbag Climber's Fund will help put skids like me back on the streets or under the boulders we crawled out from. Lord knows there are plenty of Americans out there that want to work. You can't believe the guilt I feel taking food out of their kids' mouths each month.

And it's not just they who suffer, it's you too. Just ask any card-carrying WAPMA (Women Against Parasitic Male Attitudes) member and they'll tell you it's guys like me who lay waste to the fine traditions of gender-neutral climbing prose.

Remember, I've written before and I will write again. Only the UDCF can stop me, but they can't do it without your help. So spread your checkbooks wide and ante up.

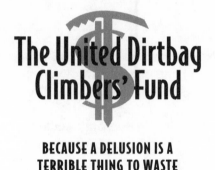

The United Dirtbag Climbers' Fund

BECAUSE A DELUSION IS A TERRIBLE THING TO WASTE

The UDCF rechannels contributors' beneficence to a plethora of worthy causes. In Verm's case, your donation will buy enough paper, crayons, and beer to keep his fecund mind occupied for days, even weeks. Send your money now. You never know when he'll write again.

Mountain Yodel, Winter 1995/96

About the Author

John Sherman is a senior contributing editor at *Climbing* magazine and author of the popular "Verm's World" column. He began his climbing career at Indian Rock in Berkeley, California, in 1975. In addition to free climbing such classics as Astroman and Tales of Power in Yosemite and Jules Verne, The Naked Edge, and The Wisdom in Eldorado Canyon, he has completed several big wall ascents as well as waterfall climbs in Alaska, Wyoming, and Colorado.

Best known for his bouldering, he played a major role in developing world-class bouldering at Hueco Tanks State Park in Texas and introduced the V-system for rating boulder climbs. He is the author of *Hueco Tanks Climbing and Bouldering Guide, Better Bouldering,* and *Stone Crusade: A Historical Guide to Bouldering in America,* which won an award at the 1995 Banff Mountain Book Festival. He lives in Estes Park, Colorado.

About The Mountaineers

Founded in 1906, The Mountaineers is a Seattle-based non-profit outdoor activity and conservation club with 15,000 members, whose mission is "to explore, study, preserve, and enjoy the natural beauty of the outdoors . . . . " The club sponsors many classes and year-round outdoor activities in the Pacific Northwest, and supports environmental causes by sponsoring legislation and presenting educational programs. The Mountaineers Books supports the club's mission by publishing travel and natural history guides, instructional texts, and works on conservation and history. For information, call or write The Mountaineers, Club Headquarters, 300 Third Avenue West, Seattle, Washington, 98119; (206) 284-6310.

Send or call for our catalog of more than 300 outdoor titles:

The Mountaineers Books
1001 SW Klickitat Way, Suite 201
Seattle, WA 98134
1-800-553-4453
e-mail: mbooks@mountaineers.org
website: www.mountaineersbooks.org

Other titles you may enjoy from The Mountaineers:

STONE CRUSADE: A Historical Guide to Bouldering in America, *John Sherman*
John Sherman's classic historical guide to the best bouldering areas in America, featuring new photographs, updated bouldering grading chart, and an author afterword.

JIM WHITTAKER: A LIFE ON THE EDGE—Memoirs of Everest and Beyond, *Jim Whittaker*
The autobiography of the first North American on Everest tells the story of big mountains, big business, and the big names—K2, REI, and the Kennedys.

THE BEST OF ROCK & ICE: An Anthology,
Dougald MacDonald, Editor
Twenty years of *Rock & Ice* magazine's finest stories collected in one volume, including insightful accounts, wicked parodies, unusual fiction, and moving reminiscences by Greg Child, Jim Bridwell, Alison Osius, and Andrew Todhunter.

CAMP 4: Recollections of a Yosemite Rockclimber, *Steve Roper*
An anecdotal chronicle of the most significant climbs and most riveting controversies of the golden age of big wall Yosemite climbing, including stories of such greats as Royal Robbins, Yvon Chouinard, Allen Steck, and Warren Harding.

THE BURGESS BOOK OF LIES, *Adrian & Alan Burgess*
The tall tales, edge-of-your-seat adventures, and poignant stories from identical twins and accomplished mountaineers Adrian and Alan Burgess.

POSTCARDS FROM THE LEDGE: Collected Mountaineering Writings of Greg Child, *Greg Child*
Selections from the best writing of elite mountaineer Greg Child. Includes humorous observations of the sport and insightful reflections on controversial climbs, plus revealing portraits of some of the biggest names in the climbing world.

ONE MAN'S MOUNTAINS, *Tom Patey*
A mountaineering classic, featuring stories, satire, and verse by the legendary Scottish climber.

ERIC SHIPTON: Everest & Beyond, *Peter Steele, M.D.*
The first biography of adventurer, explorer, and mountaineer Eric Shipton, the big name in Himalayan exploration, preceding even Hillary.